Mystery Fiction and Modern Life

Studies in Popular Culture
M. Thomas Inge, General Editor

Mystery Fiction
and Modern Life

R. Gordon Kelly

University Press of Mississippi   Jackson

Manufactured in the United States of America
01 00 99 98   4 3 2 1
The paper in this book meets the guidelines for permanence and
durability of the Committee on Production Guidelines for Book
Longevity of the Council on Library Resources.

Library of Congress Cataloging-in-Publication Data

Kelly, R. Gordon.
    Mystery fiction and modern life / R. Gordon Kelly.
        p.   cm.—(Studies in popular culture)
    Includes bibliographical references and index.
    ISBN 1-57806-005-2 (alk. paper).—ISBN 1-57806-032-X (pbk.:
alk. paper)
    1. Detective and mystery stories, American—History and
criticism.   2. Detective and mystery stories, English—History and
criticism.   3. Literature and society—United States—History—
20th century.   4. Literature and society—Great Britain—History—
20th century.   5. American fiction—20th century—History and
criticism.   6. English fiction—20th century—History and
criticism.   7. Crime in literature.   I. Title.   II. Series: Studies in
popular culture (Jackson, Miss.)
PS374.D4K45   1998
813'.087209—dc21   97-21530
                                                              CIP

British Library Cataloging-in-Publication data available

For JEL and the children

There are at least three points where chaos—a tumult of events which lack not interpretation but interpretability*—threatens to break in upon man: at the limits of his analytic capacities, at the limits of his powers of endurance, and at the limits of his moral insight. Bafflement, suffering, and a sense of intractable ethical paradox are all, if they become intense enough or are sustained long enough, radical challenges to the proposition that life is comprehensible and that we can, by taking thought, orient ourselves effectively within it. . . .*

—Clifford Geertz, "Religion as a Cultural System"

Contents

Acknowledgments

The origins of this book can be traced to a wonderfully stimulating course in popular formula fiction taught by John Cawelti one summer when I was a graduate student at the University of Iowa. It is a pleasure to acknowledge his influence as well as that of Stow Persons and Alexander Kern, with whom I also studied at Iowa. At the University of Pennsylvania, Murray G. Murphey supported my interests in popular fiction in the best possible way—by allowing me to create and teach courses on detective fiction and society.

Without institutional support from the University of Maryland, College Park, this work could not have been completed. A grant from the Research Center for the Arts and Humanities provided a semester's leave from administrative responsibilities to work on a draft. Sadly, the Research Center was one of the first casualties of budget cuts in 1990, thus depriving others of the opportunity to devote their full time to research and writing while still drawing their salary. Sabbatical leave in the spring of 1995 enabled me to complete the manuscript; I am grateful to Robert Griffith, the former dean of the College of Arts and Humanities, for approving that leave. For her support and encouragement, I am also indebted to my former colleague, Hasia Diner. My students over the years have usefully questioned and challenged my ideas. I am especially appreciative of those who read and commented on all or part of the manuscript: David Weinstein, Jenny Thompson, Jan Blodgett, Shelby Shapiro, Greg Wahl, and Tom Frank. Valerie Brown and Kathleen Waters provided invaluable secretarial assistance.

Finally, it is a pleasure to acknowledge the assistance of the personnel of the University Press of Mississippi with whom I have worked on this project: M. Thomas Inge, who first encouraged me to contribute to the series in which this work appears; Evan Young, who copyedited the manuscript with great care and skill; Seetha A-Srinivasan, whose unfailing courtesy and tact make her an author's editor, and the members of her staff, Anne Stascavage and Chimène Gecewicz; and, not least, the outside reader for the Press, who saw enough promise in the original manuscript to recommend its publication.

Introduction

An utterance is an action and hence often a move in a game.
Martin Hollis, *The Cunning of Reason*

Historically stable elements of mystery fiction, I argue in this study, are systematically linked to constitutive features of modernity involving issues of <u>knowledge</u>, <u>trust</u>, <u>risk</u>, and <u>power</u> that arise in the course of everyday social interaction. To sketch the broad outlines of this argument, let us briefly examine two stories: a recent newspaper article describing occupational risks associated with selling real estate (Bowles 1996), and John Katzenbach's *The Shadow Man* (1996), a typical mystery novel.

Real estate agents " 'get paid to meet strangers and take them to empty houses. That's your job' " (Bowles 1996). Although the vast majority of those strangers are legitimate clients, a few are not: from 1980 to 1992, seventy real estate agents were killed on the job—more than the number of prison and jail guards slain in the line of duty during the same period. Showing empty houses to strangers thus involves a measure of risk. That risk can be minimized by changes in policies and procedures—for example, declining to meet a prospective buyer after dark simply on the basis of a telephone call. Nevertheless, the job does require showing empty houses to persons an agent does not know well, and so requires agents to determine as accurately as possible the intentions of those representing themselves as prospective home buyers. [Correctly assessing the intentions of strangers with whom one must interact in the normal course of events is both a feature of modern life and a staple of mystery fiction.] Interpreting the intentions of others is the philosophers' time-honored problem of Other Minds, and a crucial issue for social scientists and historians seeking to understand and explain human action. A correct interpretation of another's intention constitutes a kind of knowledge, affords a basis for trust, and confers power. Just as the newspaper story cited above raises entwined issues of risk, trust, knowledge, and power— issues inherent in modern society—so, too, does mystery fiction, as the example from Katzenbach's *The Shadow Man* reveals.

Consider the following incident, versions of which have been a staple of mystery fiction from its beginnings in stories by Edgar Allan Poe. Katzenbach's protagonist, Simon Winter, a retired homicide detective, becomes involved, by chance, in the case of a serial killer whose victims are Holocaust survivors living in Miami. These survivors' fifty-year-old memories of Der Schattenmann, an elusive figure who served the Nazis by ferreting out Jews living in secret in Berlin as late as 1943, threaten to unmask the collaborator, who had fled to the United States after the war and assumed a false identity.

Returning to his apartment one evening, Winter is suddenly, inexplicably wary. At this point, he has no reason to think the killer even knows who he is, let alone where he lives. "There is nothing here, he told himself. Have you gone crazy? . . . He doesn't know about you . . . you are being foolish. Then he corrected himself: Being cautious is never foolish. You may embarrass yourself by trusting your instincts, but that is all you will do, and the alternative is far worse" (Katzenbach 1996, 283).

Pausing, the detective assesses the likely situation if Der Schattenmann has somehow traced him to his residence. He reasons that his assailant will be hiding inside rather than outside the apartment; that the man will expect him to "arrive home like any tired old man . . . [anticipating] that I will step inside, right into your path unawares, not seeing you until I shut the door right on my own death"; and that he will attack Winter with a knife rather than a firearm (283–86). Having formed this prediction about the situation facing him, Winter must decide on a strategy to test his suspicions, a course of action calculated both to reduce his risk and to hold out some possibility of capturing Der Schattenmann. If his assailant is waiting, confident that Winter will return to his apartment without any hint or fear of danger, then he will not expect Winter to come barreling through the patio door. In that moment of surprise and disorientation, Winter hopes to retrieve his service revolver from his nightstand and confront the intruder.

Winter discovers that his patio door has been forced, confirming, at least, that someone has been in the apartment. Winter has little choice but to assume that whoever forced the door is still inside. Slamming it open, Winter charges headlong into the darkened apartment, intent on reaching his gun, but his would-be assailant, having lost the element of surprise, escapes through the front door before Winter can retrieve his weapon. Winter "shook his head [at the intruder's escape] . . . I didn't think you'd be that smart. Or be able to move that quickly. You heard the noise behind you, and instead of letting it cripple you with surprise, you acted instantly, and you saved yourself. This impressed the old detective. Not many people can function with an animal's cunning or instinctive sense of preservation, knowing to flee at the first sound that is unexpected. . . . I'm beginning to know you, he said to himself. But the sensation was short-lived, because he realized now that the Shadow Man knew just as much about him as well" (288).

Katzenbach's detective models a particular stance in the face of consequential risk, a stance that enables effective action and minimizes the danger Winter faces. "Instinct" gives Winter, at best, a warning of possible danger. To act effectively on it requires that he appraise the situation and weigh probabilities. He must anticipate what another person can do in light of likely resources (e.g., the Shadow Man's lethal expertise) and known constraints (e.g., the layout of Winter's apartment), and fashion an appropriate strategy to deal with the situation. Finally, he must act on the basis of this plan. That action simultaneously tests the adequacy of the plan itself and confirms the assumptions on which it was formulated.

Winter's strategy—to surprise a possible assailant waiting in his apartment—requires two distinct sets of abilities and trained capacities. Effective planning requires that Winter imagine the most likely situation confronting him: if his assumptions are true, the Shadow Man has somehow identified Winter, traced him to his apartment, and now, having broken in, waits inside, intending to kill him. Central to Winter's conjecture about the situation is his prediction about how the

Shadow Man is most likely to behave in response to the unexpected—to something the Shadow Man will not have taken into account in *his* planning. Winter's prediction rests on the adequacy and reliability of what his experience has taught him about killers in general and trained killers in particular. At issue is whether Winter can come to possess knowledge of others, and if so, how such knowledge can be achieved.

Winter's effort to trap his would-be assassin yields him some useful knowledge—but at the cost of giving his adversary important information about himself. The man was hiding exactly where Winter expected, for example; Winter predicts correctly how a trained killer would evaluate and act on the possibilities and constraints afforded by the layout of his apartment. Secondly, Winter learns something from the manner of his adversary's successful escape—namely, that the Shadow Man possesses extraordinary presence of mind when confronted by sudden, unexpected danger. Like Winter, his shadowy assailant can conceive and execute an effective plan of action, in this case virtually instantaneously, based on assessing a situation accurately.

If Winter possesses a trained capacity for strategic planning in situations of high risk, he also possesses the requisite, and different, abilities that underwrite the successful enactment of the plans he has formulated. Winter's plan commits him to bursting into his unlighted apartment, where, if he has predicted correctly, an experienced assassin waits to make an attempt on his life. For his scheme to work, Winter must possess not only a measure of physical courage but a well-developed capacity for emotional control in the face of mortal threat and its accompaniment, the temptation to panic. Winter's ability to remain cool in the face of stress is thus distinguishable from, but no less important in defining his stance than, his capacity to devise strategic plans on the basis of attributing specific beliefs and intentions to an adversary. The more accurate the attribution of belief and intention, the more likely the success of the plan developed on the basis of that attribution. Winter's plan depends on his anticipating, with a very high degree of probability, where in the apartment his adversary is hiding. The quality of Winter's predictions aside, his plan, translated into action, hinges on his courage and presence of mind in the face of the uncertainty and stress of acting in situations of high-consequence risk. Winter, like fictional detectives generally, combines both sets of trained capacities.

I came across *The Shadow Man* by chance after completing *Mystery Fiction and Modern Life* in draft. Katzenbach was not an author whose work I knew, but the novel's premise—an elusive killer stalking Holocaust survivors to insure his own continued survival—suggested that its author might be using the form of the detective novel to serve several ends: as an act of memory, for example—an injunction never to forget either the victims of the Holocaust or, more particularly, the nature of its perpetrators. Throughout *Mystery Fiction and Modern Life*, but especially in chapter 7, I elaborate the view, stated succinctly by Kenneth Burke, that works of fiction "are answers to questions posed by the situations in which they arose. They are not merely answers, they ✳ are *strategic* answers" (1957, 3). A similar view informs Jane Tompkins's recent, influential study of antebellum American fiction, *Sensational Designs*: works of fiction articulate and propose "solutions for the problems that shape a particular historical moment" and provide blueprints "for survival under a specific set of political, economic, social, or religious conditions . . ." (Tompkins 1985, xi, xvii).[1]

I develop, illustrate, and support my argument about the relationship of mystery fiction and modernity with references to a relatively small number of mystery novels—small, that is, when compared to the thousands of works that make up the universe of mystery fiction. One question that necessarily arises, therefore, concerns the confidence with which inferences based on the (few) works cited can be generalized to the many works not discussed in this study.

As originally conceived, *Mystery Fiction and Modern Life* was to be a study in symbolic action. Sociologist Anthony Giddens's *The Consequences of Modernity* (1990) suggested to me a way to retain that aim while offering a framework in which to make better sense of patterns of action and consequence uncovered in my reading of mystery fiction. The work's thesis evolved as the developing conceptual framework clarified the meaning of the patterns discovered in the fiction, and as further reading, and rereading, in the fiction extended the range of the thesis. The works I cite in support of my argument are those that in my judgment best illustrate a pervasive pattern of incident and consequence characteristic of mystery fiction generally. That pattern relates mystery fiction to intrinsic features of our experience of modernity.

Readers may find my argument persuasive but judge that other works would serve as well or better to illustrate my thesis. I would be surprised—and disappointed—if that were not the case. If it has substantial merit—if it holds true for the vast majority of mystery novels—readers whose experience of mystery fiction is broader than or simply different from my own can be expected to come up with other examples in support of the argument. Other readers, agreeing with me that the works of Eric Ambler, Ross Macdonald, and Tony Hillerman deserve citation, may still feel that, for example, Ambler's *Journey into Fear* better supports the argument than *A Coffin for Dimitrios*. I will happily concede to my reader that a different work than one I cite would strengthen the argument, if doing so implicates the reader in the selection process and extends the scope of my thesis.

The principal criterion for selection of the works discussed in this study is relevance to my argument. Generalizations based on the cited works extend to most, but not all, of the much larger number of works read in preparation for this study. And of course I hope the argument does hold for the universe of mystery fiction generally.

Other considerations, however, affected the final selection of works discussed in this study. Some authors—notably Edgar Allan Poe, Arthur Conan Doyle, John Buchan, Eric Ambler, and Dashiell Hammett—created prototypical works no study of mystery fiction can ignore. Writers are readers before they are authors. As is well known, for example, Doyle drew heavily on his knowledge of Poe's "ratiocinative" stories such as "The Purloined Letter," which formed the basis for "A Scandal in Bohemia." Moreover, Poe, Doyle, and the others are among those writers with whom my readers are most likely to be familiar.

Another criterion for selection is commercial success. Many of the authors I discuss have attracted large, loyal audiences. These include, among others, Agatha Christie, Ross Macdonald, John D. MacDonald, Helen MacInnes, Patricia Cornwell, Tony Hillerman, Marcia Muller, and Sara Paretsky. Many of these authors, by virtue of their popularity, will also be known to my readers. Less well-known works or authors—the British espionage novelist Anthony Price, for example—receive attention because they are especially concerned with those issues that most interest me in mystery fiction: knowledge and the problems of interpretation, risk, trust, and power.

As noted above, this study incorporates the view that works of fiction generally can be understood as a form of human action. Characterizing fiction as a form of action implies a necessary and essential focus on writers as situated historical actors utilizing cultural resources—of language, narrative convention, and the like—to act within the complex of factors that simultaneously enable and constrain their activity. "How to Live with a Hero," John D. MacDonald's ac- ✱ count of his decision to develop a series character, analyzes the changing context for his fiction in the 1960s and describes his strategic response to those changes within self-imposed constraints stemming from his sense of vocation.

MacDonald returned to civilian life after service in World War II determined to write fiction for a living. After a brief period of discouragement, his stories began selling, and by 1960 he had published dozens of novels and more than five hundred short stories. Despite repeated suggestions from his agent and his editor, however, MacDonald had refused to develop a series character, believing that "a series would create problems I could not even define, much less feel confident handling" (J. D. MacDonald 1964, 14). By 1962, however, MacDonald had decided to try working in the series format, convinced that the market for his work was changing: "The reduced number of magazines published less fiction. Small book sales on newsstands were being diminished by three factors: New titles in excess of rack space resulted in smaller average print orders; intensive promotion on reprints of best sellers caused a squeeze from the top; semi-pornography by off-brand houses with larger retail margins caused a squeeze from the bottom" (14). Given the declining magazine market and changes in marketing and distribution, a series character made sense, but MacDonald also insisted that it fit with his aspirations as a writer: "I wanted a maximum latitude in creative invention. I did not want to be typecast" (14).

Among the series characters with whom he was familiar, only Raymond Chandler's Philip Marlowe struck MacDonald "as being a protagonist of a stature and dimension which approached valid novelistic standards"—but even in Chandler's work "certain conventions defied reality—or, at least, the novelist's imitation of reality" (14). What MacDonald sought was a series character that would do more than take "up the slack in print order quantity" and create an audience "which would lead to substantial reissues" of series titles; he wanted a character whose concept would enable him to continue producing works like *A Key to the Suite* and *Slam the Big Door*—the works of which he was proudest for "their novelistic content." "Only in this approach could I fulfill my responsibilities to all the people who had formed the habit of looking for my name and buying the books" (15).

MacDonald's initial attempt to create a series character that would meet his "novelistic" criteria resulted in failure: "My man was somber, full of dark areas, subject to moody violence." A second concept of an adequate protagonist also failed: "I swung too far the other way and ended up with a jolly, smirking jackass for my 'hero'" (16). A third effort, published as *The Deep Blue Good-by* (1963), introduced a character with whom MacDonald thought he might live comfortably and creatively for years: Travis McGee—"an individual, recognizable, independent, feisty, wry, articulate, and, bless him, reasonably mature." His concept of McGee, he acknowledged, made "shameless use of certain conventions: a variation of the Robin Hood *modus operandi*, a houseboat environment, a tropic resort flavor, a capacity for indignation." He also chose not to use other available conventions: "for example, the idea that the hero must always win." McGee emerged "an iconoclast, a critic of the cheapening aspects of his culture, an unassimilated rebel in an increasingly structured society" (16).

"How to Live with a Hero" describes what amounts to an instance of strategic planning—hardly surprising for a writer with an MBA from Harvard. The changing economic context for MacDonald's writing lay beyond his control. Responding appropriately to changing circumstances required analysis and a different approach based on that analysis, beginning with a reconsideration of his long-standing reluctance to create a series hero. That reluctance stemmed from professional and aesthetic, rather than economic, considerations—from uncertainty that his skills were equal to the technical problems posed by the series format, for example, or from apprehension that a series would threaten his standards of creativity and achievement. In the changing circumstances of the early 1960s, however, MacDonald was obliged to put aside that reluctance and accept the risk entailed in developing a series character.

Travis McGee, then, is MacDonald's strategic answer to questions posed by his situation as he understood it: how to counter the changes occurring in the market for popular fiction in general and for his fiction in particular; how to utilize the series format to mobilize an audience while still retaining his "creative flexibility." Which conventions should he retain, which discard, in creating the character? What attributes, qualities, and characteristics should he give him? What could he do and achieve in and through a character that, if all went well, he might have to write about for years to come? The process of analysis and planning that led to creating McGee parallels a process of analysis, planning, and action pervasively instantiated in mystery fiction generally.

Earlier I cited approvingly the view that imaginative and critical works are "answers" to questions posed by the situations in which they arose. John D. MacDonald's account of developing a series character suggests that this characterization, while broad, is still too narrow to comprehend the full range of actions that constitute the "doing-in-saying" of mystery fiction. Writers may equally be engaged in such actions as asserting, condemning, challenging, or exposing, to name only a few.

As a completed action that ends successfully, mystery fiction invariably links action and consequences, thereby embodying an implicit (and very often explicit) moral dimension. Inherently, mystery novels constitute arguments: murder (or treason) will out and truth prevail— but only if a sufficiently shrewd or principled or determined investigator stakes his or her reputation or life on the outcome. Occasionally, the argument *is* the work, as in the case of Josephine Tey's *The Daughter of Time* (1951), which rehearses arguments exonerating King Richard III of the charge of murdering his two young nephews to insure his succession to the throne of England. Similarly, John Le Carré's *Tinker, Tailor, Soldier, Spy* (1974) embodies an argument about how a Soviet "mole" could remain undetected for years in the highest echelons of the British Secret Intelligence Service. There can be little doubt that Le Carré had H. A. R. (Kim) Philby's perfidy in mind.

Another form of argument carried on in mystery fiction, given its inherent normative dimension, amounts to a weighing of the costs and benefits, so to speak, of engaging in homicide investigations on the one hand, or in intelligence work on the other. Le Carré's novels, as well as those of Brian Freemantle, Ted Allbeury, and Len Deighton, are notable for their consideration of the moral perils of the secret life. And mystery fiction, especially as represented by the hard-boiled detective novel and the espionage novel, is, and has been, a vehicle for social commentary in the hands of many of its practitioners. As John D. MacDonald makes clear in the essay cited earlier, Travis McGee would not only possess that "capacity for indignation" that distinguishes so many fictional private investigators; he would also be a critic of "the cheapening aspects of his culture."

The real world of real estate agents and the fictional Miami of *The*

Shadow Man share the problem of understanding another's intentions in situations characterized by high risk. Safeguards intended to reduce risks to real estate agents, particularly women, cannot eliminate completely the vulnerability arising from the conditions of their work. Agents still must show houses to individuals they do not know; procedural safeguards can at best reduce the risk. Those who are not deterred pose a threat that can only be countered by detecting their deception. This sets the agent the problem of assessing her client's intentions in every case, although statistically the risk is small in any given instance.

Assessing clients' intentions and, more generally, dealing effectively with strangers who have something to hide is the very stuff of mystery fiction, and has been throughout the century of its popularity. In Simon Winter, John Katzenbach models a stance that both enables effective action and minimizes risk in situations where deception is a variable affecting both the real nature of the situation and the degree of danger involved. Winter manages this by imagining a situation the features of which are constructed on various probabilities. Putting his conjecture to the test, Winter not only confirms the accuracy of his construction; he also learns of his adversary's formidable capacity for acting effectively in the face of suddenly altered circumstances. In short, the detective learns that he and his adversary possess the same trained capacities.

Consequential encounters with strangers involve risk and raise questions about how much trust to invest in them. Knowing more about those with whom we must interact offers a basis for assessing their trustworthiness, and hence of gauging the degree of risk involved in encounters with them. I consider this issue in chapter 2, and raise the formidable problem of Other Minds—which is especially fraught in high-risk situations. Consequential encounters with strangers are intrinsic to modern society, and I also explore why that is so.

Mystery fiction centers on consequential encounters with strangers. In pursuing their inquiries, fictional investigators of all sorts confront the problem of assessing others' trustworthiness and detecting deception. Mystery writers, given the nature of the genre, have little choice but to represent protagonists skilled at dealing with strangers in situations characterized by risk, uncertainty, and deception. In doing so, they model a stance relevant to constitutive features of modern society. Subsequent chapters consider how writers treat moral issues intrinsic to the investigative process; the idea of writers doing things in and through their fiction; and some of the things readers do with mystery fiction. In the concluding chapter, I make a connection between strategic planning, on the one hand, and the investigative stance typically modeled in mystery fiction, on the other, thus returning the discussion to the underlying issue of *Mystery Fiction and Modern Life*—namely, the relationship between mystery fiction and modern society.

Mystery Fiction and Modern Life

I

Modernity as Context

*The relations that exist between the social and political condition of a
people and the genius of its authors are always numerous . . . whoever
knows the one is never completely ignorant of the other.*
                          Alexis de Tocqueville, *Democracy in America*

*. . . it is just possible that the tensions in a novel of murder are the sim-
plest and yet most complete pattern of the tensions on which we live in
this generation.*
                                        Raymond Chandler, 1948 letter

The invention of the detective story in the 1840s and its subsequent
popularity from the 1880s on occur within the context of modernity in the double sense used by Robert Wuthnow: "Modernity . . .
is simultaneously a period of a society's history and a cultural world
distinguished by the institutional and symbolic configurations of a
technologically induced economic growth" (1984, 55). In *The Consequences of Modernity*, Anthony Giddens offers an account of modernity we can use to establish the general context in which the writing
and reading of detective fiction have flourished. In the sense I embrace
here, modernity, at the most general level, enables and constrains the
creation and reception of mystery fiction. Details of character and setting that distinguish one writer's work from another's derive straight-
forwardly from differences in individual experience. I hope to show
that the broad, stable continuities characterizing mystery fiction as a
set of related works owe their key features to the nature of modernity
rather than to the nature of, for example, democracy or capitalism, as
others have argued. That said, I am necessarily interested most in those

elements of Giddens's argument that have to do with the lived experience of modernity.

For Giddens, modernity is characterized especially by its dynamism, by the globalizing scope of its institutions, and by the degree of discontinuity it exhibits in comparison with earlier, traditional cultures; these are the characteristics he seeks to understand and explain. Looking for an appropriate metaphor with which to figure modernity, Giddens settles on the image of a juggernaut—"a runaway engine of enormous power which, collectively as human beings, we can drive to some extent but which also threatens to rush out of our control and which could render itself asunder" (1990, 139).

The dynamism of modernity has its origins in three interrelated sources. First, there is the radical separation of time and space that occurs as, for example, various technologies are perfected, permitting the coordination and control of activities over increasing distances and with greater speed. Second, modernity is characterized by, and depends upon, the creation of "symbolic tokens" and the establishment of "expert systems." The symbolic token *par excellence* is money. Expert systems are "systems of technical accomplishment or professional expertise that organize large areas of the material and social environments in which we live today" (27). Money and systems of technical accomplishment or professional expertise have two things in common. Both permit social relations to be lifted out of local contexts and restructured across indefinite areas of space and spans of time. Moreover, symbolic tokens, preeminently money, and professional expertise of whatever sort involve and depend on trust: "Trust is . . . involved in a fundamental way with the institutions of modernity" (Giddens 1990, 26; see also Misztal 1996, Silver 1985, Hardin 1993, Shapin 1994).

The essence of trust is confidence in the reliability of another person, or in the reliability of an expert system, with respect to some outcome. In either case, confidence is a function of knowledge—of how well we (think) we know another or the workings of an expert system. I have no need of trust if the other is transparent to me or if the workings of the system are fully known and understood. Under the conditions of modernity, however, I am constantly and routinely obliged to interact, often consequentially, with others about whom I know little—in a word, with strangers. Moreover, I am radically dependent on expert systems, and their practitioners, about which I can have little more than a rough-hewn sense of their respective areas of claimed expertise.

In the modern world, we are all lay persons, save in our own narrowly limited area of expertise.

Trust, in the sense defined above, involves risk. I trust someone, or some system, in an undertaking that matters to me and thereby open myself, in however small a way, to danger—to the chance of harm or damage. The more consequential the undertaking, the more I will want to know about you, and the more likely I am to take reasonable steps to insure that my confidence in your reliability to perform your part is not misplaced. My trust, in other words, involves an assessment of your trustworthiness in a given situation. That assessment, in turn, depends on my possessing or being able to obtain reliable information about you and about the expertise you claim to possess.

The risks I face under the conditions of modernity are not limited to those connected with other persons with whom I interact, whether they be representatives of expert systems or not. There are dangers of which I am aware that are truly global in scope—nuclear war, for example, or ecological disaster. The risk of either—my assessment of the probability of their occurrence (or, more likely, my assessment of the experts' assessment) contributes to my overall sense of security, which is a function generally of my trust in others and in expert systems. For a variety of reasons, modernity involves pervasive insecurity, and Giddens's image of the juggernaut—powerful but not fully or predictably controllable—is meant to capture also the insecurity and uncertainty endemic to the experience of modernity.

The conditions of modernity thus make heavy demands on us for trust while simultaneously providing us with ample cause for worry. One morning I take my car in to a mechanic, trusting him to isolate and fix a problem in the electrical system. That evening, a television news program informs me that Sears automotive stores have been engaged in what amounts to wholesale fraud, billing customers in California for unnecessary repairs or nonexistent problems. I trust my mechanic, in part because I have no real choice at this point, and in part on the basis of "weak inductive knowledge": he has successfully repaired my cars for more than a decade. That is no guarantee, of course, that he will be able to fix it this time, but my experience over the years underwrites my trust, giving me a high degree of confidence in his reliability to solve the problem and bill me fairly. On the other hand, the story on the evening news is unsettling on two grounds. I am reminded, in passing, that I am utterly dependent on whoever fixes my car, since I know next to nothing about automobile repair beyond the rudiments of changing the oil or replacing the battery. But I am also reminded that several years ago, the television program *60 Minutes* presented a story claiming to show that Audi automobiles were prone to sudden and uncontrollable acceleration. Several specialty automotive magazines subsequently disputed the allegation, and eventually the National Transportation Safety Board found no evidence of a mechanical problem. By then, however, the damage had been done. Audi sales in the United States, the company's prime market, plummeted in the aftermath of the damaging publicity (Csere 1987; Levin 1989). As these instances suggest, knowledge (or rather, knowledge claims) figures importantly in considerations of trust.

Trust is sustained or undermined in social interaction, whether fleeting, as in simply passing a stranger on the street, or more consequentially at those "access points" where lay persons encounter experts or bureaucratic functionaries in their professional or official roles. In the first instance, trust is sustained by what Giddens, following Erving Goffman, terms "civil inattention" (1990, 81). Through the management of subtle behavioral signs, two passersby on the street exchange mutual signals of reassurance, "what might be called polite estrangement. As the two people approach one another, each rapidly scans the face of the other, looking away as they pass. . . . The glance accords recognition of the other as an agent and as a potential acquaintance. Holding the gaze of the other only briefly, then looking ahead as each passes the other couples such an attitude with an implicit reassurance of lack of hostile intent" (81). Civil inattention in this example is an instance of "unfocused interaction" of the sort that goes on continually in the daily encounters with strangers that are an intrinsic feature of experience in modern society.

Trust is especially implicated, however, in the consequential encounters with others that constitute the institutional fabric of modernity. Since I can know no more than a tiny part of the specialized knowledge that underpins modern society, I am at every turn dependent on experts and professionals, and I am obliged to trust them. To be sure, the efficacy of experts and professionals resides ultimately in the scope and adequacy of their specialized knowledge and, in many cases, the particular technology at their disposal—in other words, on expert or abstract systems. Nevertheless, it is an expert, representing the body of knowledge to which he or she lays claim, with whom I must deal. My trust is partially in the expert system itself, but also and necessarily in the person who, in the final analysis, is accountable for making it work and reassuring me that it is indeed working.

Dependency, by definition, is an asymmetric relationship of power. As such, it can (and frequently does) create feelings of uncertainty, vulnerability, and resentment in the lay person seeking expert assistance or counsel. It is in the interests of both parties, therefore, to attend to the trust dimension of the relationship, however transitory the interaction may be. For my part, I need reassurance that you know what you are talking about, that you can provide the assistance or expertise or counsel I require. You, in turn, are presumably interested in convincing me, and keeping me convinced, not only of the extent and validity of your expertise but also of your trustworthiness and integrity to act appropriately and effectively on my behalf.

Trust, Giddens argues, gets negotiated and sustained in various ways at such access points as the doctor's office—through appropriate furnishings, for example, and the prominent display of professional credentials such as diplomas, licenses, and certificates, themselves carefully calculated to impress. Of critical importance, however, is the demeanor of the expert or professional in question, which prototypically combines, at a minimum, an air of assured knowledgeability with an attitude of cool "unflappability." The former points in the direction of the body of knowledge underpinning the expert's very claim to be of help, while the latter signifies the expert's capacity to deal with whatever problem or crisis may be in the offing. Learning, perfecting, and maintaining the requisite demeanor is thus a critical part of the socialization of those people who staff access points, particularly in circumstances involving risk and danger. Perfecting the requisite professional demeanor means managing one's emotions and subordinating spontaneous emotionality to rational control (Giddens 1990, 83–92). "Never let them see you sweat," the slogan for a brand of deodorant, suggests the degree to which disguising strong emotion (fear, embarrassment, surprise) has self-evident value. A demeanor of cool unflappability has near-universal applicability in modern society. I don't want to see my surgeon "sweating" any more than I want to see visible signs of distress on the faces of flight attendants preparing for landing. In these and many other instances, a show of cool confidence is intended to sustain trust. Nowhere is this display more needed than in situations of high risk and substantial danger.[1]

The foregoing has emphasized trust as played out in the inherently unequal encounters between, for example, professionals of varying sorts, representing expert systems, and their clients, who by definition lack the expertise they need. The professional demeanor of competence and unflappability is a cultural convention—learned behavior that is situationally appropriate—and, in concrete instances, an instantiation, a performance, of that convention. No matter how ingrained the habit of professional demeanor may be, however, and no matter how necessary it may be to the smooth functioning of the institutions of modernity, there is an inescapable element of staginess, of acting, about it. The dramatistic metaphor is constitutive of Erving Goffman's classic analysis of social interaction, and Giddens follows Goffman in adopting metaphors of the theater to describe encounters between lay persons and functionaries of all sorts (Goffman 1959).

Having suggested that professional demeanor is an achievement and a performance, I have little choice but to go further, to suggest as well that it is a mask, even a disguise. This in turn leads me to consider what implications that may have for trust. A demeanor intended to signal confident expertise and cool unflappability effectively subordinates spontaneous emotionality to rational control. It disguises what the expert really may be thinking and feeling in the situation. Worse, it can hide deception, even the intent to do harm. Professional demeanor may foster or sustain trust in expert systems and their personnel, but its inherent element of disguise offers grounds for skepticism and distrust. The more successful the act, the harder it is for the client to gauge what is really going on. A convincing display of professional competence may be a sign of real expertise or it may mask incompetence or worse. This poses a daunting interpretive problem for the truster, a point to which I shall return. First, however, it is worth noting that the demeanor appropriate in professional settings as an aspect of negotiated trust in expert systems cannot serve as the basis for trust in personal relations, which depends far more on openness and authenticity.

A distinction between public and private spheres is a crucial feature of modernity. In the public sphere, whether in the street or in the office or workplace, I typically encounter people in a more or less delimited role; that is to say, I encounter them partially. As we have seen, trust is inherently at issue in these encounters, and a degree of wariness, however muted, is simply prudent. In the private sphere—the world of intimate personal relationships—matters are quite different. "Modernity transforms the nature of friendship," Giddens argues, and this has important implications for personal trust (1990, 119). "Trust on a personal level becomes a project, to be 'worked at' by the parties involved, and demands the *opening out of the individual to the other* . . . trust has to be *won*, and the means of doing this is demonstrable warmth and openness," involving "a mutual process of self-disclosure" (121, italics in original). On this account, intimate personal relationships involve the whole person, rather than simply some role-specific aspect of the person, and the process of mutual discovery involves both an opening out to the other and a process of self-realization. In relations of personal trust, one is not only oneself, so to speak; one also comes truly to know oneself. Self-identity itself is achieved in and through a reflexive process of openness on the one hand, and self-inquiry on the other. The demeanor appropriate to encounters in the public sphere and at the access points to expert systems is thus antithetical to the openness required in trusting intimate personal relationships. Moreover, "ontological security"—the general, albeit largely unconscious, feeling of confidence individuals have in the continuity of their self-identity and "in the constancy of the surrounding social and material environments of action"—is closely related to trust (92).

Given the centrality of trust to both self-identity and feelings of ontological security, intimate personal relations involve hazards as well as opportunity. Trusting an intimate, for example, runs essentially the same interpretive risks, and can pose the same interpretive problem, as trusting an expert or professional encountered at an access point. If self-identity is as closely linked to open personal relationships as Giddens argues, trusting intimates and participating in a process of mutual disclosure is, by definition, highly consequential. Misplaced trust can be dangerous, in some circumstances even fatal. One wants to be sure who one's friends really are. So we return to the more general problem of knowing others as well as possible, especially in situations where the stakes are high. Under the conditions of modernity, the stakes are often high both in the public world, where lay persons confront experts and professionals on whose advice, expertise, and knowledge we all must depend from time to time, and in the private sphere of friendship and family as well.

Modernity privileges certain personal qualities and characteristics—a demeanor of unflappability, for example, which rests on a developed capacity for emotional management. In *The Homeless Mind*, Peter Berger and his coauthors, Brigitte Berger and Hansfried Kellner, explore the linkages between modernization and consciousness in ways that usefully supplement Giddens's work. In their analysis, the proto-typical institutions on which modern society rests are technological production and bureaucracy. These organize the activity of large numbers of people, and their form and structure necessarily shape not only the thinking of those who work within either sort of institutional setting, but more generally "the consciousness of the vastly larger number of ordinary people whose everyday lives involve them in various faccts of technological production [and bureaucracy]" (Berger, Berger, and Kellner 1973, 24).

Technological production involves a segregation of work from private life and fosters a distinctive cognitive style appropriate to the underlying logic of the machine process. It encourages a problem-solving inventiveness or ingenuity and a closely related tinkering attitude. The underlying logic of technological production requires control and management of emotionality, privileging the cool, low-keyed stance Giddens emphasizes as a critical aspect in those who represent and embody expert systems to lay clients. In technological production, moreover, many things typically go on at the same time, necessitating "a particular tension of consciousness characterized by a quick-alertness" to changing circumstances (Berger, Berger, and Kellner 1973, 37). These and other elements of the cognitive style appropriate to technological production appear to be intrinsic to modern society. They cannot be thought away, and although the majority of the population is not engaged directly in technological production, the cognitive style rooted in and expressive of its underlying logic is pervasive: "For better or for worse, it is not necessary to be engaged in technological work in order to think technologically" (40).

The "primary carriers" of these elements of modern consciousness are the processes and institutions directly involved in technological production; but "secondary carriers"—most notably mass education and the mass media—convey to the populace at large the "ideas, imagery and models of conduct that are intrinsically connected with technological production" (40). Thus elements of a cognitive style rooted in the logic of machine production carry over into the consciousness of people otherwise far removed from the production process itself. The problem-solving attitude required to establish and maintain ever more complex production processes has become ubiquitous, shaping our approach to everything from foreign relations (the "problem" of Bosnia) to the most intimate matters (the "problem" of male infertility). It is hardly surprising, then, that problem solving and, more generally, functional rationality are constitutive of that most popular of popular fictions, the detective story.

Like technological production, bureaucracy requires, and so fosters, a distinctive cognitive style. Problem solving is common to both technological production and bureaucracy, but bureaucracy involves correctly classifying and categorizing phenomena—putting things in their proper boxes, so to speak—while technological production typically requires analysis of a different sort, especially synthesis in the service of coordinating complex activities in time and over distance. Presupposing a general "organizability" in human affairs, bureaucracy encourages organization, system, meticulous attention to detail, and a preoccupation with procedure. Like technological production, bureaucracy requires its functionaries to exhibit and maintain emotional control. Ideally, bureaucracy treats every client equally, which requires, among other things, "the bracketing of personal bias, the objective assignment of cases into their appropriate boxes, the painstaking adherence to proper procedure even in situations of great stress" (Berger, Berger, and Kellner 1973, 57). That bureaucracy will operate fairly and with regular procedures is thus both a constraint within which its functionaries must operate and a normative expectation clients bring with them to encounters with those functionaries, whatever their institutional location. Equal treatment, however, virtually assures depersonalization in any given instance, since the case in hand must first be assigned to a more encompassing category of similar instances and then dealt with in terms of established procedures appropriate to that category. The potential for threat to the client's self-esteem or, in the extreme case, the individual's subjective identity is clear: "in encountering bureaucracy there is always a potential emotional strain. Put differently, bureaucracy has a strong propensity to make its clients nervous," the more so because of the asymmetry of power between expert and client, which can engender feelings of vulnerability, frustration, and resentment, in addition to nervousness (59).

The demands of modern society for individuals with highly developed "technological egos" is aptly summarized in a passage from Kenneth Kenniston's *The Uncommitted*, a study of alienated American young people premised on essentially the same analysis of modernity presented in *The Homeless Mind* and *The Consequences of Modernity*:

> [E]ven to survive for one day, the average urban American requires a kind of personality organization that in many societies even the most outstanding individual does not possess: a capacity to govern his own behavior, to make his way in a world of strangers, to do a job requiring years of training in the basic skills of literacy, to cope with unexpected situations and unfamiliar people. . . . [M]ost desirable positions in our society require advanced and specialized training, and, with it, high levels of dispassionateness, ability to remain cool under stress, capacity to concentrate, to maintain long-range goals yet to adapt rapidly to new conditions, to deal with remote and distant situations, to abstract, to co-ordinate complex operations, to synthesize many recommendations, to plan long-range enterprises, to resist distraction, to persevere despite disappointment, to master complex conceptual assignments, to be impartial, to follow instructions. (Kenniston 1970, 318–19).

Many, perhaps most, of these trained capacities and characteristics may be found in successful individuals—generals and administrators, for example—whose exploits and achievements in some cases predate modernity by centuries, even millennia. But the widespread need for large and ever growing numbers of persons with these skills and capacities appears to be a relatively recent historical phenomenon intrinsically connected to the spread and underlying dynamism of modernity. That dynamism, in turn, depends on the increasing power and control stemming from scientific discovery and the development of technology that have occurred over the last century and a half particularly.

The features of modernity to which writers of detective fiction have responded were emergent phenomena in this country in the antebellum period and were pervasive by the turn of the century, by which time the detective story had achieved the widespread popularity it has enjoyed ever since. In antebellum America, two forces combined in profoundly altering the face of society. The egalitarian ideal was working its way into every aspect of the young nation's life, from political practice to the very structure of citizens' notions of self and identity. Everywhere the world of colonial privilege and hierarchy was on the defensive, crumbling before the relentless leveling tendencies of democracy. In the emerging "horizontal" society, the locus of opportunity—economic, social, and intellectual—lay in the rapidly expanding cities, first of the eastern seaboard, then the Midwest and the west coast, as the center of population shifted ever westward over the course of the century. In the process, the relatively autonomous "island communities" typical of the eighteenth and early nineteenth centuries gradually gave way to an integrated and interdependent national economy whose organization and functioning both involved and depended on the defining elements of modernity: greater predictability, system, control, rationalization, expertise, improved communications, bureaucracy, pluralism, professionalization, standardization, and the like (Wiebe 1967). The rapidly growing urban centers were the most visible sites of modernity, just as they were the loci of economic, social, and cultural opportunity. In the island communities, "people at least thought they knew all about each other after crossing and recrossing paths over the years" (1967, 2). In the rapidly growing cities, on the other hand, residents encountered strangers at every turn. "Fearful of each other's competition and ignorant of each other's ways, [people] lived in mutual suspicion" (1967, 14). By the mid-1880s, more and more urban residents had come to believe "that people they could neither trust nor understand were pressing upon them" (1967, 96).[2]

Fear of urban growth and the conditions associated with urban living are evident in the antebellum advice books aimed at young men intent on seeking their fortunes in the burgeoning cities of the eastern seaboard, especially New York. In these books, the recurring figure of the confidence man symbolizes and condenses the dangers that threatened newcomers to the urban world of strangers. A skilled actor and dissembler, adept at the art of disguise, and a master of human psychology, the confidence man threatened to corrupt and betray impressionable youth and ultimately to subvert the American republican experiment. Typically the work of clergymen, advice books such as William Alcott's *The Young Man's Guide* (1834) warned readers of the wiles and stratagems of the principal types of con men—the untrustworthy urban companion, the demagogue, and the gambler (Halttunen 1982, 10–20).

To counter the blandishments of those who preyed on the innocence and vulnerability of the newly arrived, the advice books urged their readers to develop "character," understood broadly as self-possession, self-government, and self-reliance, which rested on and embodied fixed principle. The youth who held fast to fixed principle "could not be led astray by false companions" (Halttunen 1982, 26). More importantly, a firm character was held up as the basis for success and accomplishment in the fluid, competitive world of the expanding cities. A firm character represented both the youth's best defense against the confidence man's attempts to manipulate and betray him and the young man's most secure foundation for realizing his ambitions. But despite the sharp distinction drawn in the advice books between the individual with fixed principles and the unprincipled and predatory confidence man, the two had much in common. Both were trying to get on in a world of strangers competing with one another for economic success and social distinction. The social and economic fluidity of the city, combined with its anonymity, made trust a crucial issue. Not surprisingly, then, the advice books of the antebellum period focused especially on a single evil trait—hypocrisy (33).

The urban world of strangers posed two fundamental problems for those seeking to make their way in it. For members of the emerging urban middle class, there was the question of how to succeed without adopting the confidence man's cynical manipulation of appearances to his own ends. This was, at bottom, a moral dilemma. As Halttunen has shown, the advice books of the antebellum period advocated sincerity as the answer to the pervasive hypocrisy observable in urban social relations (1982, 34ff). The second, and closely related problem, was less moral, more interpretive, and at bottom epistemological. It had to do with how to gauge or assess the reliability and trustworthiness—in a word, the character—of another, a stranger, especially in consequential circumstances or encounters. In their emphasis and preoccupation with sincerity as the answer to hypocrisy, the antebellum guide books spoke primarily to the first of these questions: how to get on in a world of competing strangers without sacrificing principle.

Hypocrisy represented the studied disjuncture of outward appearance and the individual's true nature, his or her true moral character and real plans, purposes, intentions, and beliefs. Sincerity, on the other hand, constituted a link, observable in principle, between one's true (but unobservable) inner nature and one's outward manner and appearance; the sincere individual was transparently who and what he or she appeared (and claimed) to be. Sincerity thus promised a basis for reliably assessing others and so gauging their trustworthiness; sincerity was a guarantor of the genuineness of appearances, which in the urban setting took on new and critical importance.

The increased frequency of transitory encounters with strangers, typical of the urban experience, enhanced the importance of appearances as the basis for forming impressions of others. The authors of advice books paid special attention to the face as an index to character: " 'the habits of the soul become written on the countenance; what we call the expression of the face is only the story which the face tells about the feelings of the heart. . . . The expression of the countenance is a record which sets forth to the world the habitual feelings, the character of the heart' " (Halttunen 1982, 40–41). Such statements imply both a moral injunction (attend to your habitual feelings because they will inevitably and unambiguously determine your appearance) and an interpretive imperative (master the typology of physiognomies). Undercutting both, however, was the specter of the confidence man's proven skill at severing the connection between his inner corruption and his appearance of winning sociability. In the urban world of competing strangers, the cultivation of appearances, on which impressions depended, was thus fraught with ambiguity and consequence. "The youth had to learn to cultivate good surface impressions in order to make his way in the city. But by doing so, he was learning the arts of the confidence man, whose 'fair exterior and winning manners' were designed for deception" (42–43). How to succeed without resorting to hypocrisy?

Young men were counseled never to lie. Sincerity required of them candor and a frank and open countenance in which all could read their character. The sincere youth was in reality what he appeared to be. Transparency of character held out a solution to the moral problem posed by the anonymous and fluid world of the cities. The sincere person was an open book, whose trustworthiness could be quickly and reliably assessed. To the extent that sincerity itself could be feigned, however—and there was abundant evidence of the confidence man's skills in this regard—the injunction to be open, candid, and frank left one vulnerable to manipulation by others. Moreover, it offered no solution to the interpretive problem of determining, for example, the trustworthiness of another, given the possibility that they were not what they appeared or claimed to be.

The competitiveness, anonymity, and deceptive appearances of the city fostered suspicion and skepticism among many of its residents. If being transparent and trusting meant running the risk of being manipulated and corrupted, then suspicion and wariness, whatever their appeal on grounds of prudence, threatened to destroy the bonds of trust on which both the economics and the politics of the republic ultimately depended. Foreign travelers such as Frances Trollope, Harriet Martineau, and Charles Dickens all commented on the degree of distrust to be found in the new nation (Harris 1973, 70–71). The potential for isolation and alienation amid the transformative changes of the age especially worried Alexis de Tocqueville: "Thus, not only does democracy make every man forget his ancestors, but it hides his descendants and separates his contemporaries from him; it throws him back forever upon himself alone and threatens in the end to confine him entirely within the solitude of his own heart" (quoted in Halttunen 1982, 193).

By the 1870s, Halttunen argues, the single-minded emphasis on sincerity so evident in the antebellum advice books gave way to counsel of a different sort. The advice and success books published after 1870 typically advocate aggressiveness and charm and the skillful management of appearances. "The central skill demanded within the new success formula was the art of social manipulation that had been cultivated to perfection by the antebellum [confidence man]" (1982, 207). Meanwhile, the specter of the confidence man himself all but disappears from the post-Civil War advice literature. What did not disappear, however, and what is still with us, as Giddens stresses again and again in his analysis of modernity, is what I called earlier the interpretive or epistemological problem as distinct from the moral or pragmatic problem of how to behave amid the leveling tendencies and urbanization of the early nineteenth century on the one hand, and in the emerging corporate world of the later nineteenth century on the other. It may be that "In the success mythology of twentieth-century corporate America, the confidence man has been effectively welcomed into the mainstream of American middle-class culture," as Halttunen concludes; but one may be permitted one's doubts (210).

The interpretive problem of reliably assessing what another is up to not only is not resolved by advocating and cultivating the arts of deception; it is exacerbated. The interpretive problem is inherently formidable. Encounters with strangers in situations of high risk make the problem as consequential as it is epistemologically daunting. Consequential contact with strangers presumed skilled in the arts of deception makes reliable assessment of their true motives and plans as difficult as it is imperative. Discovering and implementing reliable techniques of penetrating deliberate deception is thus big business—and has been for well over a century. At bottom, the quest for those techniques aims at connecting aspects of "interiority" with visible behavioral correlates in a systematic and predictable way.[3] Ideally, such correlates would be immune to conscious manipulation. Before looking briefly at the history of those efforts, however, I first want to touch on some other responses to the problem of trust posed by the democratizing and urbanizing trends of the antebellum period; then I will examine briefly Erving Goffman's analysis of "relations in public."

In *Humbug: The Art of P. T. Barnum*, Neil Harris describes the success of Barnum's American Museum, "the most popular institution of its kind in the country" by 1851, and offers an explanation for its popularity in terms of an "operational aesthetic" emergent in the 1830s and 1840s. Barnum's American Museum combined exposure and deception, and its appeal, Harris argues, rested on the willingness of large numbers of Americans to seek amusement admixed with deceit and to find pleasure in experiencing deception while learning its mechanics. Barnum's museum, as well as his hoaxes, Harris asserts, "trained Americans to absorb knowledge. This was an aesthetic of the operational, a delight in observing process and examining for literal truth" (1973, 79). This taste for exposure and problem solving appears throughout the fiction of the day, most notably, as Harris acknowledges, in Poe's "famous studies of criminal detection" (85). Like Barnum, Poe acts simultaneously as an exposer and a deceiver in such stories as "The Murders in the Rue Morgue," and both men were responding to and exploiting the problematic relationship between appearance and reality as experienced particularly in the growing cities. The implications of pervasive suspicion for the issue of trust, or what Harris calls "social confidence," are also thematized in fiction by Cooper and Hawthorne, but especially in Melville's last novel, *The Confidence Man* (1857), which focuses explicitly on the problem— maintaining confidence in the face of deceit and deception—that exercised so many of his contemporaries.

Both sociological theory, at the high level of abstraction offered by Giddens, and the circumstantial historical evidence contained in nineteenth-century advice books suggest the scope and consequentialty of the problems associated with trust under the conditions of modernity. Our understanding of these problems is enriched by Erving Goffman's fine-grained analysis of behavior in public places, especially his chapter on "normal appearances" in *Relations in Public* (1971). The settings for Goffman's account, the sites for his "naturalistic observations," are those urban spaces and places where most of the persons encountered are strangers. The overall conceptual framework for Goffman's analysis is explicitly Darwinian. The world divides into predators and quarry. Their respective survival depends on different skills, but both groups have a common stake in, and share common skills associated with, monitoring what Goffman calls "normal appearances": "When the world immediately around the individual portends nothing out of the ordinary, when the world appears to allow him to continue his routines . . . we can say that he will sense that appearances are 'natural' or 'normal.' . . . normal appearances mean that it is safe and sound to continue on with the activity at hand with only peripheral attention given to checking up on the stability of the environment" (1971, 239).

Survival requires that the individual monitor his environment for signs of danger and be appropriately responsive when such signs are perceived. "If individuals were not highly responsive to hints of danger or opportunity, they would not be responsive enough; if they carried this response far on every occasion of its occurrence, they would spend all their time in a dither and have no time for all the other things required for survival" (239). Normal appearances, so long as they remain so, need only minimal monitoring, allowing the individual to get on with his other projects; the perception that things are as expected facilitates "disattention." It goes without saying that normal appearances are relative and context specific; "whatever range of risk and opportunity an environment contains, the individual exposed to these considerations typically comes to terms with them, making what adjustments are necessary in order to routinely withdraw his main attention and get on with other matters" (239–40).

Normal appearances arise in, and are sustained by, the actions and interactions of individuals engaged in the normal round of day-to-day routine. Over time, the individual comes to possess a finely tuned sense of normal appearances, but one that is typically unconscious in the sense of being taken for granted. To make the constitutive details of normal appearances the object of consciousness requires effort and training. Such training is required of those who would utilize normal appearances to disguise the true nature of their activities—"agents of deceit," whether spies, forgers, con artists, or whatever; and such training is equally required of those who would penetrate their disguises—counterespionage agents and law enforcement officers, for example. The particulars that constitute normal appearing will thus be of crucial concern to those who wish to avoid giving alarm or arousing suspicion about the nature of their activities, whether they be predators or hunt-ers of predators. Mastery of normal appearances offers the best disguise: "To disappear from sight, to melt from view, is not, then, to hide or to sneak away; it is to be present but of no concern"—that is, to be thoroughly and unambiguously (hence safely) "disattendable" (Goffman 1971, 257; Hood 1990, 179).[4]

To carry off a disguise of this sort successfully, particularly over a long period of time, is demanding work. "Those who conceal matters under what is normal appearances for another will have two different things to conceal: the facts of the matter and the fact that they are making an effort to conceal them" (Goffman 1971, 261–62).[5] The latter requires finely honed skills of emotional control and management in addition to presence of mind capable of coming up quickly with "the kind of accountings that allow a disturbing event to be assimilated to the normal" (263; Le Carré 1974, 39–41).

Alternatively, the individual who suspects something is up may find it necessary to conceal his suspicions as well as to suppress any anxiety arising from those suspicions, lest he reveal them and in doing so possibly endanger himself. He may need to become conscious of his routines without betraying that he has become so, on the one hand, and without sinking into a debilitating preoccupation with self-presentation, on the other. Both acts, if they are to be successful, require presence of mind and well-developed skills and competence in emotional control in order to sustain the normal appearances that will insure that the individual remains safely "disattendable" and so able to carry on with his own projects, whatever those may be.

In Goffman's analysis, everyday encounters with strangers in public places demand of individuals some of the same personal qualities and traits linked by other analysts of modernity to the requirements of bureaucracy and technological production. Peter Berger's account of the impact of technological production on consciousness places special emphasis on the control of spontaneous emotionality required by production-line work, for example, and argues that the complexity of the production process also "necessitates a particular tension of consciousness characterized by a quick alertness to ever-changing constellations of phenomena" (Berger, Berger, and Kellner 1973, 37). Similarly, Kenneth Kenniston, in assessing the demands of modern work, particularly in the professions, emphasizes the salience of dispassionateness: the trained capacity to remain cool under stress, to be able to adapt rapidly to changing circumstances, and the ability to concentrate and resist distraction. To these qualities can be added the skills in impression management Giddens emphasizes in his analysis of behavior at those access points where experts or bureaucratic functionaries interact with clients.

Impression management in these settings involves a measure of acting, in the theatrical sense, and hence a measure of deception; but the deception involved is generally benign and ordinarily makes limited demands on the experienced individual. However, for those whose business it is to mask their nefarious purposes with innocent appearances, the demands of impression management are very great, requiring, as Goffman remarks, "the [constant] production of normal appearances under freshly difficult circumstances" (1971, 260). For those whose business it is to penetrate the systematic counterfeiting of normal appearances, the demands are arguably even greater, since one must not only allay the enhanced wariness expected of one's duplicitous quarry, but also contend with the interpretive problem at its most difficult—namely, when an actor is engaged in doing everything in his power to prevent others from understanding what he is truly up to. For the time being, it is enough to say that investigators, whether in fiction or in real life, are especially subject to these demands. Put differently, "investigation," as a process, effectively condenses essential and intrinsic elements of modernity. Before I explore that, however, I want to consider in more detail the intensive efforts, extending over more than a century, to discover reliable techniques of "deception detection," given the scope modernity affords for the practice of deception.

The paradigmatic problem, as noted earlier, is to establish reliable linkages and their indices between "interiority" and the external, observable "surface" of another's behavior. The most useful linkages, offering the most reliable indices, would be those not subject to the control of the will. In the antebellum period, phrenology offered a persuasive answer, if only for a short time, to the challenge of linking mind and behavior so that the former could be read off the latter with some confidence. Assuming that the mind was divided into discrete faculties, theorists of phrenology like Franz Joseph Gall further argued that the contours of the skull mirrored the contours of the brain, which in turn displayed the relative presence or absence of the various mental faculties. The more "amativeness" possessed by a subject, for example, the greater the bulge in the brain at the point believed to be the localized seat of that faculty. Conversely, a depression on the brain's surface revealed a deficiency in a given faculty. Assuming that the skull exhibited the contours of the brain, phrenologists were prepared to read a subject's mental endowment from a close and systematic examination of the configuration of the subject's head. Popularized in this country by Orson and Lorenzo Fowler and their brother-in-law, Samuel Wells, phrenology offered a means for improving self-knowledge, a basis for counseling (a betrothed couple could assess their mutual compatibility, for example), and insight into the great men of history, whose cranial endowments explained the basis of their achievements (Hanson 1993, 200–205).[6]

The knowledge claims of phrenology were short-lived, but the impetus behind phrenology endures, as the work of Paul Ekman and others amply demonstrates. Dedicated to Erving Goffman, *Telling Lies* (1985) summarizes Ekman's years of research aimed at answering such questions as: Are there behavioral clues to deceit? If so, what are they? And how reliable are they? Ekman's choice of epigraphs is suggestive. His first, from Goffman's *Strategic Interaction*, bears directly on the matter of normal appearances: "When the situation seems to be exactly what it appears to be, the closest likely alternative is that the situation has been completely faked; when fakery seems extremely evident, the next most probable possibility is that nothing fake is present" (Ekman 1985, 7). The second, which echoes Goffman's deepest commitments in *Relations in Public*, is from critic George Steiner's *After Babel*: "The relevant framework is not one of morality but *survival*. At every level, from brute camouflage to poetic vision, the linguistic capacity to conceal, misinform, leave ambiguous, hypothesize, invent is *indispensable* to the equilibrium of human consciousness and to the development of man in society" (Ekman 1985, 7; emphasis added). On the other hand, if everyone could lie perfectly, "If treachery was as easy with emotions as with ideas, if expressions and gestures could be disguised and falsified as readily as words, our emotional lives would be impoverished and more guarded than they are" (283). Our imperfect ability to lie sets two puzzles: one interpretive, one finally and inescapably moral. The first is neatly captured in a "crucial problem in detecting deception: it is next to impossible to distinguish the innocent boy's *fear of being disbelieved* from the guilty boy's detection apprehension. The signs of fear would be the same" (51). The moral issue has to do with the power conferred by the ability to detect deception, the uses to which such knowledge might be put, and the potential, perhaps inevitable, violation of another that is entailed in successful detection.

Reflecting on the deeper interest of his project beyond the purely pragmatic uses to which his research findings might be put, Ekman suggests its implications for sorting out the voluntary from the involuntary "parts of our own life, to learn how well we can deliberately control the outward signs of our inner life" (1985, 281). The capacity to accomplish this sorting out predictably and reliably, however, raises moral issues that, in the end, cannot be evaded: "*sometimes* lie catching violates a relationship, betrays trust, steals information that was not, for good reason, given. The lie catcher should realize at least that detecting clues to deceit is a presumption—it takes without permission, despite the other person's wishes" (282). In short, skill at the detection of lying confers power, as does skill at deception. "Natural liars, highly skilled in deceit *but not without conscience*, should be able to capitalize upon their talent in certain professions—as actors, salesmen, trial lawyers, negotiators, spies, or diplomats," Ekman notes without hint of irony (57, emphasis added). Those who come to possess superior skills at deception or its detection may thereby become suspect. How will they use the power their skills give them? "Such stability as the individual has in his *Umwelt*," Goffman reminds us, "derives from the fact that the right information is not in the wrong hands" (1971, 319).

The emergence of the detective in the nineteenth century as someone whose occupation inescapably involved penetrating deception was fraught with moral ambiguity. It could hardly have been otherwise. The emergent occupation—its defenders and advocates such as Allan Pinkerton would call it a "profession"—posed acutely the dilemma that underwrote the antebellum advice books: how to act effectively, successfully, in the new world of the cities without becoming corrupted in the process. For those charged with organizing metropolitan police forces, the question was as important as it was vexing. The problem, Carl Klockars writes, "was to construct an image for the new role of detective that would be acceptable to the public," given the contempt in which the entrepreneurial, avocational police of the early nineteenth century were held, particularly in England (1985, 65).

Using the rise of the metropolitan police in London as a case study, Klockars argues that the new role of detective had to be carefully and persuasively distinguished from the despised roles traditionally associated with private policing: those of police informer, of thief taker, and of agent provocateur. The first was essentially a police spy, paid to betray others. Objections to the police informer, rooted in widespread hostility to the harshness of English criminal law, created sympathy for criminals. The architects of the New Police countered the objection by tying the idea of the police detective to the crime of murder, the most serious of crimes and hence the least likely to create sympathy for its perpetrator or to perpetuate objections to the detective as informer. Objections to the role of thief taker centered on their skills in blackmail, perjury, and receiving stolen property, but especially on their unwillingness to work unless their fees were guaranteed (Klockars 1985, 66). The latter objection was met by making detectives salaried public officials.

Of the three stereotypes of police detective, the most contemptible of all, hence the most important to counter, was the agent provocateur, the police agent who led innocent individuals into criminal activity in order to arrest them for the reward offered for their capture (1985, 65–66). "What could prevent the new detective from creating crimes and criminals for personal, political, or financial reasons?" (79). Klockars argues that the solution to the problem lay in the convention of the *case*: "the defining attribute of the idea of the detective, case imposed a temporal barrier between the detective and the crime" (80). The detective would act only in response to the commission of a crime. The case not only made it possible to distinguish absolutely the new detective from the despised figure of the agent provocateur; it also gave police detectives two important rights that qualified them for professional status: control over the organization of their working time and a large measure of personal discretion in the conduct of their cases (81). In these ways, the architects of the New Police successfully countered the existing negative stereotypes associated with what the newly established police detectives would do: investigate crimes, especially murder, and apprehend those committing them. The means by which those ends might be accomplished, however, were and remain intrinsically problematic and susceptible of abuse.

The moral ambiguity associated with detective work in the nineteenth century is evident in the memoir of George S. McWatters, *Knots Untied; or, Ways and By-ways in the Hidden Life of American Detectives*. McWatters served for twelve years as a detective with the New York City metropolitan police before he resigned in 1870. Prior to that, he had worked as a private detective after returning to New York from a brief stint in the California gold fields during the height of the gold rush. In offering *Knots Untied* to the public, McWatters hoped to enlarge "the security of the innocent from the machinations of the depraved,—by the detail of certain wily 'offenses against the law and good order of society,' while demonstrating therein how sure of final discovery and punishment are the criminally vicious, however crafty and subtle, in these days, when the art of police detection has become almost an exact science" (1871, iv; Gilbert 1976).

In his final chapter, "The Detective System," McWatters defends detective work as a necessary and decisive contribution to maintaining social order. "Society creates, for the most part, the crimes it punishes," he acknowledges (643). It was the lax morality of business life, the hypocrisy of society, and the driving preoccupation with wealth that created the social dislocations the detective was then called upon to alleviate. The real law of society, the highest practical morality, is simple: "buy cheap and sell dear," a principle manifest in stock manipulations, in landlords charging all that the traffic would bear regardless of the value of their investment, and in monopolistic practices designed to reduce competition and drive wages as low as possible. Society consisted of the "tramplers and the trampled," and the detective, McWatters admitted, belonged among the former: "He is dishonest, crafty, unscrupulous, when necessary to be so. He tells black lies when he cannot avoid it; and white lying, at least, is his chief stock in trade. He is the outgrowth of a diseased and corrupted state of things, and is, consequently, morally diseased himself. His very existence is a satire upon society" and defensible only to the extent that his "rogueries and villainies" are done in the name of the people's security (648–49). The detective's calling is the only one in which "hypocrisy is elevated into a really useful and beneficent art" (649). Resort to devious means in the service of a good end might be less corrupting than engaging in falsehood and deception for mere self-aggrandizement, but the conditions of the detective's life would never elevate or ennoble him, although he might ease his conscience in the knowledge that he is "operating as an aid to justice" (649). McWatters was unwilling, however, to let the matter rest there. The detective, he recognized, helped to sustain the status quo and was tainted by that very fact. He was necessary, for the most skillful among the criminal classes had become too cunning for ordinary police procedures, but he was also the inevitable consequence of a system that placed a premium on results over means.

McWatters's detective is cunning and subtle, possessing a general and accurate knowledge of "human nature"—a characteristic he shared with the confidence man of the antebellum advice books. The detective is knowledgeable about business practices, and has acquired a broad understanding of the "criminal classes." He is ever alert for the unexpected, "for however deep his theories, or well laid his plans, some accident or incident, apparently trifling in itself, may occur to give him in a moment more light than he might otherwise obtain in a month's searching and study" (1871, 115). In recounting various cases, most of them involving crimes against property—fraud, forgery, theft, embezzlement—McWatters shows himself to be adept at disguise, undertaken sometimes on short notice, and clever at impersonation. He is, in fact, an accomplished actor in the theatrical sense and skilled at improvising on the spot when the occasion demands. He clearly possesses that presence of mind Goffman properly regards as crucial to someone feigning the role of another as well as counterfeiting the normal appearances involved in that role. In short, a master of plausible dissembling, McWatters is, and knows himself to be, indistinguishable, in terms of his skills and knowledge, from the confidence men he hunts, save for one thing: "operating as an aid to justice," the detective could ease his conscience to the degree that his efforts resulted in justice (649). McWatters remained ambivalent, however, about the disjuncture between ends and means required in detection—the unavoidable black lies, the routine white lies.

Not so Alan Pinkerton, whose *Thirty Years a Detective* echoes McWatters's description of the detective—but without a trace of ambivalence. Since mid-century, the American detective "has undergone a complete metamorphosis," Pinkerton proclaimed. "His calling has become a profession, and himself an intelligent, keen sighted and accomplished gentleman, relying upon his own high moral character, his superior intelligence and his indefatigable energy for the success which he has attained" (1886, 16–17). The successful criminal, anticipating efforts at detection, will have solved the crucial problem of "how to accomplish their objects, and yet succeed in shrouding themselves from detection" (18). The detective, therefore, "must be possessed of a mind which is the equal, and, if possible, the superior of his antagonist" (18).

Elaborating on the qualities of the effective detective, Pinkerton portrays a skilled manipulator of appearances in a passage Goffman might have cited in support of his dissection of normal appearances:

> [The detective] must appear the careless, ordinary individual, particularly to those upon whom he is to operate. Assimilating, as far as possible, with the individuals who are destined to feel the force of his authority, and by appearing to know but little, acquire all the information possible to gather from every conceivable source, and in the least curious or inquisitorial manner.
>
> Possessed of an ability to adapt himself to every association in which he may find himself, and at the same time prolific in resources, he must be prepared at all times when emergencies arise which require quick conceptions and ready subterfuges. To-day, his associates may be the lowest orders of humanity, and to-morrow he mingles with the best elements of the social community. He must at all times be upon his guard, ever ready to take advantage of the most trifling circumstances, and yet, with an outward demeanor that dispels suspicion and invites the fullest confidence.
>
> The profession of the detective is, at once, an honorable and highly useful one. . . . He is an officer of justice, and must himself be pure and above reproach. (1886, 18–19)

Pinkerton's detective is equally a master dissembler and a man of honor, quick to react to an emergency with "ready subterfuges," but at heart "pure and above reproach" (cf. Aubrey and Caputo 1980, 79ff). In the quick shift from the one to the other, Pinkerton invokes the terms of the dilemma that exercised the authors of antebellum guide books: namely, how to get on safely and successfully in a world where charlatanry is common without succumbing to charlatanism oneself. But Pinkerton appears to have had no interest in exploring the issue. Pinkerton headed the nation's largest and best known (and, in some quarters, most notorious) private detective agency. His interest clearly lay in defusing a deeply unsettling issue and in asserting the trustworthiness of his operatives, whose skills in the arts of the confidence man could be put to good use without moral qualm or suspicion. George McWatters, on the other hand, was much freer to explore the moral ambiguity associated with detection in general and private detection in particular. He had resigned from the New York police force over a matter of principle prior to publishing *Knots Untied*. A self-made man, like Pinkerton, although on a lesser scale, McWatters bespeaks his deep ambivalence about the basis and meaning of success in general and his own in particular in his stark division of society into the (few) tramplers and the (many) trampled. He and his former colleagues and associates belonged to the former, as did their masters, the men of property and wealth who needed the services of detectives; but McWatters's sympathies lay with the latter, from whose ranks he had himself come. The moral ambiguity inherent in being an effective detective has exercised many writers of detective fiction, a matter I take up in chapter 6.

Modernity poses a problem of meaningfulness for individuals and groups alike, growing out of its characteristic features of pluralism and secularism. Under the conditions of modernity, the more or less unified "life-world" of the premodern individual gives way to the experience of plural life-worlds that resist unification, and therefore meaningful integration. The dichotomization of modern life into public and private, together with the withdrawal of religion into the private sphere and the domination of the public sphere by the scientific and the rational requires that the individual move between two different, "often severely discrepant worlds of meaning and experience" (Berger, Berger and Kellner 1973, 64). To revert to a general example already given, the prudent and pragmatic wariness appropriate to the public sphere of competitive endeavor is, in Giddens's analysis, dysfunctional in the world of intimate personal relationships.

Functional rationality bestows the capacity to do something without endowing the activity with meaning. Over the last century, our capacity to do has expanded enormously, in large measure driven by scientific discovery and technologically induced economic growth. But in Murray Murphey's tart formulation, we now confront "the paradox of a society in which the capacity to do is developed beyond any historical example, but in which no one is certain what is worth doing" (1979, 163). Neither before nor after the fact is functional rationality much use, it turns out, in rendering activity meaningful. That requires setting the activity in some wider context. Traditionally, religion provided the basis for meaningfully integrating the various sectors of social life, but the gradual withdrawal of religion into the private sphere—the secularization of the public sphere—means that the integrative function of religion, its capacity to locate phenomena in a comprehensive overarching framework, is greatly reduced in modern society, in part because religious belief is seen to be in competition with other belief systems, notably science, in the business of understanding and explaining phenomena and events (Berger 1967; Berger, Berger and Kellner 1973, 63–82). Particularly in need of explanation, at the individual level, are the unexpected events that seriously harm persons who appear neither to have brought the injury upon themselves nor to deserve it. Stories of seemingly inexplicable personal tragedy are a staple of feature journalism; they insistently raise the question: Why? In doing so, they call into question the taken-for-granted reality of everyday life and our capacity to understand and explain certain classes of events—namely, those in which "bad things happen to good people." Put differently, these events, and the stories we tell about them, raise unsettling questions about meaning. What is the meaning of a particular instance of unexpected, uninvited, seemingly unmerited suffering? Solving a murder—the central convention of detective fiction throughout its history—illuminates central features and tensions of modernity. Works of detective fiction—"murder mysteries"—are never simply "whodunits." They are always "whydunits." However perfunctorily, works of detective fiction explicate motive, the psychological rationale underlying the act that brings the case into being. As works of detective fiction have become more "novelistic," the emphasis on motive has become more explicit.

2

Knowing Others Better (than They Know You)

> *The first condition of having to deal with somebody at all is to know with whom one has to deal.*
>
> Georg Simmel, "Knowledge of One Another"

> *The good news is that I know why I do things. The bad news is—so does everyone else.*
>
> overheard by the author outside the Stouffer Hotel, Nashville, 30 October 1994

The "realist" in murder, according to Raymond Chandler, writes of a world characterized by deceptive appearances: "a world in which the nice man down the hall is a boss of the numbers racket" (Chandler 1995). In such a world it becomes crucially important to know the motives and intentions of those with whom one interacts and to be careful in disclosing oneself to others: whatever stability "the individual has in his *Umwelt* derives in part from the fact that the right information is not in the wrong hands" (Goffman 1971, 319). In such a world, the problem of other minds looms large indeed. That problem, "premised on the separateness of persons, is how one mind can know what is in the mind of another," if all we have access to is their behavior (Hollis 1994, 146). Writ large, the problem of other minds is the problem of understanding another culture. Whether posed with respect to an individual or to another culture, it is the generic epistemological problem of the social sciences, and as Goffman's work reveals, it is a problem of everyday life (Goffman 1971; Hollis 1987; Murphey 1994). It is also an issue that lies at the heart of much detective fiction, including especially works by Edgar Allan Poe, Dashiell Hammett, and

John Buchan—exemplars and prototypes, respectively, of the ratiocinative detective story, the hard-boiled detective novel, and the espionage thriller.

Modernity exacerbates the problem of other minds generally, for the reasons explored in chapter 1: increasing interdependence requires trust, which in turn hinges on an assessment of the real motives and intentions of others. The problem becomes especially acute, however, when someone purposefully engages in deception, for whatever reason. And when deception is undertaken to mask criminal or hostile intent, the problem of other minds can become consequential indeed. That is the form the problem typically takes in mystery fiction.

To deal effectively with the problem of other minds in this acute form, the fictional detective or agent relies on two broad sets of skills and related knowledge that make up an essential aspect of his or her stance in the particular fictional world the writer has created. On the one hand are the skills involved in reading others accurately. These skills have both a methodological and a cognitive dimension—comprising techniques of observation as well as knowledge of what to look for. Both are culturally constrained, and over the history of the detective story, we would expect to see some variation in the cognitive component particularly. When phrenology was in vogue and credible, for example, it made perfect sense to pay close attention to the contours of someone's head, and consequently to describe a fictional detective as doing so. A writer today, fresh from a reading of Paul Ekman's *Telling Lies*, might have his or her fictional detective looking for telltale signs of deception in facial expression: a false smile, pupil dilation, mistakes in coordinating gesture and expression.[1] However the feat is accomplished, reading the other aims at understanding them; it aims at penetrating or unmasking deception to ascertain the true nature of the other's motives and intentions. Understanding the other well renders that person transparent and thereby permits one to anticipate and predict how that person will behave in certain circumstances.

Reading others and reading physical clues have this much in common: both aim at linking the visible and observable with the invisible and unobservable by means of what amounts to a causal theory. In the case of the former, observable features of behavior—a shift of the eyes, a quick intake of breath—are taken as manifestations of some interior state (e.g., guilt or apprehension) that is otherwise accessible only to the individual who experiences it. Seeking to make sense of behavioral clues, the observer construes the observable feature as the effect of the unobservable cause—in short, as an index of the other's otherwise inaccessible interiority.

Similarly, physical clues are the observable residue of events or processes that occurred in the past and so cannot be observed directly. Correctly interpreting physical clues assumes a <u>causal connection between what remains physically in the present and some (postulated) past activity</u>. The detective is perforce a historian of sorts, and the historian something of a detective—an analogy that has not been lost either on historians or on writers of detective fiction (Winks 1969).[2] William Sanders extends the analogy to sociology and concludes his study of police investigation with this observation: "every finding about detective investigation came to be a finding about sociological research" (1977, 207; see also Sanders 1974).

In addition to skills and knowledge associated with penetrating and unmasking deception and interpreting physical evidence, the detective, and especially the secret agent, possesses skills, and the requisite knowledge, to frustrate an adversary's efforts to understand him or her. These are skills of acting and dissembling that render the detective opaque to the other's best efforts at discovering what he or she suspects or knows or intends to do.

In the analyses presented here of selected works of mystery fiction, the fundamental stance of the detective or investigator involves an <u>asymmetrical relationship of knowledge, and hence of power</u>.[3] The detective must come to know the other better than the other is allowed to know the detective. Establishing and maintaining that asymmetry enables the detective to identify, unmask, and entrap the other and simultaneously permits the detective to survive in a tricky and dangerous world of predators—tramplers, as George McWatters called the forgers, embezzlers, counterfeiters, and confidence men he hunted successfully in the 1850s and 1860s. Knowing the other involves knowledge and understanding of individuals both as individuals—that is, in their rich circumstantiality and idiosyncrasy—and as members of particular groups or occupants of particular social roles, who thereby possess the special knowledge associated with the group or role—especially the knowledge of the cultural rules that structure and inform role-specific behavior.

Murray Murphey's "Explanation, Causes, and Covering Laws" (1986), on the explanatory potential of cultural rules, is relevant to my argument. Murphey is interested in determining whether cultural rules, properly understood, can be said to function as laws in explaining human action, the way scientific laws explain natural phenomena. Cultural rules, Murphey acknowledges, appear at first glance to have little in common with natural laws. Cultural rules are human constructions. They are learned and transmitted by way of symbol systems, especially in and through the medium of language; and they are normative and prescriptive. They define what ought to be done, not what people actually do. Thus, knowing that a cultural rule exists in a particular society "does not tell us what behavior is actually performed" (1986, 52). Deviance from cultural rules tends to create a record, however, and where they exist, Murphey argues, we can use these records to estimate and state the degree of conformity to the rule in question, sometimes with a very high probability "that a given individual actor in that society acted according to that rule, *or will so act*" (52, emphasis added). When "conformity statements," as Murphey calls them, carry a high enough probability, they may serve as "covering" generalizations that have explanatory force. This is so because an individual's conformity to a cultural rule involves both knowing and deliberately following it. In other words, following a cultural rule is the outcome of a rational decision process within a structure of well-understood expectations and sanctions.

Murphey concludes that conformity statements—statements, based on adequate deviance data, that a particular individual actor in a given society acted, or is likely to act, according to a particular cultural rule—permit prediction, support counterfactuals, and explain human behavior as voluntary rule conformity. Such conformity statements, or covering generalizations, thus have explanatory power and can perform the function of general laws in history: "That such generalizations do in fact explain human behavior has been demonstrated by many works in anthropology, which without discussing covering laws or other such matters have utilized cultural rules to account for behavior of people in societies all around the world" (1986, 57).

As a simple illustration, consider the cultural rule (in the United States at least) that people drive on the right-hand side of the road. The rule prescribes—it does not describe—the behavior of American drivers; but deviance data—police and accident records, for example—suggest that conformity with this rule is very high. Drivers knowingly, and with a very high probability, conform to this rule, and their behavior is thereby explained. If that probability of rule compliance were to decline, however, it would be cause for concern. Indeed, such was the case several years ago when there appeared to be evidence of a decline in compliance with respect to traffic signals in the District of Columbia. Several well-publicized accidents and newspaper accounts of drivers ignoring red lights documented increasing deviance from the rule. For a time, there was something approaching a crisis of confidence in the behavior of other drivers in the District, and an accompanying sense of heightened risk at the diminished predictability of others' behavior.

It is their predictive power that makes Murphey's cultural rules most relevant to detective fiction. As noted earlier, close similarities exist between the task of the historian, seeking to explain past behavior on the basis of presently observable evidence, and that of the fictional detective, who is typically attempting to reconstruct the circumstances surrounding a crime, almost invariably murder, on the basis of surviving clues, knowledgeable individuals, or both. Moreover, detective fiction typically involves two stories or sequences of action. One is historical, involving the reconstruction and chronological ordering of past events in a causal sequence that accounts for whatever evidence exists in the case; the other involves efforts to apprehend the guilty party. The latter story may, and frequently does, turn on the detective's predictions of how that person is likely to act in certain circumstances. Murphey's conformity statements not only account for or explain past behavior with varying degrees of probability; they also support predictions of future behavior. To the degree that they carry a high degree of probability, such predictions constitute a powerful resource with which to manipulate a person's actions. In much detective fiction, predictions of future actions play a central role in the apprehension of the guilty party. Such predictions rest, finally, on knowing, with a high degree of probability, how a particular person will act in a given situation. Put differently, those predictions of future actions, if confirmed, constitute practical, context-specific solutions to the general problem of other minds.

In three stories written in the 1840s, Edgar Allan Poe introduced the prototypical fictional investigator, C. August Dupin.[4] Every subsequent fictional detective has a bit of Dupin in his makeup, although that is not to claim that every writer of detective fiction has necessarily read or is consciously indebted to Poe's stories (although many assuredly are). The first of these stories, "The Murders in the Rue Morgue," appeared in *Graham's Magazine* in April 1841, and brought Poe some attention for its "ingenuity." A year later he published "The Mystery of Marie Roget," based closely on the murder of Mary Cecilia Rogers, a case that had received extensive coverage in the New York press in the weeks following the discovery of her body on July 28, 1842. "The Purloined Letter," Poe's third tale featuring Dupin, was published in *The Gift*, a giftbook annual, for 1845.

Each of the stories illustrates and dramatizes the mental activity Poe called "analysis." "Analysis, or the *Analytic Method*," Charles Hutton wrote in a mathematics text Poe would have known, "is the art or mode of finding out the truth of a proposition, by first supposing the thing to be done, and then reasoning back, step by step, till we arrive at some known truth.—This is also called the *The Method of Invention*, or Resolution" (Hutton 1812, I:3). Like other mental phenomena, analysis was associated with its own specific faculty, the analytic faculty, and according to Poe could be known only in and through its effects. Exercising the analytic faculty afforded its possessor pleasure and enjoyment. Like other faculties, the analytic could be strengthened and invigorated by appropriate exercise. Wanting to make a sharp distinction between analysis and calculation, however, Poe discounted the value of mathematical study and dismissed the game of chess as unsuited to strengthening the analytic faculty. Chess, he argued, demands attention and concentration but does not depend on acumen and so cannot develop that invaluable trait. To foster acumen, Poe recommended checkers and especially the card game whist. The former required the winning player to identify with his opponent and thereby discover the means to outwit him. Whist, however, offered the best exercise of the analytic faculty. It not only demanded memory and a mastery of the rules of the game but required subtle observational skills that in turn depended on knowing what to look for in an opponent's behavior: "The necessary knowledge is that of *what* to observe," Poe insisted (1938, 51). What the analyst seeks to identify in the behavior of the other are those indexical gestures that reveal what the opponent is truly thinking. Poe implied that mental activity "leaks" into behavior as a matter of course, despite even the most careful monitoring of such disclosure on the part of the individual.

To illustrate the ability of the analyst to follow another's thoughts, Poe's narrator recounts an earlier incident with Dupin. On one of their walks, their conversation had flagged and each became lost in his own thoughts. After a period of fifteen minutes, however, the narrator was astonished at Dupin's making a remark that chimed with his own thinking at that moment, and he asked his companion for an explanation. Dupin obliged by reminding the narrator of the point at which they broke off their conversation and then went on to describe the various subtle behavioral clues, together with the inferences he drew from them, that led to his apposite remark.

Dupin's "method" crucially involves an intimate knowledge of the narrator as a particular individual as well as a theory of mental activity in general. In the incident described, the former—Dupin's intimate knowledge of his friend's history—amounts to a description of initial conditions, while the latter—Dupin's understanding of mental activity as an associative process—functions as a scientific law. Dupin's remark, which breaks their mutual silence, implies a correct description of the end conditions of the (lawlike, hence predictable) mental process in which his friend was engaged. The narrator's thinking, set in motion by a particular remark, can be expected to develop in and through a regular process of predictable association, the general outlines of which Dupin has mastered. Dupin is able to track the unfolding process of mental association by paying attention to subtle changes in his friend's demeanor and gait within the context of his knowledge of his friend's beliefs and experience. His theory of how the mind works, together with his understanding of his companion's particularity, permits Dupin to predict his companion's thoughts at a particular instant in time. In this situation, Dupin is on thoroughly familiar ground, while the narrator, oblivious to Dupin's scrutiny, has made no effort to monitor or control the behavioral clues that afford Dupin the basis for predicting the nature and pace of his companion's train of associations.

With the savage and initially inexplicable murder of two women in their apartment in the Rue Morgue, however, Poe's analyst is confronted with a situation in which his adversary, the unknown murderer, not only is absent but may have tried to eliminate any traces of his presence in the apartment. The rich stream of behavioral clues available at the whist table or over the checker board is drastically thinned out. Dupin is left to make do with newspaper accounts and observations and discoveries made during a visit to the crime scene. The introduction of murder into the story greatly increases the stakes associated with the exercise of analysis, and serves to define an essential feature of Dupin's world. In his world, as in the growing cities of the 1840s, violent crime is a predictable, recurrent feature, bringing demands for its control, questions about its etiology, and debate about how and with what techniques and at what costs violent crime might be reduced.

In the final scene of "Murders in the Rue Morgue," Poe demonstrates that Dupin's command of analysis is equal to the challenge posed by the murders. Dupin's method, to repeat, is partly a matter of knowing what to look for, of how to structure observation. At the whist table, for example, he knows to pay attention to the manner in which a trick is played or a hand is sorted. In the physical absence of his opponent, he looks for "peculiarities," for the "outre" aspects of the crime, for what distinguishes this crime from others of which he has detailed knowledge. The solution depends on isolating the unique aspects of the case, which Dupin summarizes in a series of questions: What explains the witnesses' disagreement over the nature of a second voice heard at the time of the crime? How did the murderer exit an apparently locked room and then reach ground level if not by means of the staircase? What explains the violence of the crime? Nothing was missing from the apartment, and the women had led seemingly blameless lives. What then was the motive for, or the meaning of, the crime, if not robbery? Dupin seeks an explanatory argument that will organize the various peculiarities of the case, relate them systematically to each other, leave nothing material out, and specify a unique solution. Dupin's method also involves devising a means to confirm his inferences, which remain tentative and speculative until put to the test. Having concluded that the women were almost certainly killed by a large ape that had escaped from his master, very probably a sailor, Dupin places a newspaper advertisement claiming to have captured such a beast. A sailor turns up at Dupin's door in response to the ad, and Dupin persuades him to tell his story. The sailor's tale certifies the validity of Dupin's reasoning and his conclusions about what must have happened in the women's apartment.

In the wake of appreciation and admiration for "Murders in the Rue Morgue," Poe dismissed the apparent ingenuity displayed by his investigator, Dupin. In 1846, he wrote to the Southern author Philip Pendleton Cooke: "[my] tales of ratiocination owe most of their popularity to being something in a new key. I do not mean to say that they are not ingenious—but people think them more ingenious than they are. . . . In the 'Murders in the Rue Morgue,' for example, where is the ingenuity of unravelling a web which you yourself (the author) have woven for the express purpose of unravelling?" (Ostrom 1948, 2:328). "Murders in the Rue Morgue," Poe's first effort to dramatize the principles of detection, makes a claim about the efficacy of what he called analysis, but it is a limited claim, as his letter to Cooke makes clear. The mystery is one of his own devising and its details are wholly within his control as the author of the tale. The murders reported in the story merely resemble the sorts of crimes that were beginning to receive extensive newspaper coverage in New York and elsewhere, and any resemblance to an actual murder disappears when Poe reveals the identity of the murderer, an orangutan.

In "The Mystery of Marie Roget," however, Poe took the extraordinary step of trying to demonstrate that the principles of analysis introduced in "The Murders in the Rue Morgue" were sufficient to solve an actual murder. "I am just now putting the concluding touch to . . . 'The Mystery of Marie Roget'—a Sequel to 'The Murders in the Rue Morgue,' " Poe wrote to Joseph Snodgrass on June 4, 1842.

> The story is based upon that of the real murder of Mary Cecelia Rogers, which created so vast an excitement, some months ago, in New-York. . . . [U]nder the pretence of showing how Dupin . . . unravelled the mystery of Marie's assassination, I, in fact, enter into a very rigorous analysis of the *real* tragedy in New-York. No *point* is omitted. . . . I really believe, not only that I have demonstrated the falsity of the idea that the girl was ⟨not⟩ the victim of a gang ⟨as supposed⟩, but have *indicated the assassin*. My main object, however . . . is the analysis of the *principles of investigation* in cases of like character. (Ostrom 1948, 1:201–2; emphasis in original)

Poe's claim to have solved the Rogers case has been challenged by John E. Walsh, who concludes that between the initial publication of the story in *The Ladies' Companion* (November and December 1842 and February 1843) and its reprinting in his *Tales* (1845) Poe made a series of revisions intended to strengthen the probability that Mary Rogers had died as the result of a bungled abortion attempt rather than at the hands of a naval officer or a roving gang. Poe made these changes, Walsh argues, because new evidence in the case became public in mid-November of 1842, by which time the second installment of "Marie Roget" was already on sale. Whether Poe actually made changes in the final installment, which appeared not in January as scheduled but in February, remains unclear, but the unusual delay in the publication of the third installment may have been caused, Walsh suggests, by Poe's making a handful of final, strategic revisions so as to suggest that he had, in fact, reasoned to the probable circumstances of her death as indicated by the new evidence.

In "The Purloined Letter," Poe again located and defined the methodological center of "analysis" in a game analogy and in the achievement of imaginative identification with one's opponent. The premise of the story is well known: a courtier, the Minister D——, has managed to steal an indiscrete letter from a member of the royal family and is using the threat of disclosure to further his own political ends. The problem confronting Dupin is twofold. First he must discover the location of the letter Minister D—— has stolen and secreted, almost certainly somewhere in his living quarters. Second, having located it, Dupin must devise means to retrieve it and return it to its rightful owner. Despite the fact that the police have repeatedly searched the minister's apartment with no success, Dupin is convinced the letter must be readily available to the minister and consequently must be hidden in the minister's living quarters.

Dupin's conviction regarding the likely whereabouts of the letter rests more on his understanding of the situational constraints facing the minister than on his knowledge of the minister per se; but his plan to discover the location of the letter in the minister's apartment depends crucially on his understanding of D—— as a man having certain traits and possessing knowledge associated with specific cultural roles. The minister is bold, daring, and accustomed to intrigue—someone "who dares all things, those unbecoming as well as those becoming a man" (Poe 1938, 209). In addition to being a bold courtier, however, the minister combines the talents of both mathematician and poet. It is the combination of these two talents that Dupin recognizes as crucial to understand and take into account in attempting to defeat the minister.

Dupin's knowledge, perhaps even his observation, of the minister's past actions presumably provides the basis for his assessment of D——'s salient personality traits—the degree of boldness and daring typical of a wily, ambitious, and experienced court politician. But any predictions about how the minister will act in a given situation depend crucially as well on Dupin's recognition of the minister as an accomplished mathematician and poet. Dupin understands the minister most importantly in terms of his cultural roles and attainments, which involve specific training, knowledge, modes of expression, and especially patterns of thinking. "Such a man," Dupin reasons, "could not fail to be aware of the ordinary policial modes of action. He could not have failed to anticipate . . . the waylayings to which he was subjected. He must have foreseen . . . the secret investigations of his premises" and planned accordingly to defeat the anticipated search of his dwelling (1938, 218). Dupin concludes that the minister would necessarily be driven to "simplicity" in hiding the stolen letter and that, most probably, simplicity would take the form of "the comprehensive and sagacious expedient of not attempting to conceal [the letter] at all" (1938, 220).

If his assessment of the minister is correct, Dupin's conclusion that he will act in a certain way is reasonable; but Dupin's informed guess requires confirmation if it is to serve as the basis for a plan calculated to bring the minister down. Dupin proceeds to test his theory by calling on the minister in his apartment on a pretext. Wearing dark glasses so that the minister will not be able to see what he is looking at, Dupin carefully and systematically surveys the interior of the apartment and is gratified at last to see a letter, in plain view, that in the very degree of "radical difference" from the original invites suspicion "of a design to delude the beholder into an idea of the worthlessness of the document" (1938, 220–21). Dupin concludes that this is indeed the letter he seeks, and he proceeds to devise and execute a strategy designed to retrieve it for his royal patron.

During a second visit to the minister, a diversion planned by Dupin and timed to coincide with his visit distracts the minister's attention sufficiently for Dupin to replace the stolen letter with a facsimile without the minister's being aware of the switch. Dupin restores the original letter to a grateful prefect of police, thereby demonstrating his superiority both to the prefect and the minister. The prefect remains blind to the limitations of the unimaginative and unreflective measures of which he is so proud. Minister D—— proves to be insufficiently wary of Dupin, carelessly or arrogantly forgetful of having done Dupin a disservice on an earlier occasion. Dupin's defeat of the minister's plans is an act of revenge as well as fealty.

It should be noted that Minister D—— and Dupin both possess essentially the same skills of analysis or investigation. The process of inference by means of which the minister established the significance of the letter in the first place is identical with the process Dupin employs to reason to its probable hiding place in the minister's apartment.

The theft occurred during a meeting between the queen and the minister, which had been interrupted by a messenger bringing her the letter. She had read it immediately, and the minister, observing her expressions, concluded that the letter was a potential source of embarrassment to her. Acting boldly on his conviction, and without any opportunity to test his inference, D. had casually appropriated the letter when his hostess was momentarily distracted. Her failure to protest the theft reassured the minister that he now possessed a powerful hold over her. Whatever the letter's exact contents, she had good reason to keep them from her husband.

Analysis, Poe asserts at the beginning of "The Murders in the Rue Morgue," can only be approached in and through its effects. Like the faint star, it is most clearly seen out of the corner of the eye rather than confronted directly. As an experience, analysis is a pleasurable mental activity that "disentangles." Dupin, however, is less engaged in disentangling than in tracing, establishing, or divining the causes that account for the behavior of others or for the existence of physical evidence. Put differently, he is typically engaged in correctly determining the relationship of appearances to the underlying, hidden causes of which those appearances are the outward and necessary effects. The minister alters the appearance of the stolen letter so as to thwart the anticipated searches by the police. Dupin's achievement is to see through the minister's manipulation of appearances and to recognize the letter he seeks, despite its radically altered appearance. Similarly, in the locked apartment in the Rue Morgue, Dupin "sees" that the window must have provided the only possible means of escape available despite its appearance of being closed and securely locked. He confirms his theory by trying to raise the window and discovers that it only appeared to be nailed shut. Analysis rests on a "strict analogy" between the material and the immaterial, Dupin asserts in "The Purloined Letter," but given the manipulability of appearances, Poe's investigator is obliged to be cautious about how things seem, since they may have been arranged deliberately to mislead; at the same time he must be self-conscious about how his own behavior may inadvertently reveal his thoughts (1938, 219). Dupin dons dark glasses for his visit to the minister in order to conceal his careful inventory of his adversary's quarters.

In Dupin's world, then, every effect, correctly understood, has its true cause and every appearance its "reality." But that connection must be established in the face of appearances that always admit of at least two interpretations: things really are as they seem, or they have been carefully arranged to convey that (misleading) impression. It follows that for any particular "appearance," there are at least two causes, one of which is the deliberate manipulation of appearances for effect. In this instance, the letter on the minister's rack may be, in fact, the soiled, carelessly saved bit of correspondence it appears to be—or it may be the purloined letter. The altercation outside the minister's window may be spontaneous or it may be staged. The interpretive problem lies in determining which it is; and the starting point, for the investigator, is an attitude of skepticism, a recognition that while things may be what they seem, they also may not be. As the minister's insufficient wariness suggests, the safest stance in high stakes games is to assume that little, if anything, is as it seems and to remain alert and wary.

To the investigator's habitual skepticism about appearances must be added knowledge, something with which Poe did little in these stories but which subsequent writers have developed enormously. In "The Murders in the Rue Morgue," for example, bystanders reported a second voice coming from the women's apartment during the attack and speaking what seemed a foreign language, although there was no agreement among the witnesses as to which language was spoken or whether it might be the language of a madman. In describing his reconstruction of the crime, Dupin rejects the latter interpretation. Poe offers no justification but the inference seems clear: Dupin knows enough about the speech of madmen to conclude that a different explanation is needed to account for the features of the second voice heard by the bystanders. Dupin also knows something about poets generally and hence about the minister as a member of the class of poets, just as Dupin knows something about police search procedures and their limitations, and hence their exploitable weaknesses. Knowledge of the other involves knowing what roles they occupy as well as something about the knowledge specific to those roles. Dupin knows the prefect as a policeman and knows a good deal about police procedure as well. The prefect, like Dupin, knows the minister to be a poet, but, contemptuous of poets, he fails to appreciate how this aspect of the minister's identity might make him a particularly formidable adversary. Beyond his knowledge of how poets or mathematicians think, Dupin knows that mental activity proceeds by what amount to laws of association such that if sufficient particulars are known about a person, the analyst can effectively follow the exact course of the other's thinking, given a known stimulus or starting point.

In the same passage in "The Murders in the Rue Morgue" in which Poe spoke of the analytic as "disentangling," he also characterized it as a "moral" activity. Solving murders and releasing one's sovereign from the clutches of a ruthlessly ambitious courtier prepared to resort to blackmail would seem to qualify as moral acts, at least for those concerned with public safety or those of royalist persuasion. There is little in these stories, however, to suggest that Poe was troubled by any moral issues that might be associated with Dupin's investigative prowess; but the fact that Dupin and the minister are both accomplished practitioners of "analysis" suggests where a difficulty might lie. Poe characterizes the minister finally as "an unprincipled man of genius." By implication, Dupin is the converse, a principled man of genius. On the other hand, if it takes a thief to catch a thief, then Dupin's evident powers raise a question about means and ends. That question will be raised repeatedly by later writers of detective fiction, and it was a central issue raised in connection with the creation of police detective bureaus and with the operation of private detective agencies such as the Pinkerton agency throughout the latter part of the nineteenth century. It is an issue, too, in much espionage fiction. Finally, it is worth noting that if Poe played Dupin in the stories discussed above, he may be said to have played the Minister D—— in some of his other writings, notably the hoaxes for which he was well known in his day. Those hoaxes depend for their effect on "entangling" the reader in misleading but seemingly plausible appearances rather than illustrating and dramatizing the principles by which the "strict analogy" between the immaterial and the material can be revealed by analysis, despite deception and dissimulation.

Few writers of detective fiction have had as much to say about methods of investigation as Sir Arthur Conan Doyle in the four novels and fifty-six short stories that detail the exploits of Sherlock Holmes. "You know my methods, Watson" must be among the most widely recognized quotations from fiction. References to Holmes's methods are scattered throughout the stories, but most can be discussed under three headings: observation, knowledge, and that process of reasoning usually referred to in the stories as "deduction" but more properly understood as a form of abduction.[5]

Like Poe, whose work he knew well, Doyle distinguishes between observing and merely looking or seeing. The former is actively interpretive and meaning-seeking. It is the very basis for successful investigation. The latter is passive and unreflective, blind to the telling details of the world. "You see, but you do not observe," Holmes chides Watson on one occasion, pointing out that although he has climbed the stairs to Holmes's rooms numerous times, his companion cannot recall the number of stairs. "You have not observed. And yet you have seen. That is just my point" (Doyle 1927, 162). Observation is sometimes directed by expectation born of theory, as when Holmes finds a clue overlooked by the police. " 'I cannot think how I came to overlook it,' said the inspector with an expression of annoyance.' 'It was invisible, buried in the mud. I only saw it because I was looking for it,' " Holmes responds (1927, 343).

Observation is akin to curiosity, and both contribute to the vast and heterogenous knowledge on which Holmes depends for his successes. Some of this knowledge consists of an encyclopedic familiarity with other criminal cases: " 'As a rule . . . I am able to guide myself by the thousands of other similar cases which occur to my memory' " (1927, 176–77). Much of what Holmes knows has to do with the habitual, the customary, the typical, the usual, the probable, or the "natural." It has to do with knowledge of occupation, class, and gender. "When you see a man with whiskers of that cut and the 'Pink 'un' protruding out of his pocket, you can *always* draw him by a bet" (1927, 253; emphasis added). Visiting Watson at the beginning of "The Crooked Man," Holmes remarks that his friend has had that token of evil "the British workman" in the house: " 'He has left two nail-holes from his boot upon your linoleum just where the light strikes it' " (1927, 411). In "The Stock-broker's Clerk," Holmes becomes suspicious when his client reports that in joining a company he had been asked for a written declaration: Why? "Not as a business matter," Holmes suggests, "for these arrangements are usually verbal" (1927, 371). And in "A Scandal in Bohemia," Holmes relies upon his knowledge of female nature to discover where Irene Adler has hidden a compromising photograph he means to retrieve for his client: "When a woman thinks that her house is on fire, her instinct is at once to rush to the thing which she values most. It is a perfectly overpowering impulse, and I have more than once taken advantage of it. . . . A married woman grabs at her baby; an unmarried one reaches for her jewel-box. Now it was clear to me that our lady of to-day had nothing in the house more precious to her than what we are in quest of. She would rush to secure it" (1927, 173).

At its most specific, Holmes's knowledge is of the habits and tendencies of a particular individual. Holmes knows Watson well enough to break in on his thoughts, relying on the same combination of shifting facial expressions to reveal probable mental associations that Dupin utilized. " 'So, Watson,' said he, suddenly, 'you do not propose to invest in South African securities?' I gave a start of astonishment. Accustomed as I was to Holmes's curious faculties, this sudden intrusion into my most intimate thoughts was utterly inexplicable' " (1927, 511).

At its most general, Holmes's knowledge is of the hereditarian determinants of human features, behavior, and moral nature. His identification of the murderer in *The Hound of the Baskervilles* occurs when he recognizes the resemblance between a seventeenth-century portrait and the man who calls himself Stapleton: "The face of Stapleton had sprung out of the canvas. 'Ha, you see it now. My eyes have been trained to examine faces. . . . It is the first quality of a criminal investigator that he should see through a disguise. . . . [This] is an interesting instance of a throwback which appears to be both physical and spiritual' " (1927, 750). Professor Moriarty, at whose hands Doyle sought to rid himself of Holmes in "The Final Problem," is described as having "hereditary tendencies of the most diabolical kind. A criminal strain ran in his blood, which, instead of being modified, was increased and rendered more dangerous by his extraordinary mental powers" (1927, 470–71). In "The Reigate Puzzle," Holmes finds "traces of heredity . . . in the *p*'s and in the tails of the *g*'s" in a letter he concludes was written by two persons who were blood relatives. Holmes describes himself and his brother Mycroft in hereditarian terms in "The Greek Interpreter." Responding to Watson's suggestion that his skill at observation and deduction are the result of training, Holmes agrees that they are "to some extent," but goes on to explain: " 'My ancestors were country squires, who appear to have led much the same life as is natural to their class. But, none the less, my turn that way is in my veins, and may have come with my grandmother, who was the sister of Vernet, the French artist. Art in the blood is liable to take the strangest forms.' 'But how do you know that it is hereditary?' 'Because my brother Mycroft possesses it in a larger degree than I do,' " Holmes responds (1927, 435).

In addition to his knowledge of the habitual, customary, and natural

in human affairs, Holmes is knowledgeable about a wide range of arti-
facts and processes. He has a printer's knowledge of typefaces, for example, and a tobacconist's knowledge of cigars: " 'Oh, this is a
Havana, and these others are cigars of the peculiar sort which are im-
ported by the Dutch from their East Indian colonies. They are usually
wrapped in straw, you know, and are thinner for their length than
any other brand' " (1927, 432). He is an expert on tattoos, footprints,
handwriting, and perfume: " 'There are seventy-five perfumes,' he tells
Watson, 'which it is very necessary that a criminal expert should be
able to distinguish from each other, and cases have more than once
within my own experience depended upon their prompt recognition' "
(1927, 765). He knows that suicide most commonly occurs around 5
A.M. (1927, 432) and that pipes, like shoelaces and watches, are une-
qualled for providing insight into "individuality." And he can tell by
looking at the pattern of mud spattered on a woman's jacket that she
must have been recently a passenger in a dog cart: "There is no vehicle
save a dog-cart which throws up mud in that way, and then only when
you sit on the left-hand side of the driver" (1927, 259). Holmes has
almost no interest, however, in the natural world, divorced from
human activities. He finds no pleasure in contemplating either countryside or sea, preferring to "lie in the very centre of five millions of people, with his filaments stretching out and running through them,
responsive to every little rumour or suspicion of unsolved crime"
(1927, 423).

Although Doyle refers to Holmes's inferences as "deductions," he
rarely has his detective reason from the general to the specific. Typically, Holmes reasons backward from effect to cause: from facial expression to thought; from a corrupt moral nature to its origin in
biological transmission; from a particular pattern of spattered mud to
the process by which it came to assume that distinctive pattern; from a
calloused thumb to the work conditions that tend to create just such a
callous; or from a marred floor to the sullen workman who must have
deliberately left his mark in a conspicuous place. "In the everyday affairs of life it is more useful to reason forward," Holmes declares.
"There are fifty who can reason synthetically for one who can reason
analytically. . . . There are few people . . . who, if you told them a
result, would be able to evolve from their own inner consciousness
what the steps were which led up to that result. This power is what I

mean when I talk of reasoning backward, or analytically" (Eco and Sebeok 1983, 39).

In reasoning from effect to cause, Holmes is dependent on his knowledge of the normal, the customary, the habitual, and the "natural" in social practice and in human nature. To the extent that a particular feature or phenomenon is linked invariably, or with a high degree of probability, with a specific cause, his method promises success. If sitting beside the driver of a dog cart invariably, or generally, results in a unique pattern of mud spatters, Holmes's recognizing that pattern leads to the correct conclusion that a person has recently been in a dog cart. If different causes lead to identical or indistinguishable effects, however, the analyst must be prepared to entertain alternative theories or hypotheses: "One should always look for a possible alternative and provide against it. It is the first rule of criminal investigation" (Truzzi and Morris 1971, 66). Holmes's inferences, then, almost invariably have the provisional, inherently corrigible and tentative status of hypotheses or theories that need to be tested and confirmed if they are to be useful; and some stories, such as "The Adventure of the Speckled Band," "The Red-headed League," or *The Hound of the Baskervilles*, conclude with Holmes putting his reasoning to the test and predicting what is most likely to happen, given his reconstruction of what must have happened.

Working backwards from effects to causes, Holmes establishes connections between effects (or appearances) and the processes that created them—connections that were everywhere being severed or obscured in the urban world of the late nineteenth century. Factories engrossed and hid the processes of production of goods at the same time that households engaged in fewer forms of production. The emerging urban world, as Allan Trachtenberg argues in *The Incorporation of America*, was increasingly "opaque" to its inhabitants, who beheld an ever increasing variety of goods but possessed a diminishing sense of the processes in and through which those goods were created. Holmes's mastery of his world, then, depends in part on his maintaining a wide and varied knowledge of the processes of production, habit, custom, and nature that create the material features of the world. Individuals bear the marks of their experience, and human activity invariably leaves traces, "abrasions," or residues the investigator must identify and connect with the activity or processes that produced them. The most dangerous criminal, by implication, was the individual who knew how to manipulate appearances so as to obscure or destroy the traces of activity and intention on which the investigator depended in working backward from effect to cause. Among the most difficult crimes "to track is the one which is purposeless," the one in which the act has no motivating intention, thus eliminating the link between effect and cause (1927, 457). In such cases, the act and any clues that remain for the investigator to ponder have no meaning as a sign of human purpose and rationality.

Working forward, from his reconstruction of an opponent's activity and his assessment of his abilities and intentions, Holmes predicts what the person is likely to do: "I put myself in the man's place, and, having first gauged his intelligence, I try to imagine how I should myself have proceeded under the same circumstances" (1927, 395). Like Poe, Doyle reserved an essential role for the "scientific" use of imagination in investigation. Without imagination, the investigator could never rise beyond a limited competence: "Inspector Gregory . . . is an extremely competent officer. Were he but gifted with imagination he might rise to great heights in his profession" (1927, 338–39). Later Holmes exclaims: "See the value of imagination. It is the one quality which Gregory lacks. We imagined what might have happened, acted upon the supposition, and find ourselves justified" (1927, 344). Left out of this calculus is the possibility that his opponent may be engaged in the same process of imaginative projection in order to thwart Holmes. In "A Scandal in Bohemia," Holmes successfully predicts Irene Adler's behavior and tricks her into betraying the hiding place of the photograph he seeks by staging a diversion designed to panic her. When she suspects that he may have created the incident for just such a purpose, she dons a disguise to put her theory to the test. Holmes fails to recognize her, and hence fails to anticipate her fleeing the country before he can attempt to retrieve the photograph from its hiding place. She defeats him by his own methods: "I have been trained as an actress myself," she later writes to Holmes, who is himself a notable actor and a master of disguise (1927, 174). And this skill is dependent on knowledge of the typical, the customary, the usual, and the normal for the type of individual the actor chooses to play.

Holmes's mastery of disguise is more than a matter of knowledge, however. It involves a capacity for iron self-control: "He had, when he so willed it, the utter immobility of countenance of a red Indian, and I could not gather from his appearance whether he was satisfied or not with the position of the case" (1927, 460). His composure and capacity for control are evident, too, in the several stories, notably "The Adventure of the Speckled Band," which end with tense vigils in utter darkness, waiting, in this case, for the first hints that a poisonous snake is slipping down a bell rope, as Holmes has predicted. Watson remarks several times in the stories on his friend's lack of emotion and the degree to which Holmes approached being a "perfect reasoning machine." "All emotions . . . were abhorrent to his cold, precise but admirably balanced mind. . . . He never spoke of the softer passions, save with a gibe and a sneer. They were admirable things for the observer—excellent for drawing the veil from men's motives and actions. But for the trained reasoner to admit such intrusions into his own delicate and finely adjusted temperament was to introduce a distracting factor which might throw a doubt upon all his mental results" (1927, 161).

In addition to making a sharp distinction between the rational and the emotional, Doyle drew an equally sharp distinction between the detective's work and his leisure habits. Immersed in the details of a case, Holmes is single-minded, tireless, and intense, possessed of an enormous capacity for sustained, concentrated attention to every detail of the investigation. He is a "fox-hound" on the scent or a "reasoning machine" immune to distraction. When not working on a case, however, Holmes is prey to boredom and ennui. He chafes restlessly at inactivity and seeks refuge from monotony in music or, on occasion, cocaine. Moreover, "although in his methods of thought he was the neatest and most methodical of mankind . . . he was none the less in his personal habits one of the most untidy men," given to keeping "his cigars in the coal-scuttle, his tobacco in the toe end of a Persian slipper, and his unanswered correspondence transfixed by a jack-knife into the very centre of his wooden mantlepiece" (1927, 386).

Doyle made Holmes a card player, perhaps another echo of Poe's Dupin, as well as a fencer and a boxer, but failed to show a connection between these interests and Holmes's investigative prowess. He worked, Watson assures the reader, for "the love of his art" or for "the game's own sake," finding his reward in the exercise of his methods in solving a difficult problem; but in "The Adventure of the Dancing Men," having failed to act quickly enough to save the life of his client, he continues working on the case to avenge the man's death. As he prepares to take on Moriarty in "The Final Problem," Holmes tells

Watson, "The air of London is the sweeter for my presence. In over a thousand cases I am not aware that I have ever used my powers upon the wrong side" (1927, 477). Holmes and Moriarty, like Dupin and Minister D——, are virtually indistinguishable except for the crucial difference in motivation. If Moriarty sat "motionless, like a spider in the centre of its web . . . [knowing] well every quiver of each of them" (1927, 471), Holmes "loved to lie in the very centre of five millions of people, with his filaments stretching out and running through them" (1927, 423). Motivated by a desire for power and control, Moriarty mounts a malign surveillance. Holmes has no such ambitions.

The Holmes stories demonstrated convincingly the flexibility and adaptability of the story form created by Poe, and provided a ready model for subsequent writers. But the stories also model a rational process of inference in an appealing and accessible way, inviting the thought that the process might be learned and applied to endeavors other than simply creating similar stories. Like Poe, Doyle sought to apply his detective's methods to mysteries in the real world. In this, Doyle was more successful than was Poe with "The Mystery of Marie Roget," and it may be that his well-publicized intervention in real cases lent additional credibility to Holmes's methods beyond the persuasiveness of the stories themselves. Readers of the Holmes stories continue to claim that they learn important lessons from the stories, which still draw praise and comment for their accurate representation of rational methods in inquiry and inference (Williams 1987; Ashton-Wolfe 1932; Berg 1970; Hogan and Schwartz 1964).

Dupin and Holmes are amateurs in one sense. They work for the pleasure derived from the exercise of their skills. Nevertheless, both are recognizably experts of a sort, possessing the trained capacities described in the previous chapter as the hallmarks of modern professionalism. With only minor modifications, either character would be a formidable police detective. With the publication of John Buchan's *The Thirty-nine Steps* in 1915, there appeared another amateur, this one fit for the world of dangerous and deceptive surfaces associated with international intrigue and military rivalry.[6] Serialized in 1915 in the venerable *Blackwood's* magazine, from whose pages Poe had earlier drawn inspiration, *The Thirty-nine Steps* was published as a novel the following October to wide notice and popular appreciation (Atkins 1984, 31).

Buchan's protagonist is Richard Hannay, a Scot by birth, who had emigrated with his family to South Africa at the age of six. A successful mining engineer, Hannay is visiting London for the first time since leaving Britain thirty years before. Bored with English life and English weather after three months, and with neither friends nor family there, he is about to return to South Africa when he is approached by an American who occupies a flat in the same building. Franklin Scudder confides to Hannay that he has stumbled on evidence of an international conspiracy to bring about war between Russia and Germany. Fearing for his life, Scudder asks Hannay to put him up. Four days later, Hannay finds Scudder stabbed to death on the floor of his living room. Concluding that he could very well stand accused of Scudder's murder, and feeling obligated to carry on Scudder's efforts to try to avert whatever incendiary international incident was being plotted, Hannay decides to go into hiding for the three weeks remaining before the expected incident. He leaves his flat the next morning disguised as a milkman in case the building is being watched by whomever had killed Scudder. With him, Hannay takes Scudder's notebook, which he had found hidden in the dead man's flat, intending to "keep vanished till the end of the second week of June. Then I must somehow find a way to get in touch with the government people and tell them what Scudder had told me" (1963, 23).

In creating *The Thirty-nine Steps*, Buchan confronted several problems that did not exist in the writing of detective fiction as Doyle and others had been practicing it. How was Hannay to come by the dangerous knowledge that puts his life at risk? The consulting detective has no such problem. Someone brings him the "case," to which he adds whatever facts and observations his own researches may bring to light. By trusting him, for reasons Buchan fails to make clear, Scudder gives Hannay the equivalent of the detective's case—but with a twist, as it turns out. Deciphering Scudder's coded notebook entries, Hannay discovers that Scudder had lied to him about the nature of the conspiracy. He had trusted Hannay only to hide him from his pursuers, nothing more. By killing off Scudder, Buchan makes Hannay the sole remaining obstacle to the success of the conspirators. A prudent tourist, finding a body on his living room floor, might consider calling in the authorities. Buchan solves the problem of keeping the story Hannay's by having him conclude that he would be the prime suspect in Scudder's murder. At the risk of impugning British justice with the unflattering suggestion that it would convict an innocent man on circumstantial evidence, Buchan sets Hannay on the run from both police and conspirators.

Keeping Hannay on the run becomes the relatively straightforward problem of engineering a chase, but at some point Buchan must answer two questions: first, how will Hannay get in touch with the proper authorities? and second, how can he be kept at the forefront of the action, once he has done so? Buchan gets out of the first difficulty through providential occurrences that probably strike most readers today as the very definition of coincidence. He solves the second difficulty with some question-begging reasoning. The overriding technical problem, however, is to imagine a protagonist equipped to survive in a world of deceptive appearances and mortal danger.

A self-made man, Hannay is in his late thirties, active, vigorous, accustomed to challenge and to working outdoors. An ex-intelligence analyst and sometime soldier, he has "seen men die violently . . . and even killed a few [himself] in the Matabele War," but he is revolted by the "cold-blooded indoor business" of Scudder's murder (1963, 21). He speaks enough German to think about passing himself off as a German tourist but decides instead to rely on his Scots ancestry and to go to ground in Galloway, in southeastern Scotland. Captured by his enemies, Hannay fashions a crude bomb out of materials found in the storeroom in which he has been locked, blows out the door, and makes good his escape.

Complementing Hannay's practical expertise are his skills at disguising himself, improvising a role, and penetrating the disguises of others. In the final analysis, Hannay owes his survival to his ability to manipulate appearances rather than chemicals. He eludes his pursuers at one point by carefully disguising himself as a road mender: "My boots did not satisfy me, but by dint of kicking among the stones I reduced them to the granite-like surface which marks a roadman's foot-gear. Then I bit and scraped my finger-nails till the edges were all cracked and uneven. The men I was matched against would miss no detail. I broke one of the bootlaces and retied it in a clumsy knot and loosed the other so that my thick grey socks bulged over the uppers" (64). His attention to detail pays off when his disguise stands up under the intense scrutiny of two of his pursuers.

Later, it is Hannay who spots one of the conspirators posing as a high-ranking British naval officer.

He walked past me, and in passing he glanced in my direction, and for a second we looked each other in the face. Only for a second, but it was enough to make my heart jump. I had never seen the great man before, and he had never seen me. But in that fraction of time something sprang into his eyes, and that something was recognition. You can't mistake it. It is a flicker, a spark of light, a minute shade of difference, which means one thing and one thing only. It came involuntarily, for in a moment it died, and he passed on. (1963, 113)

Acting on his surmise, Hannay confirms that the man he has just seen is an imposter, an enemy agent. In the final confrontation with the conspirators, it is a similar fleeting, involuntary bit of behavior that permits Hannay to unmask the conspirators.

Buchan has difficulty justifying a central role for Hannay at the end of the story. Once Hannay has discovered a plausible explanation for Scudder's cryptic reference to "thirty-nine steps," there is little reason to keep him around, by his own admission: "It was ridiculous in me to take charge of the business like this, but they didn't seem to mind, and after all I had been in the show from the start. Besides, I was used to rough jobs, and these eminent gentlemen were too clever not to see it" (1963, 122). It thus falls to Hannay to confront his adversaries alone and to try to accomplish what they had failed to do in the roadmending incident, when Hannay's performance as a Scots countryman was sufficiently convincing to allay their suspicions. Watching the men he suspects of being enemy agents and Scudder's murderers, Hannay at first sees only normal appearances: "It was simply impossible to believe that these hearty fellows were anything but what they seemed—three ordinary, game-playing, suburban Englishmen" (1963, 130). Still, the stakes are very high in the situation, with "all Europe trembling on the edge of an earthquake," and Hannay concludes there is only one thing for him to do—"go forward as if I had no doubts, and if I was going to make a fool of myself to do it handsomely" (1963, 130–31).

These normal appearances seem unshakable until Hannay remembers something he had been told by a canny old Rhodesian scout, Peter Pienaar:

Peter once discussed with me the question of disguises. . . . He said, barring absolute certainties like finger-prints, mere physical traits were very little use for identification if the fugitive really knew his business. He laughed at things like dyed hair and false beards and such childish follies. The only thing that mattered was what Peter called 'atmosphere.' If a man could get into perfectly different surroundings from those in which he had been first observed, and—

this is the important part—really play up to these surroundings and behave as if he had never been out of them, he would puzzle the cleverest detectives on earth. . . . A fool tries to look different; a clever man looks the same and *is* different. (1963, 131–32).

Bolstered by Pienaar's theory of acting, Hannay confronts the three seemingly innocent Englishmen in their house, announcing that he has come to arrest them for Scudder's murder. Their protests seem utterly guileless and shake Hannay's confidence in their guilt: "It couldn't be acting, it was too confoundedly genuine. My heart went into my boots, and my first impulse was to apologize and clear out" (1963, 136–37). Stymied in his initial effort to confirm his suspicions, Hannay accepts their invitation to play bridge. "I accepted as if it had been an ordinary invitation at the club. The whole business had mesmerized me. . . . I took my place at the table in a kind of dream." Now thoroughly on the defensive in the situation, Hannay clings "desperately to the words of Peter Pienaar." In the midst of the play, one of the men makes a fleeting, unconscious gesture that "awakens" Hannay and confirms his suspicions: "A little thing, lasting only a second, and the odds were a thousand to one that I might have had my eyes on my cards at the time and missed it. But I didn't and, in a flash, the air seemed to clear. Some shadow lifted from my brain and I was looking at the three men with full and absolute recognition" (1963, 139).

It is tempting to credit Buchan with alluding to Poe and Doyle in this final scene. The clue that brings Hannay to the house ("thirty-nine steps—I counted them") suggests the passage in which Holmes distinguishes observing from (mere) seeing by asking Watson how many steps lead to the Baker Street flat; and Poe, it will be recalled, thought whist, the forerunner of bridge, to be superior to either chess or checkers in developing acumen. Both Poe and Doyle emphasized the crucial importance of subtle behavioral signs as evidence of an opponent's real intentions. What occurs over the bridge table is a momentary lapse into the unconsidered and the habitual, a relaxation of reflexive monitoring that triggers a reorientation of Hannay's perception of the situation: "Now I saw cruelty and ruthlessness where before I had only seen good-humour" (1963, 139).

Like his predecessors in the field, Buchan defines the effective investigator as a consummate role player. Hannay possesses the knowledge requisite to the roles he assumes, and the emotional control and composure both to improvise in a given role and to prevent any betrayal of his own true intentions through a slip, however briefly, into habitual patterns associated with his real identity. In Buchan's hands, the amateur secret agent is thus indistinguishable in essential ways from the prototypical investigator or detective introduced in Poe's tales of detection and subsequently elaborated in Conan Doyle's immensely popular and influential stories of Sherlock Holmes.

Hannay's success certifies the efficacy of the various traits and skills that make up his character, among the most important of which are his courage, resourcefulness, presence of mind, and ability to dissemble convincingly. Buchan finds his sturdy resoluteness and uncomplicated patriotism admirable and sufficient in the end to counter the brilliant masquerade of the German agents; and he clearly intended Hannay to exemplify commonplace virtues that were equal to the challenge of empire building or to its defense, when needed. Subsequent writers—Helen MacInnes, for example—have created characters like Hannay to achieve similar ends, while others, such as Eric Ambler, have used the conventions of the innocent swept up in a bewildering and dangerous conspiracy for quite different ends. But these are matters for another chapter.

To return to Poe briefly, "The Purloined Letter" depicts a clear relationship between knowledge of another on the one hand, and power—in the sense of the capability bestowed by that knowledge to predict, and hence to manipulate, another's actions—on the other. It follows that "unpredictability," understood as the capacity to anticipate and then act to confound another's expectations, should constitute an effective strategy for avoiding manipulation by someone else. Unpredictability, it should be noted, is parasitic on knowledge of another. One is unpredictable in relation to another's expectations. Thus, to be unpredictable involves knowing how one is perceived by another and then acting in ways that disconfirm and unsettle that perception. A stance of studied, calculated unpredictability involves acting so as to deny the other access to the true nature of one's plans, purposes, and intentions. It means, in short, that one must know the other while maintaining one's own opacity in the face of the other's determined efforts to penetrate it.

As a case in point, consider Dashiell Hammett's *The Maltese Falcon* (1930).[7] Unpredictability is central to the fable Sam Spade tells Brigid O'Shaughnessy early in the novel about a Tacoma businessman, Flitcraft, who had disappeared suddenly and inexplicably one day and was not found until Spade discovered him living in Spokane five years later. Attempting to persuade Spade that his sudden disappearance was "reasonable," Flitcraft described how he was nearly killed in a freak accident. The incident convinced Flitcraft, with the force and certainty of revelation, that he had gotten out of step with the reality of things, with how the world really was. To conform his life to his newfound conviction that chance ruled reality, Flitcraft abandoned his job and family on the spot and took to behaving in a deliberately random fashion. Gradually, however, he slipped back into his old ways: "He adjusted himself to beams falling," Spade explains, "and then no more of them fell, and he adjusted himself to them not falling" (1964, 57).

Spade says nothing about the means he used to locate Flitcraft, but the implication of the story seems clear enough. Flitcraft made himself locatable when he reverted to being the person he had been before his brush with death: a small businessman with a home in the suburbs and a habit of playing golf "after four in the afternoon during the season" (1964, 56). In slipping back into his old ways, Flitcraft became predictable once again. And in that predictability lay the increased probability that he could be located by someone willing to learn the patterns and habits of his life.

Spade, by contrast, survives by keeping his adversaries off guard—in a word, by being as unpredictable as possible. "My way of learning," he tells Brigid O'Shaughnessy at one point, "is to heave a wild and unpredictable monkey-wrench into the machinery" (1964, 77). In the final scenes of *The Maltese Falcon*, Spade puts on a virtuoso performance in unpredictability, thwarting first Caspar Gutman, who expects to trap him in his apartment and force him to give up the falcon, and then Brigid O'Shaughnessy, who expects Spade to let her go free, despite her having murdered his partner, Miles Archer.

Accompanied by Brigid, Spade returns to his apartment late at night. There he is surprised by Gutman, Gutman's associate Joel Cairo, and Gutman's young bodyguard, Wilmer Cook. By the end of the scene, however, Spade has regained control of the situation by manipulating Gutman to make decisions typically framed in terms of two mutually exclusive alternatives: Gutman can order Wilmer to search Spade and risk getting Spade shot—or he can forgo the search. Gutman forgoes the search. Spade then sets about persuading Gutman that there must be a fall guy, someone who can be given over to the police as responsible for at least two of the three killings that have occurred. The essence of his argument is: either give the police a fall guy or you will never be safe to make a fortune from the falcon. Spade suggests handing over Wilmer as the necessary fall guy. "By Gad, sir, you're a character," Gutman replies after a pause; "Yes, sir, there's never any telling what you'll do or say next, except that it's bound to be something astonishing" (1964, 160).

Counting on Gutman to be both rational and greedy, Spade grounds his argument, first, in his knowledge of how the legal system works in San Francisco: "[The DA] is like most district attorneys. He's more interested in how his record will look on paper than anything else" (1964, 162). Spade then works on the assumption that greed is the key to Gutman's character, taking precedence, for example, over loyalty to his associates. Getting Gutman even to consider giving up Wilmer to the police gives Spade an opening: he can suggest to Wilmer, with some plausibility, that Gutman is selling him out. Wilmer's self-control cracks, as Spade doubtless expected it to, and he threatens to kill Spade. When Gutman intervenes to prevent that from happening, Spade exploits the opportunity. He knocks Wilmer unconscious, disarms him, and announces that they now have their fall guy, adding: "Don't be a damn fool again. . . . You let Cairo whisper to you and you held the kid while I pasted him. You can't laugh that off and you're likely to get yourself shot trying to." Spade follows this up immediately with another forced choice: "you'll either say yes right now or I'll turn the falcon and the whole damned lot of you in" (1964, 167–68).

In the final scene with Brigid O'Shaughnessy, Spade is equally disconcerting—from her point of view. Despite the fact that she murdered his partner, Brigid is hopeful, even confident, that Spade will spare her out of love—or infatuation. He is determined to turn her in to the authorities, however, and offers a variety of reasons for doing so, ranging from the obligation (any)one owes to a partner to his own unwillingness to think "that there might be one chance in a hundred that you'd played me for a sucker." As a final reason, he returns to the issue of predictability: "I won't [let you go] because all of me wants to—wants to say to hell with the consequences and do it—and because . . . you've counted on that with me the same as you counted on that with the others" (1964, 194). In other words, I won't run the risk of being manipulated—played for a sap—by doing what I know you expect me to do.

These stories by Poe, Doyle, Buchan, and Hammett throw into especially sharp relief some of the constitutive elements of detective and espionage fiction. They are prototypes or models, and as such constitute cultural resources with which subsequent writers have worked their variations on the form. Writers are readers first, and one student of Poe's stories has summarized, in the form of a list of "firsts," the usable elements Poe bequeathed to subsequent writers, including the companion narrator, the eccentric detective, the unjustly suspected person, the "scientific" investigator, the series detective, and so forth (Lowndes 1970). It is well known that Raymond Chandler was an appreciative reader of Hammett, praising him for his realism and for giving murder back to the people who did it well, thereby making the detective story something that readers with a "sharp, aggressive attitude to life" could enjoy (Chandler 1995, 989). But Chandler saw in Hammett's model not simply something to follow, but something to improve upon, and he added an element of "redemption" he thought Hammett's work lacked. By the mid-1940s, when Ross Macdonald was beginning to write, the form in which Chandler excelled—the "California crime novel"—was a recognized variant on the hard-boiled detective novel. In Chandler's wake, Macdonald conceded that the master "wrote like a slumming angel" and distinguished his own work from Chandler's in terms of its greater social realism, thus invoking the same criterion Chandler had employed in contrasting the work of Bentley and Milne with Hammett's (Macdonald 1971, xvi).

Before discussing how various subsequent writers have handled the problem of knowing others while at the same time resisting others' efforts to know them, I want to offer a somewhat broader framework in which to locate that issue. Fictional detectives attempt to solve mysteries or problems by first identifying the person or persons whose acts, culminating typically in murder, created the mystery or the problem and then apprehending the perpetrator(s). Put differently, fictional detectives seek first the truth of the matter (not Truth) and then "justice," although the latter often turns out to be more variable in form than simply remanding the culprit to the proper authorities. Justice in detective fiction is not always or simply to be found in courts of law. On occasion it involves hiding the truth discovered in the process of investigation—or parts of it—and may involve failing to turn the perpetrator over to the proper authorities for various good reasons—in order to protect other individuals who might be injured by the public identification of the perpetrator, for example, or to guarantee that the perpetrator does, in fact, pay for their acts, given the uncertainties of the judicial system. On the other hand, truth—the facts of the matter—rarely admits of ambiguity in detective fiction. The detective's investigation leads to the unequivocal identification of the perpetrator and provides convincing proof regarding the facts of the matter. Justice can and does take various forms in the hands of different writers, but truth is ever a matter of discovering causal linkages and offering proof of those beyond any reasonable doubt.

Given the foregoing, how do fictional detectives go about their twin tasks of "identifying" and "apprehending?" At the most general level of abstraction, they do so by "interrogating" physical evidence or individuals or both and by acting, under conditions of uncertainty and risk, on the information received. At its most basic, interrogating physical evidence involves discovering causal connections between presently observable "residues" or traces and the past activities or processes of which they are the necessary consequences, hence evidence. Interrogating individuals entails, most basically, asking questions and assessing the answers provided. The detective typically deals with two broad groups. The first are those informants or experts on whom he or she must depend, on occasion, for specific information—a network of persons, sources, and experts, created and maintained by the detective to provide access to knowledge or expertise that lies outside his or her experience or is otherwise unavailable. Modern society requires knowing how to access expertise, and investigators are no exception. The second broad grouping with whom the detective typically must deal consists of those persons who have or seem to have a material connection to the case in hand.

Interrogating the observable surviving traces of past activity is grounded both in technical knowledge and in trained capacities such as the ability to concentrate over long periods of time, the capacity to work accurately and efficiently against deadlines, the ability to avoid distraction, to remain composed in the face of intense stress. The character of modern society requires and privileges these trained capacities as well as others discussed in the previous chapter. Searching for and analyzing physical evidence may require imagination and resourcefulness, but it seldom involves risk or danger, except in cases where the evidence may be hazardous in its own right.

Questioning individuals is the investigator's stock in trade. Effective questioning requires knowledge about who individuals are, in terms of their personal histories, intentions, motives, plans, and purposes, and to whom they are related in what ways. In the quasi-official capacity of a "private" investigator, whether duly licensed as such or not, the detective routinely confronts the general problems of <u>interpretation</u> and <u>persuasion</u> in questioning any of the persons connected with a given case. Those most closely connected with the case may have reason to dissemble or lie, whether they are suspects or not, making an accurate assessment of their answers vital. But before their answers can be assessed, persons involved in the case must be persuaded to answer the detective's questions in the first place. Moreover, questioning suspects, unlike interrogating physical evidence, may be distinctly dangerous, especially in the final stages of an investigation when the detective may be focusing increasingly on a single (presumably guilty) individual.

As an interrogator of persons, rather than of surviving traces of past activity, the detective must interact effectively with a wide range of individuals. He or she must possess a memory for details, the ability to synthesize and connect bits and pieces of information gleaned from a variety of sources, a capacity for careful observation, an eye for telling detail, and skill at formulating and, when necessary, modifying explanatory hypotheses in light of new information. Moreover, in questioning individuals, the detective is routinely required to act a part, play a role, assume an identity, sometimes on very short notice, and to carry the deception off without arousing suspicion. Acting a part, especially as Hannay, for example, does, in high-risk situations, requires that the detective possess the trained capacity to maintain emotional control, highly developed and finely calibrated skills of self-presentation, and substantial improvisational skills.

The centrality of interrogation in detective fiction is evident in its form—typically a series of conversations, episodes of questions and answers, punctuated by actions that link the sequence of interviews, establish connections, and test the emerging explanatory hypothesis that will, in the end, order the true facts of the matter. As a series of interrogations, the form of detective fiction is remarkably flexible, allowing for enormous variation as to who is questioned and with what consequences.

There are two general sources of (potential) frustration of the investigator's goal of identifying and apprehending the perpetrator(s). The first rests in the perpetrator's skills at lying, dissembling, covering his or her tracks, and in general successfully hiding from the investigator. These skills are the "defensive" equivalents of the detective's skills at penetrating deceptive appearances; both parties possess similar talents for manipulating surface appearances in order to disguise the reality of their respective plans, intentions, and suspicions. Indeed, Irene Adler, Holmes's adversary in "A Scandal in Bohemia," is more accomplished in this regard than the Great Detective himself.

A second threat to the detective's investigation lies in the power—economic, technological, or broadly political—possessed by the perpetrator to thwart first the process of identification and then the process of apprehension, if the detective is successful in establishing the identity of the perpetrator. Thus the fictional detective emerges as a specialist of sorts, an expert in his or her own right, who is skilled at penetrating deception, on the one hand, and at resisting, evading, or neutralizing threats to the integrity of the investigative process, on the other. At the heart of detective fiction there is always at least one fact (of the matter) someone wants kept hidden as much as someone else—the investigator—wants it disclosed.

3

Detectives Reading the Other

The hidden feeling betrays itself often against the will of the best actor in life.

George Young, *Elementary Course of the Principles of Detection*

If we cannot find the truth, what is our hope of justice?

Scott Turow, *Presumed Innocent*

Few writers of detective fiction are better known than Raymond Chandler, and none, with the possible exception of Dashiell Hammett, has received greater critical recognition.[1] Nevertheless, there is nothing in his best regarded work—*The Big Sleep* (1939); *Farewell, My Lovely* (1940), his personal favorite; or *The Long Good-bye* (1953)—that has methodological interest and significance for the problem of other minds comparable to that of the Flitcraft episode in *The Maltese Falcon*. Like Hammett, Chandler served his apprenticeship in the pulp fiction market of the 1930s, earning a penny a word for his efforts, before *The Big Sleep*, his first novel, was published by the distinguished New York publisher Alfred Knopf. Reviewers, whose reactions to that novel were mixed, recognized Chandler as following in the tradition of James M. Cain and Hammett. A year later, Knopf published *Farewell, My Lovely* to more favorable reviews and eventually sold over a million copies, establishing Chandler's reputation as a practitioner of the hard-boiled detective novel.

Like any writer choosing to work within a set of conventions, Chandler faced the problem of differentiating his approach from other writers. Creating a suitable protagonist was crucial to that process of individuation. Chandler developed his version of the private detective hero, Philip Marlowe, in the short stories he published in *Black Mask* and other pulp fiction magazines, and retained him as the protagonist of his novels, beginning with *The Big Sleep*. Where Hammett chose to define Sam Spade in terms of his <u>unpredictability</u>, his capacity to avoid others' efforts to manipulate him, Chandler chose to define Philip Marlowe primarily in <u>moral</u> terms—as an honest man in a corrupt world that made honesty look "in the end either sentimental or plain foolish" (Gardiner and Walker 1962, 233). The detective, he wrote in the oft-quoted closing sentences of his 1944 *Atlantic Monthly* essay "The Simple Art of Murder," must be

> a man of honor, by instinct, by inevitability. . . . He must be the best man in his world and a good enough man for any world. . . . He will take no man's money dishonestly and no man's insolence without a due and dispassionate revenge. He is a lonely man and his pride is that you will treat him as a proud man or be very sorry you ever saw him. He talks as the man of his age talks, that is with rude wit, a lively sense of the grotesque, a disgust for sham, and a contempt for pettiness. The story is his adventure in search of a hidden truth, and it would be no adventure if it did not happen to a man fit for adventure. (1995, 992)

John Houseman, for whom Chandler salvaged the screenplay for the film *The Blue Dahlia*, recalled Chandler defending Marlowe and "his kind" as "the last honest men left in our society; they did their assigned jobs and took their wages; they were not acquisitive nor did they rise in the world by stepping on other people's faces. . . . Marlowe's was, in fact, the only attitude that a self-respecting, decent man could maintain in today's rapacious and brutal world" (Houseman 1965, 61). In *The High Window* (1940), Marlowe defends his moral stance to two Los Angeles police detectives: "Until you guys own your own souls you don't own mine. Until you guys can be trusted every time and always, in all times and conditions, to seek the truth out and find it *and let the chips fall where they may*—until that time comes, I have a right to my conscience, and protect my client the best way I can" (Eames 1978, 190; emphasis added). In light of his emphasis on honesty as Marlowe's constitutive and defining characteristic, it is hardly surprising that Chandler once characterized *The Maltese Falcon* as "the record of a man's devotion to a friend" (Eames 1978, 203), notwithstanding Spade's own words to the contrary about his dead partner: "Miles was a louse . . . [but] When a man's partner is killed he's supposed to do something about it" (Hammett 1964, 193).

Chandler's condemnation of the British ratiocinative tradition of detective fiction, like his conception of the detective hero, turned to a large extent on the issue of honesty. Writing in 1940 to his *Black Mask* crony George Harmon Coxe, who had recommended that Chandler read Agatha Christie's *And Then There Were None*, he said the experience "finally and for all time settled a question in my mind. . . . Whether it is possible to write a strictly honest mystery of the classic type. It isn't. To get the complication you fake the clues, the timing, the play of coincidence, assume certainties where only 50 per cent chances exist at most. To get the surprise murderer you fake the character" (Gardiner and Walker 1962, 48). Four years later, in "The Simple Art of Murder," Chandler developed this line of criticism in detail. And in the ten guidelines he set down in 1949 for writing detective fiction, "Casual Notes on the Mystery Novel," he emphasized the matter of honesty again and again: credible motivation, sound methods of detection, accuracy of detail, and fair play for the reader, for example. "It is the basic theory of all mystery writing that at some stage of the proceedings the reader could, given the necessary astuteness, have closed the book and revealed the essence of the denouement." Granting that, the facts of the case should be presented "fairly," and they should be the kind of facts from which the "ordinary lay reader" could honestly be expected to draw the right conclusions: "The reader cannot be charged with special and rare knowledge nor with an abnormal memory for insignificant details" (Gardiner and Walker 1962, 63–70).

As a hero conceived and defined primarily in terms of pride, loneliness, and honesty (on occasion to the point of moral arrogance), Chandler's detective, in the abstract, could serve equally as a vehicle for social commentary and criticism and as a character in and through which a writer might explore the epistemological and moral ambiguities associated with detection. Chandler was disinclined to use Marlowe for the latter purpose, preferring rather to use him to voice—however uneasily—his own criticism of all he thought meretricious and corrupt in the southern California society in which he had spent his adult life. Nevertheless, the interpretive problem posed by having to question others about whom one knows little or nothing, together with the issues of risk and trust involved in such interactions, could not be evaded, at least at the surface level of describing interactions and their outcomes. Marlowe may be "the best man in his world," but Chandler's preoccupation with his man's pride and moral stature frequently comes at the expense of Marlowe's effectiveness as a questioner.

Two conversations in *Farewell, My Lovely* illustrate the point. Toward the end of that novel, Marlowe and a Los Angeles police detective, Lieutenant Randall, discover the body of Jessie Florian, one of the principals in the case on which Marlowe has been working. Back at his office, Randall offers Marlowe an account of the investigation into Florian's death "[j]ust so maybe for Christ's sake you will let this one lay" (Chandler 1964, 167). Both agree that Florian's killer is almost certainly Moose Malloy, recently released from prison after eight years and looking for a young woman who used to work in Florian's bar. Marlowe goes on to suggest that Malloy probably did not mean to kill her: "He's just too strong." Randall responds, "That won't help him any." Marlowe proceeds to argue the point with him, prompting Randall to remind him pointedly, "We got friendly this morning. Let's stay that way" (168). After Randall has given Marlowe everything he is willing to, Marlowe asks him about an apparent loose end in the case. "I have a theory about that," Randall says, and proceeds to outline it for Marlowe. When Randall is finished, Marlowe ignores Randall's theory of the case and points to a pink-headed bug he has noticed:

> "Look," I said, "This room is eighteen floors above ground. And this little bug climbs all the way up here just to make a friend. Me. *My* lucky piece." I folded the bug carefully into my pocket. Randall was pie-eyed. His mouth moved, but nothing came out of it. "I wonder whose lucky piece Marriott [Marlowe's murdered client] was," I said. "Not yours, pal." His voice was acid—cold acid. "Perhaps not yours either." My voice was just a voice. I went out of the room and shut the door. (170–71)

Marlowe's response to Randall is a textbook case of "flouting," a deliberate rejection of the implicit rules governing conversation (Murphey 1987, 218). "Marlowe wouldn't be Marlowe, if he could really get along with policemen," Chandler remarked in a 1958 letter (Gardiner and Walker 1962, 248).

Leaving Randall's office, Marlowe visits John Wax, chief of police in Bay City, a coastal town controlled by a local gambling czar and racketeer, Laird Brunette. Two of Wax's men, moonlighting for a sinister psychic, Jules Amthor, had earlier beaten Marlowe and then left him in a private psychiatric clinic in Bay City that served as a front for various criminal activities. Chief Wax agrees to let Marlowe talk to one of the two policemen, a Sergeant Galbraith, after Marlowe tells Wax he is working on a case for one of Bay City's wealthiest residents. Marlowe wants to know why he was put in the clinic and kept there for two days against his will. Galbraith can tell him and knows that Chief Wax expects him to cooperate with Marlowe. Early in the ensuing conversation, Marlowe's wisecracks merely annoy Galbraith, but later Marlowe's approach nearly goads Galbraith into ending their talk on a note of hostility and threat—and without giving Marlowe the information he wants.

Galbraith has tried to explain to Marlowe why police corruption occurs: "Cops don't go crooked for money. Not always, not even often. They get caught in the system. . . . A guy can't stay honest if he wants to" (1964, 182). The answer, Galbraith confides, is M.R.A., the Moral Rearmament movement: "There you've got something, baby." To this Marlowe replies, " 'If Bay City is a sample of how it works, I'll take aspirin' . . . 'You could get too smart,' [Galbraith] said softly. 'You might not think it, but it could be. You could get so smart you couldn't think about anything but bein' smart' " (182). Having used the exchange primarily to affirm again Marlowe's integrity, Chandler concludes the conversation between the two men on a gesture of conciliation: "[Galbraith] put his big hand out. 'No hard feelings?' 'M.R.A.' I said and shook the hand. He grinned all over. He called me back when I started to walk away." Galbraith then obliquely suggests a way Marlowe might approach Bay City's "owner," Brunette. Marlowe's reply, however, seems calculated to destroy the mutuality of the handshake and to reassert Marlowe's superiority: " 'I get it,' [Marlowe] said. 'I had the same sort of idea. I don't know why I bothered so much to get you to have it with me' " (185–86)—yet another of Chandler's reminders that his detective, "the best man in his world," works alone, works honest, and, especially, works proud. Favoring scene over plot, and preoccupied with displaying the incorruptibility of his detective, Chandler elides the problem of other minds that had exercised Hammett, to whom Chandler felt superior for having transcended Hammett's realism with the "redemption" implicit in Marlowe's moral stature.

Ross Macdonald, creator of the series detective Lew Archer, began writing mystery fiction in the shadow of Chandler's early work after returning from duty with the U.S. Navy in World War II and settling, with his wife Margaret Millar, in Santa Barbara, California.[2] Just as Chandler wrote partially in reaction both to the British ratiocinative tradition and to Hammett, Macdonald was obliged to distinguish his own approach to the hard-boiled detective story from Chandler's. "Raymond Chandler," he acknowledged, "was and remains a hard man to follow. He wrote like a slumming angel and invested the sun-blinded streets of Los Angeles with a romantic presence. While trying to preserve the fantastic lights and shadows of the actual Los Angeles, I gradually siphoned off the aura of romance and made room for a more complete social realism" (Macdonald 1971, xvi). By 1957, with the publication of *The Doomsters*, Macdonald felt he had made "a fairly clean break with the Chandler tradition, which it had taken me some years to digest." He distinguished his approach to the hard-boiled novel in terms of both his attitude toward plot and his conception of the detective. "Chandler described a good plot as one that made for good scenes, as if the parts were greater than the whole. I see plot as a vehicle of meaning. It should be as complex as contemporary life, but balanced enough to say true things about it. The surprise with which a detective novel concludes should set up tragic vibrations which run backward through the entire structure. Which means that the structure must be single, and *intended*" (1970b, 303; italics in original).

Macdonald conceived of Lew Archer as a "catalyst" rather than a prickly moral paragon—less a doer than "a questioner, a consciousness in which the meanings of other lives emerge" (Macdonald 1970b, 304). Moreover, he gave Archer qualities possessed by "the two best private detectives I personally know . . . their intelligent humaneness, an interest in other people transcending their interest in themselves, and a toughness of mind which enables them to face human weakness, including their own, with open eyes" (1970b, 305). Singling out Chandler by name, Macdonald argued, "An author's heavy emotional investment in a narrator-hero can get in the way of the story and blur its meanings, as some of Chandler's books demonstrate. . . . I don't have to celebrate Archer's physical or sexual prowess, or work at making him consistently funny and charming. He can be self-forgetful, almost transparent at times, and concentrate as good detectives (and good writers) do, on the people whose problems he is investigating. These people are for me the main thing" (1970b, 304). Macdonald rejected out of hand the notion of the redemptive hero with which Chandler had sought both to distinguish himself from and elevate himself above Hammett: "The detective-as-redeemer is a backward step in the direction of sentimental romance, and an oversimplified world of good guys and bad guys" (1970b, 300).

The Galton Case, published in 1959 (coincidentally the year of Chandler's death), marked a turning point in Macdonald's career as a writer of mystery fiction. "Ten years and ten novels [after settling in California], seismic disturbances occurred in my life. My half-suppressed Canadian years, my whole childhood and youth, rose like a corpse from the bottom of the sea to confront me" (Macdonald 1970a, viii). Macdonald moved his family from their home in Santa Barbara to the Bay area for a year. "There I went through belated mental growing pains, trying to understand the peculiar shape of my life," for "the inner shape of a man's life . . . if he is a writer . . . is what he writes from and about. . . . Since I couldn't change the shape of my life, I decided to make the best of it" (1970a, viii). He began a new novel, the writing of which raised a crucial question: whether he could be faithful to the inner shape of his life while continuing to work within the conventions of the hard-boiled detective novel. His "answer," *The Galton Case*, convinced Macdonald that he could do both, thereby making good "the right to my inheritance as an American citizen and writer, while bringing into unsparing view the poverty and brokenness of my worst days" (1970a, ix).

The Galton Case involves several mysteries—the unsolved disappearance years before of Anthony Galton, his wife, and infant son; the recent murder of a houseman employed by Galton's mother's attorney, Gordon Sable; the question of whether a young man, who calls himself John Brown Jr., is truly Mrs. Galton's grandson; and how the foregoing are related—if they are. The genesis of the novel lay in a brief notebook entry of Macdonald's: "Oedipus angry vs parents for sending him away into a foreign country" (Macdonald 1969, 151). Into the book went also the major legacy of Macdonald's impoverished Canadian childhood—his sense of a profoundly divided world. With many others during the Depression, Macdonald "shared the dilemma of finding myself to be at the same time two radically different kinds of people, a pauper and a member of the middle class" (1969, 152). The doctrine that poverty is deserved was common in the world in which Macdonald grew up: "In a puritanical society the poor and fatherless, suffering the quiet punishments of despair, may see themselves as permanently and justifiably damned for crimes they can't remember having committed" (1969, 152). Even after moving back to the United States after his war service, and despite his moderate success as a writer in the following decade, Macdonald had not dealt with the problems of his origins. He did so only when those problems could no longer be avoided. "My mind," he later admitted, "had been haunted for years by an imaginary boy whom I recognized as the darker side of my own remembered boyhood. By his sixteenth year he had lived in fifty houses and committed the sin of poverty in each of them. I couldn't think of him without anger and guilt," or of the father who had early abandoned Macdonald and his mother, for that matter (151).

The focal character of the novel—John Brown Jr., or John Galton—is a version, at the emotional level, of Macdonald himself, but "my nature," he cautioned, "is probably better represented by the whole book than by any one of its characters" (Macdonald 1969, 153). In writing *The Galton Case*, Macdonald demonstrated to his own satisfaction that he could fuse his hard-won knowledge of the conventions of the hard-boiled detective novel with the painful truths of his boyhood and youth. Macdonald would have abandoned those conventions only in the face of overwhelming necessity. "There is more to our use of the convention," he has argued, "than meets the eye. . . . the literary detective has provided writers since Poe with a disguise, a kind of welder's mask enabling us to handle dangerously hot material" (1969, 147). An authorial disguise like Lew Archer allows the writer to half divulge his own crucial secrets "while deepening the whole community's sense of its own mysterious life" (1969, 148). An "imaginative catalyst," Archer made it possible for Macdonald

> to dredge up material I wouldn't be able to dredge up writing in my own person. He embodies a tradition. If I tried to write this stuff straight, I couldn't do it. . . . But Archer is more than that. He represents modern man in a technological society, who is, in effect, homeless, virtually friendless, and who tries to behave as if there is some hope in society. . . . He's a transitional figure between a world that is breaking up and one coming into being in which relationships and people will be important. (Sokolow 1971, 108)

"From Poe to Chandler and beyond, the detective hero has represented his creator and carried his values into action in society" (Macdonald 1970b, 295–96).

In *The Zebra-Striped Hearse*, published three years after *The Galton Case*, Lew Archer describes another investigator, Arnie Walters, as having "the qualities of a first-rate detective: honesty, imagination, curiosity, and a love of people"—qualities he shares with Archer and, as noted earlier, with the best private investigators Macdonald knew personally (1964, 97; 1970b, 305). *The Galton Case* also shows Archer to be a skilled, effective, and persuasive questioner of people, some of whom find themselves, to their surprise, being more open with him than they intended, and all of whom possess information, secrets, that they reveal to him reluctantly, fearing the risks involved in disclosure. Archer, in Macdonald's view, is—and needs to be—a capable, sensitive reader of people. His effectiveness as an investigator depends on that skill.

When it suits his purpose, Archer is adept at deception. He misrepresents himself as a corporate investigator on one occasion; or, more subtly, he allows others to think he is acting in an official rather than a private capacity. He resorts to a small, strategic lie once in *The Zebra-Striped Hearse* to preserve the pride of a police officer he meets on the case. In the course of his investigation, Archer reveals a flexible, pragmatic intelligence, changing his mind in the face of new findings and formulating new, but tentative, explanatory hypotheses in response. These serve to shape his inquiries only so long as they prove useful or adequate to the facts of the case as he understands them at the time. In his search for the truth, Archer is unencumbered by the political ambitions that make one police official reluctant to consider an individual as a suspect in one of the novel's two murders; and he is resolute in pursuing his inquiries, even in the face of extreme physical intimidation. Despite the strategic deceptions his detective practices, Macdonald shows Archer to be transparently, hence convincingly, honest and trustworthy, motivated by a desire to pursue the truth wherever the investigation may lead, all the while remaining mindful that discovering the truth often creates risk for individuals peripheral to a case and so requires of Archer both discretion and compassion.

The Galton Case involves discovering the circumstances surrounding two murders separated in time by more than twenty years, but the deeper mystery of the story, and the last to be resolved, concerns the identity of a young man who represents himself as the son of the murdered Anthony Galton and the heir to the Galton fortune. Is the young man, who has gone by various names—John Brown Jr., John Lindsay,

Theodore Fredericks—an imposter, a gifted actor trying to parlay a physical resemblance to Anthony Galton into a fortune? Or is he John Galton, a talented actor to be sure, but nevertheless the legitimate son and heir of Anthony Galton? The issue is complicated by various factors that emerge in the course of Archer's investigation. Initially convinced that the young man is John Galton, Archer subsequently becomes persuaded that he is an imposter and sets out to expose him. Confronting him in the final scene of the novel, Archer gradually abandons his suspicions, however, and concludes that John Galton is in fact who he claims to be.

The puzzle of Galton's identity is more than usually complicated because he is genuinely uncertain himself as to whose son he is. His mother has lied to him throughout his life, first to protect him from his stepfather, Fred Fredericks, who turns out to be Anthony Galton's killer, and then to protect herself from being left alone should her husband's crime be discovered and he be convicted and imprisoned. When John was sixteen, Peter Culligan, a boarder in the family rooming house, told him his stepfather had killed his real father, an allegation Culligan later retracts. Acting on Culligan's allegation that Fredericks had killed his father, John had attacked Fredericks with a knife, left him for dead, and fled to Detroit and subsequently Ann Arbor, where he was taken in by a sympathetic high school teacher who gave him a home. Eventually Culligan finds him and involves him in a scheme to pass him off as the son of Anthony Galton and the heir to a fortune, intending to blackmail John out of a substantial portion of his inheritance. John admits to Archer that he played along with the scheme: "I didn't know which of [Culligan's] stories was true, or if the truth was something else again. I even suspected that Culligan had killed my father himself. How else would he know about the murder?" (1964, 184).

In the novel's final scene, John Galton explains to Archer why he believes he really is Anthony Galton's son. His conviction rests almost entirely on feelings and perceptions: his feeling that Fredericks never treated him as a son; that the high school teacher John Lindsay saw something in him that he didn't know was there; that the doctor who had delivered him recognized a resemblance to Anthony Galton; that the young woman who has fallen in love with him believes his story; and that a story his mother used to tell him was not simply a "fairytale" but " 'a story about myself. . . . She said that I was a king's son

. . . and she showed me a gold ring with a little red stone set in it that the king had left her for a remembrance.' He gave me a curious questioning look. Our eyes met solidly for the first time. I think the reality formed between us then" (1964, 183). In a reversal of roles, Archer answers John's remaining questions, convinced that no barrier of deliberate deception separates them from each other or from the facts of the matter. A final confrontation with his mother confirms the truth of the story he and Archer have constructed.

In concluding that John is Anthony Galton's son, Archer assesses John's account of himself not simply for how it accords with the facts as Archer knows them, but for John's sincerity and authenticity, his transparency. Archer's skepticism yields to whatever it is he recognizes in Galton when "their eyes met solidly for the first time." Part of what Archer recognizes in John's "curious questioning look" is surely the young man's determination to face and understand the true nature of his past. That tough-minded stance, Macdonald insists in this pivotal work, is the identity-defining act *par excellence*—the necessary basis for elaborating identity in other terms—and an essential quality for the investigator, real or imagined, to possess. He makes it central to his conception of Lew Archer, and he singled it out, as I noted earlier, in characterizing the best real private investigators he knew. In facing the truth of his own past in the act of writing *The Galton Case*, Macdonald did for himself what his fictional detective accomplished for John Galton.

In the unfolding of the Galton case, Archer variously invites, per-suades, cajoles, and, on occasion, bullies or threatens individuals into confronting facts—truths—they have been evading or lying about. The effect of acknowledging truth is almost always salutary in Macdonald's later work, freeing the individual from the isolating consequences of maintaining secrets, especially from intimates. The nurse hired by An-thony Galton to help care for his infant son, for example, had been present but not an eyewitness to Galton's murder. Until Archer finds her and interviews her, she had kept silent about what she had heard for twenty years: "I was afraid of the truth," she confides to Archer. "I didn't want to believe what happened, I guess. . . . I couldn't face my own part in it. . . . I was the one responsible for the whole thing. I've lived with it on my conscience for over twenty years" (1964, 83). Later, after she has talked to John Galton about the circumstances of his father's death and to her husband about the past she had never confided to him, she tells Archer, "It's all right. I've talked it out with [my husband]. Whatever comes up . . . we can handle it together. My husband is a very good man" (1964, 178).

Macdonald defines Archer as a questioner, a "catalyst," a consciousness in which the meanings of other lives emerge—three ways of describing Archer's role that assign to him rather different degrees of activity. The outcomes of his interviews, the nature of the meanings that emerge in and through his consciousness, the substance of his investigations, consist finally in the connections he makes—between past and present, or the living and the dead, for example—that have been rendered invisible by lies and deception. In *The Instant Enemy* (1970c), Archer reflects on the exhilaration and deeper function of this activity: "I had to admit to myself that I lived for nights like these, moving across the city's great broken body, making connections among its millions of cells. I had a crazy wish or fantasy that someday before I died, if I made all the right neural connections, the city would come all the way alive" (1970c, 106).

As noted above, the lies within which Theodore Fredericks/John Galton was raised complicate his efforts to understand who he really is since, in a basic sense, he does not know himself. He agrees to "play" John Galton in Culligan's scheme hoping to discover who he is. In trying to determine the young man's identity, Archer confronts the difficult interpretive challenge posed by the conjunction of Galton's acting skills, his evident self-interest in being taken for Anthony Galton's son, and his uncertainties about his origins. These factors combine to make *The Galton Case* an especially complicated meditation on the problem of other minds.

The problem of other minds is endemic to mystery fiction, but the work of Tony Hillerman is especially interesting for his treatment of it. *Skinwalkers* (1986) is the eighth in Hillerman's series of mystery novels featuring Navajo Tribal police officers Jim Chee or Joe Leaphorn or, as in *Skinwalkers*, both. Hillerman's setting is the sprawling Navajo reservation of New Mexico's Four Corners area and the Anglo culture that surrounds it. To be effective investigators, Chee and Leaphorn need to have mastered two very different cultural worlds characterized by different ontologies and different interpretive frameworks. The Navajo world, for example, contains witches, the skinwalkers of the title—beings that are unknown, even unimaginable, in the ontology of Dilly Streib, the FBI agent assisting Leaphorn and Chee in the investigation of three seemingly unrelated homicides. Cultural differences in etiquette further complicate what Jim Chee, for example, must both learn and unlearn, if he is to be effective as an investigator in both worlds. A Navajo lawyer, "studying Chee's face" during a conversation, reminds him that attending to another in this way "was a habit that [he] had learned slowly, and come to tolerate slowly, and that still sometimes made him uneasy." In the Navajo world, "Only the rude peered into one's face during a conversation . . . [a woman friend] had asked him how this worked for a policeman. Surely, she'd said, they must be trained to look for all those signals facial expressions reveal while the speaker is lying, or evading, or telling less than the truth. . . . Like police academy, Chee thought, law schools teach interrogators a different conversational technique than Navajo mothers. The white way. The way of looking for what the handbook on interrogation called 'nonverbal signals.' Chee found himself trying to keep his face blank, to send no such signals" (1986, 193–94).

If Chee must unlearn elements of his own culture, he must also learn elements of Anglo culture that have no analogue in his own. As a Navajo, Chee does not understand revenge as a motive, but his effectiveness in his world requires that he understand beliefs and values that motivate others, and hence enter into explaining their behavior—or manipulating it, as occurs in the final scenes of *The Dark Wind* (1982). Threatened by a corrupt DEA agent ("He should have expected [agent] Johnson"), Chee saves his own life by manipulating the man accompanying him, a vengeful father, into attacking the agent, whom the father blames for his son's murder (1983, 204–10).[3]

Early in *Skinwalkers*, someone tries to kill Chee by firing a shotgun into the small house trailer in which he lives. Cleaning up after the attack, he discovers a small bone bead in his bed. An Anglo investigator might easily have missed it, given its size, or, having found it, discarded it as of no consequence. Within Anglo culture, the bit of bone is not a sign and hence is meaningless. To Chee, however, it signifies witchcraft: someone has taken him for a witch. Of human origin, the bone bead is intended to induce the fatal illness "corpse sickness" in the putative witch (1986, 66–67). Leaphorn, Chee knows, "had no tolerance for witchcraft," even less in a case in which the FBI is involved (1986, 72). Chee, on the other hand, retains a measure of traditional belief, accepting, for example, the "poetic metaphor" of the Navajo creation story, with its explanation of witchcraft. He believes "in the lessons such imagery was intended to teach;" and he is sufficiently a Navajo traditionalist, as Leaphorn is not, to train as a Yataalii, a ritual healer, even while he pursues a career in the tribal police (1986, 73). If he does not believe in witches per se, Chee understands that beliefs, whether false or true, underwrite action and so enter into the explanation of action. The bone bead, understood in its appropriate context (i.e., as a Navajo sign), orients Chee's investigation.

Gradually the investigation reveals the three murders to be related and the instigator, if not the perpetrator(s), of the killings to be a Native American of another tribe who has established a medical clinic that blends elements from Anglo and Navajo culture. " 'People come to me at the clinic,' " its owner, Yellowhorse, tells Leaphorn. " 'I tell 'em what's wrong with 'em. What kind of cure they need.' . . . 'If they have been fooling with wood that's been struck by lightning, or been around a grave too much, or have ghost sickness, then I tell them whether they need a Mountaintop sign, or an Enemy Way, or whatever cure they need. If they need a gallstone removed, or their tonsils out, or a course of antibiotics to knock a strep infection, then I check them into the clinic for that' " (1986, 29–30). To keep the clinic going in the face of financial difficulties, Yellowhorse had resorted to fraud. When a social services investigator, herself a Native American, was on the verge of exposing the fraud, Yellowhorse arranged her murder and the murder of two others by manipulating Navajo traditionalists into believing their victims to be witches responsible for harming them. Yellowhorse arranged the attack on Chee in the same way—by convincing a young woman whose child had been born with a severe brain disease that Chee was the witch responsible for the child's condition. Killing the witch, according to traditional belief, would restore the child to health. Given the young mother's beliefs, Yellowhorse expected her to act predictably, once she knew the identity of the witch. To insure the witch's death, she had added the bone bead to the shotgun shell, believing it would induce fatal corpse sickness. Chee's discovery of the bit of bone, together with his recognition of its likely meaning within Navajo belief, leads him to specific inferences—that traditional beliefs about witchcraft were involved in the attack on him, and, even more specifically, that he is suspected of being a witch.

Just as Yellowhorse was able to manipulate several Navajo through their belief in witchcraft, Chee's well-known desire to become a Yataalii leaves him open to manipulation. Luring him to a secluded place on the pretext of wanting a Blessing Way performed, the young woman whose baby is dying ambushes Chee a second time, wounding him and trapping him inside a deserted hogan. The problem Chee faces, in general terms, is not unlike the one faced by Sam Spade in the closing scenes of *The Maltese Falcon*: how to survive in the face of deadly threat under the constraint of time (Chee is bleeding) by manipulating one's adversary through knowledge of the adversary. "He had to keep her here. Had to keep her talking until he could make his mind work. Until he could learn from her what he had to learn to save his life" (1986, 244).

Confirming his guess that she thinks him a witch, Chee thereby understands, with a high degree of probability, what her belief entails about his alleged powers. Questioning her about how she became convinced he was a witch, more to confirm what he has come to suspect than out of genuine puzzlement, Chee gets the answer he expects, and with it the outlines of a strategy to stay alive by enlisting her help in getting him to a hospital: he promises to tell her who the "witch" really is, using her term but meaning by it something else: "[Chee] knew witchcraft in its basic form stalked the Dinee. He saw it in people who had turned deliberately and with malice from the beauty of the Navajo Way and embraced the evil that was its opposite. . . . He saw it . . . in those who sold whiskey to children, in those who bought videocassette recorders while their relatives were hungry, . . . in beaten wives and abandoned children" (1986, 246). Chee seeks first to reassure the young woman by demonstrating that he is not armed and then invites her to join him in the hogan, out of the rain, where he will identify the real witch, and " 'where you can look at my face while I tell you. That way you can tell whether I speak the truth' " (1986, 247). Hearing her walking in the mud outside the hogan, Chee gathers his thoughts: "He had to know exactly what to say" to persuade her to help him (1986, 247). Chee saves his life by quickly fashioning a strategy calculated to manipulate his assailant's beliefs to his advantage.

That Chee was merely wounded, rather than killed outright, in the attack testifies to other skills that make him an effective investigator. "Chee's intelligence," Hillerman informs his reader, "had its various strengths and weaknesses—a superb memory, a tendency to exclude new input while it focuses too narrowly on a single thought, a tendency to be distracted by beauty, and so forth. One of the strengths was an ability to process new information and collate it with old unusually fast. In a millisecond, Chee identified the missing odor, extracted its meaning, and homogenized it with what he had already noticed about the place . . . all this changed him, mid-stride, from a man happily walking through the rain toward a long-anticipated meeting, to a slightly uneasy man with a memory of being shot at. It was just then that Chee noticed the oil" (1986, 240–41).

Hillerman's extensive knowledge of Navajo culture has made his work an accessible source of information about Navajo (and Hopi) ways and beliefs, but the investigative skills possessed by Leaphorn and Chee, the more traditional of the two, are not finally rooted in their culture. Chee's superb memory is "Navajo-trained," to be sure. He possesses unusual observational skills. He synthesizes information quickly and accurately, and he is adept at understanding others and using that knowledge to his advantage, as needed. Chee correctly explains his assailant's attack on him as a consequence of her traditional belief in witchcraft and her conviction that Chee is the witch responsible for her baby's condition. His knowledge of her rests on correctly understanding the nature of her beliefs and using that understanding to persuade her that, by the very logic of those beliefs, Chee cannot be a witch and that she has been lied to and manipulated by Yellowhorse. Chee's insight, his understanding of his assailant's beliefs, owes something to his being Navajo; but it owes more to his ability to set aside or bracket his personal belief in order to identify with the other. The process of interpretation itself is independent of any given cultural content; it is neither Anglo nor Navajo. Through Chee, Hillerman suggests that understanding belief makes it possible to understand action as rational; simply judging or characterizing belief, as distinct from understanding it, renders action opaque and hence inexplicable.

At the end of *Skinwalkers*, the identities of Yellowhorse's two proxy killers remain unknown. " 'I guess we could find them now,' Chee said. '. . . Just work down through the records of the caseload here, looking at them the way Yellowhorse would have looked. . . . 'You think [FBI agent] Streib will think of it?' 'I doubt,' Leaphorn said . . . 'People say I hate witchcraft. [Streib], he hates to even think about witches.' 'Doesn't matter, anyway,' Chee said. 'It's finished,' " since Yellowhorse is dead. On that note, Hillerman ends the story. Understanding action begins with taking others' beliefs seriously, not because the beliefs in question are true but because they inform action and hence feature in its explanation. Unwilling even to think about witches, the FBI's Dilly

Streib can never close the case because he cannot perform the requisite imaginative identification with beliefs so far from his own. Presented first in Poe's "Murders in the Rue Morgue" and "The Purloined Letter," the critical importance of being able to identify with one's adversary remains basic to the writing of mystery fiction, despite the enormous variety, especially since 1980, in the gender and ethnic identity of the detective.

Robert Campbell's series character Jimmy Flannery, introduced in his Edgar-winning first novel *The Junkyard Dog* (1986), is a notable case in point. Flannery is not cast as a private detective as such but as a Democratic precinct captain in Chicago, an accomplished Irish "pol." He holds a patronage job reading meters for the city's water department, but most of his time is spent on constituent service. Sometimes that service involves him in the investigation of murder. Like Lew Archer, Flannery works in a large city; like Jim Chee, he is a visible, familiar, and well-known figure in a particular locale, in this instance the near West Side ward in which he lives and works. Occupying a visible position in a large and complex political organization, Flannery works within a framework of accountability and constraint that is looser than if he were a police detective but tighter than if he were a self-employed private investigator. Flannery manages to be a skillful political operator on the one hand, and a tenacious and resourceful investigator on the other.

In *The Junkyard Dog* Campbell tells two stories: one political, the other a conventional murder mystery involving the deaths of two women in the bombing of an abortion clinic located in Flannery's ward. Flannery's successful resolution of the challenges to both his political and his investigative resources rests on a familiar set of skills. Strategic lies, "white lies," are Flannery's stock in trade: "I will lie at the drop of a hat if it don't do no individual any harm, prevents hysteria, or cuts through the crap," he admits (1986, 14). Flannery reads others well; he knows that "every soul has a soft spot," (1986, 71) which, if identified, can be exploited when necessary; and he can assume, when required, the investigator's studied opacity to mask his thoughts or true feelings: "She's standing there staring at me, looking for signs. I stare right back. People who give you surprises like that think they can read the truth of your feelings in your eyes" (1986, 45). Flannery's knowledge of social customs and social roles permits him to move with equal ease in the "horizontal" world of Chicago's ethnic neighborhoods and in its hierarchical world of wealth and power. Finally, Campbell shows Flannery to be absolute in his refusal to drop an investigation in the face of escalating threats and intimidation. In *The Junkyard Dog*, these include a severe beating and a murderous attack on his fiancee that kills a woman mistaken for her.

The final test of Flannery's sure-footed sense of the world in which he works occurs in a scene toward the end of *The Junkyard Dog*. He has gone to confront Daniel Tartaglia, son-in-law of Chicago's syndicate boss, Carmine DiBella, but instead encounters DiBella himself. Gauging just how far he can go with DiBella, Flannery adroitly maneuvers the don into confirming the hypothesis Flannery has pieced together. "He stares at me as though I could be a devil, or maybe I could be the priest who's hearing his last confession. 'I hate this,' he finally says. 'I hate that you put me in a place where I got to explain myself. I'm not used to having to explain myself . . . [but, Flannery,] 'You're entitled' " (1986, 176).

By the time DiBella's son-in-law joins the conversation, DiBella has grudgingly acknowledged Flannery as an equal of sorts: this isn't "lawyer talk," DiBella snaps at his son-in-law; " 'this is talk between honorable men' "(1986, 179). In the course of the ensuing conversation, Flannery gets an accounting of the abortion clinic bombing and the subsequent cover-up, but he still has no evidence on which charges can be brought against anyone. " 'I found out some things. I can maybe find out more.' DiBella shakes his head slowly. 'No, no. Mr. Flannery. Don't you see you got nobody to take it to even if you dig up any gold? Don't you see there are too many people involved now who can't back down? Be smart. Better. Be wise' " (1986, 180–81). In short, forget about the whole thing. Drop the case. Flannery's fiancee and father also advise him that he has no prosecutable case, his conversation with DiBella notwithstanding. " 'There's three people dead,' I says. 'You can't leave me with just that and six bits for the altar candles.' 'That's what they left you with, Jimmy,' [his father] says, 'just a prayer' " (1986, 183).

Convinced that the case will never be brought to court, Flannery seeks an alternative resolution of the situation. Approaching a lawyer, ostensibly a friend of Tartaglia's (but who has an interest in seeing Tartaglia compromised), Flannery suggests a trap. " 'You know and I know that your friend Danny ain't going to stay home and true-blue forever. He's got an appetite and it don't go away. He'll be buying ass again.' . . . [the lawyer] leans forward a little. What he wants and what I want is making us partners, if not pals" (1986, 185–86). The lawyer will find a suitable young woman to introduce to Tartaglia, "maybe even loan them your apartment the first time," Flannery suggests. "Along the way we move them to a flat, a little place with a hidden mike. A flat where we can take pictures if we have to. And then, one day, I put out the word. It whispers through the town. It gets to the ears of a man like DiBella, who makes it his business to hear everything and . . ." (1986, 186; ellipses in original). Predicting how the lawyer will respond to his proposal, banking on Daniel Tartaglia's known sexual appetites, estimating the likely limits of DiBella's tolerance of his son-in-law's infidelities, Flannery calculates the most likely outcome—Tartaglia's execution at DiBella's order, once Tartaglia has been discovered *in flagrante delicto.*

Weeks later, at ceremonies honoring the deceased firefighter for whose widow he has been trying to obtain full pension rights, Flannery is approached by the Democratic party chairman, Ray Carrigan: " 'Ain't it terrible what I read in the paper about Daniel Tartaglia?' . . . 'Ain't it ironic he should get shot down in a house, in which working girls was allegedly plying their trade, by a pair of thieves?' " (1986, 188). Flannery's predictions of how others will act, based on his knowledge of them, are thus confirmed by the outcome Flannery sought to bring about. What the city's legal system could not deliver in this instance—the restoration of the "honor of his house"—Flannery achieves by understanding the motives and beliefs of others sufficiently well to manipulate their actions with a high degree of confidence.

Flannery knows that " 'Nobody does nothing for nothing' " (1986, 111). He also knows things that uniquely characterize a particular individual: "And [Bo Addison's] brother the pimp don't forget [one of the murder victims] because he was using her to maybe bring Tartaglia down, which would maybe bring [a judge] down, which would maybe put the squeeze on [an Italian alderman] so that the mayor and the party chairman figures it's time for a black alderman, like Addison, in the Twenty-fifth" (1986, 184). Between these two extremes lies a wealth of understanding about individuals classified in terms of social role: "He makes [Tartaglia's wife] sound like a clay pot. I don't think she's a clay pot. She was raised like a Sicilian princess. I figure she's a woman with hot blood. I think she puts up with what she's got to put up with when Tartaglia starts to stray. She puts up the good front as long as he don't make her lose honor" (1986, 159). Flannery persuades a prostitute to talk to him by appealing to a fear he attributes to street-walkers generally: " 'What happened to her [another prostitute] could happen to you someday . . . Wouldn't you want somebody to care how you got there?' She's quiet a minute, her eyes going soft and afraid while she thinks about the many bad ways whores come to the end of the line. 'Okay,' she says, her voice husky all of a sudden" (1986, 169). Moreover, Flannery knows how individuals are related in the complex interdependency of the city's economic and political life. In short, he knows how the system works, and knowing that, can manipulate the individuals whose everyday activities constitute the workings of the system.

Marcia Muller is widely credited with modifying the conventions of the hard-boiled novel to make private investigation a suitable job for a woman (Brainard 1994). *Wolf in the Shadows* (1993), her thirteenth mystery novel featuring Sharon McCone, an investigator for San Francisco's All Souls Legal Cooperative, finds McCone involved in a highly personal case in which she risks her future with All Souls to undertake a search for her lover, Hy Ripinsky, who has disappeared while working for an international security consulting firm. Like her male counterparts, McCone is adept at deception and quick to lie or misrepresent herself, however reluctantly, when strategy or necessity require her to do so: "I felt uncomfortable lying so badly, especially to an old friend of my brother, but this was a situation where I couldn't be straightforward" (1993, 179). Over the years, McCone has built up a network of useful, reliable contacts—police officers, a telephone company employee, a former employer with whom she has retained good relations—upon whom she can call for advice but especially for information to which she otherwise would not have ready access. Like her male counterparts, she possesses the presence of mind, the quick, sure adaptability to uncertain situations, and the acting and improvisational skills that characterize fictional investigators generally but are the hallmarks of the hard-boiled private detective in particular. These skills are tested early in *Wolf in the Shadows* when McCone arranges an appointment with Gage Renshaw, the head of the security firm Ripinsky was working for when he disappeared. She knows Renshaw only by reputation as ruthless, dangerous, and obsessively secretive.

Renshaw and McCone begin their conversation by fencing, each trying to draw out the other, while giving nothing away in the process.

McCone wants to know what Ripinsky was working on; Renshaw wants to know what McCone is up to. Neither wants to give away any more than is necessary, and each is suspicious and wary of the other, alert for the smallest gesture that will signal a lie or betray what the other is really thinking. "Something in the way he said Hy's name put me on my guard. I saw a tightening of his mouth, a telltale whiteness of the skin. This man was angry at Hy—very angry" (1993, 57). McCone tries to manipulate Renshaw's anger by telling him Ripinsky cheated her in a business deal, but "[he] didn't believe my story of the business deal any more than I believed his abrupt shift to the role of confidant" (1993, 57). Unwilling to tell him her real motives for wanting to find Ripinsky but needing to break the stalemate of their mutual distrust, she resorts to another lie: "All I can tell you is that when I find Ripinsky, there'll be nothing good in store for him." To that Renshaw replies: " 'Either you're telling me the truth or you're a very good actress . . . [adding], When I find [Ripinsky], I intend to kill him.' Now I had to call upon all my acting skills. With an effort, I kept my voice level as I asked, 'What did Ripinsky do to you?' " (1993, 58–59).

Renshaw refuses to say, and McCone, concluding that he really has no idea where Ripinsky is, tries a bluff: " 'If you tell me what went down, I can find him. You see, Ripinsky and I used to be lovers; I know how he thinks.' Two lies there, McCone" (1993, 59). Renshaw, however, remains unconvinced: "You realize I don't believe a word of your story. . . . All of this seems like a smoke screen for some private agenda that I'm not going to try to guess at" (1993, 60). McCone ventures another move, part argument, part challenge: "My motives don't matter. What does is that I can be bought to do what your operatives so far haven't managed" (1993, 60). After a brief "internal debate," Renshaw accepts McCone's challenge, if not the details of her story, and fills her in on what Ripinsky was doing when he disappeared and why Renshaw is determined to kill him when he finds him. In her interview with Renshaw, then, McCone succeeds in concealing her true feelings about Ripinsky—her real motive for wanting to find him—while getting from Renshaw the information she must have to begin her search.

Wolf in the Shadows concludes with McCone, Ripinsky, and a business executive they have rescued from kidnappers attempting to cross back into the United States from Mexico, using a route (and a guide) relied on by illegal immigrants. Not fully trusting their guide, however, and sensing that something is amiss as they are about to enter a storm drain traversing the border, McCone lets the two men, both wounded, continue on while she climbs an embankment to look for an ambush. Her fears are confirmed; she spots the novel's principal villain, Marty Salazar, armed and poised near the entrance of the drainage pipe, ready to shoot whoever emerges. McCone, armed herself, must decide very quickly on a course of action. Earlier in her career, she had resorted to deadly force while on a case and discovered that doing so had isolated her from those to whom she was closest, including her older brother. She briefly weighs the risk of alienating him anew against the clear and present threat to her lover's life. She knows Salazar is a killer, but there is a further consideration: she is preparing to shoot someone in the back without warning, a situation arising infrequently in detective fiction and almost never with female protagonists: "Everything I believed in told me this was wrong. Everything I cared about told me this was right. One shot, two at most. Shoot to kill. A gun has only one purpose: if you use it, be prepared to kill." McCone pulls the trigger when Salazar, settling into position, makes his deadly intention unmistakable.

McCone's shooting is ruled self-defense, although she reacts to it as "murder: it was just that, no sugar-coating the fact . . . I'd shot a man in cold blood. Taken his life to get my people through" (1993, 360). Her fears about the impact of the event on her brother prove groundless, however: "I'd feared the killing would reerect the barrier between John and me. But he'd seen Salazar, seen the evil I was up against; taking him along while I'd investigated had allowed him a glimpse of the realities of my world that he would never forget, and created a stronger bond between us" (1993, 360). Moreover, Renshaw and his partner are impressed enough with her work to offer her a position: "[we] doubt any of our operatives would have handled this situation better—or more, shall we say, creatively" (1993, 365).

McCone shares with other fictional investigators a finely honed ability to read other people and a talent for deception. She is unusual, however, in the degree to which Muller makes feeling the basis for her knowing things, often of crucial importance to her case. Visiting the site where she has every reason to believe Hy Ripinsky had been murdered, she comes away convinced instead that he remains alive: "When I finally began to feel, the emotions were not the ones I'd anticipated. . . . I'd come here this morning on a pilgrimage, thinking everything was over, finished. Now I realized my search was only beginning"

(1993, 5, 177). At another site, trying to establish whether Ripinsky might have been there shortly before his disappearance, she concludes, "this, then, had not been Hy's destination. . . . Logic told me so, but I also knew it on a deeper, more elemental level. . . . he had not come to this lonely place, not ever. If he had, I would have known. It was that simple" (1993, 42–43). Renshaw recognizes this distinctive aspect of McCone's makeup: "You strike me as someone who works on instinct. Your impressions of the people you're dealing with meld with the facts you're presented. Sometimes your conclusions aren't strictly logical, but they feel right. And nine times out of ten they turn out to *be* right" (1993, 95). It is feeling that makes the difference at the conclusion of *Wolf in the Shadow*, warning McCone that she and her companions may be entering a trap: "There might not be any people in [the drainage pipe] now, but I could smell their leavings, feel remnants of their fear and despair. I could also smell the faint trapped odor of cordite. I stiffened. . . . 'Something *is* wrong,' I whispered" (1993, 356). Acting with conviction on her feeling, McCone slips out of the pipe to reconnoiter and discovers the impending ambush.

Reading the other is central to other recent works of detective fiction, such as Jeremiah Healy's *Act of God* (1994), the ninth in his series about Boston private investigator John Cuddy. Following the fatal bludgeoning of an elderly Jewish furniture store owner and the subsequent disappearance of one of his secretaries, Cuddy agrees, reluctantly, to work for both the victim's widow and the brother of the missing young woman, since the murder and the disappearance may be linked. Cuddy soon establishes that the missing secretary was both something of an actress and a close observer of men: " '[from a young age] . . . she wasn't just watching them, she was . . . studying them, maybe? Trying to figure out what they were like, maybe *what* they liked' " (1994, 109; ellipses in original). By the end of the case, Cuddy has discovered that Darbra Profit's manipulative skills had led, directly or indirectly, to the deaths of two men and the wife of a third man, with whom she was having an affair.

Cuddy's ability to read others accurately is especially clear on two occasions. Following up a lead in a New Jersey resort town, Cuddy encounters a young man, a college football player, physically abusing his female companion. Cuddy steps into the situation to prevent his hitting her again, despite a physical disparity favoring the younger man: "her boyfriend had me by about two inches, twenty years, and forty pounds." Cuddy gives his young adversary something to think about: "Around the time you were learning how to throw up, the Army spent a lot of tax dollars training me to hurt people. Touch her again, and we'll see if Uncle Sam got his money's worth" (1994, 212). As the momentum of the situation shifts to Cuddy, he plays on the athlete's likely weak spot: "Wouldn't sit so well with the coach, your hitting a woman, all these witnesses and a formal complaint to boot" (1994, 213). Cowed by the threat, the belligerent young man retreats. Worried that an injured knee and shoulder have reduced his ability to deal with physical threat, Cuddy must depend, in this instance, on knowing how to manipulate another in order to intervene successfully in the chance encounter.

At the end of *Act of God*, Cuddy is equally successful in reading and manipulating another. Convinced that Roger Houle murdered his wife so that he could be with Darbra Profit, Cuddy goads Houle into a murderous assault, thus giving himself an excuse to shoot Houle in self-defense: "I wasn't sure [Houle] was seeing his chance. 'What say you pick up one of those long-handled shovels, Rog, and we do some archaeology?' I'd tipped him, but the way he kept his eyes on me while reaching out and grabbing the handle told me he'd been thinking it before I said it" (1994, 310). Houle attacks Cuddy with the shovel, prompting Cuddy to fire three times.

Later, under questioning from police officers openly skeptical of his account of the events leading up to the shooting, Cuddy successfully obscures precisely how Houle came to attack him. " 'You say he came at you with a shovel.' 'Right,' [Cuddy replied] 'And you didn't have time to show your gun before you had to use it?' 'He'd knocked me down and was standing over me, about to split my head open.' The townie lit a cigarette. 'Doesn't say much for your agility, you can't clear your holster before a guy with a shovel gets close enough to whack you' " (1994, 311–12). At the end of the interview, another officer asks Cuddy who killed the furniture store owner, whose widow hired him. " 'Can't tell by me,' " Cuddy lies (1994, 313), having decided that compassion for the living, who would be hurt by the truth of the matter, weighed more than identifying and bringing the perpetrator to justice—a point to which I return in chapter 5, "Costs and Benefits."

4

Tradecraft: The Systematization and Professionalization of Duplicity

Belief in a colleague in an intelligence agency is to some degree an act of will; you don't know a man is to be trusted; you believe he is to be trusted, and decide to trust him.

Thomas Powers, *The Man Who Kept the Secrets*

K nowing the other better than the other knows you defines intelligence work, both in the real world and in the worlds of fictional agents, from such amateur spies as Erskine Childers's Carruthers (*The Riddle of the Sands*, 1903) and John Buchan's Richard Hannay to the professional agents of John Le Carré, Len Deighton, Ted Allbeury, Charles McCarry, William Hood, and countless others.[1] A textbook example of this asymmetrical relationship, and the potential for manipulation arising from it, occurs in W. Somerset Maugham's *Ashenden* (1928) in the chapter "The Traitor." *Ashenden* draws extensively on Maugham's own experiences as a British agent during World War I, first in Switzerland and then in Russia, where he was sent in 1917 as part of a British effort aimed at preventing the Bolshevik revolution and keeping Russia in the war (Morgan 1980; Atkins 1984, 164–69; Masters 1987, 35–65).

Set earlier in the war, "The Traitor" finds Ashenden dispatched to Lucerne, where an expatriate Englishman, Grantly Caypor, lives with his German wife. Caypor has been spying for the Germans, but what has particularly drawn the attention, and the abiding enmity, of Ashenden's controller is Caypor's responsibility in the death of a young Spanish national recruited by British intelligence. "Ashenden's instructions were to get acquainted with Caypor and see whether there was any chance that he would work honestly for the British; if he thought there was, he was entitled to sound him and if his suggestions met with favour to make certain propositions. It was a task that needed tact and a knowledge of men" (Maugham 1943, 128). On the other hand, if he concludes that Caypor will not work honestly for the British, Ashenden is to get him to leave Switzerland so that he can be apprehended by the British and shot for causing the death of their agent.

Ashenden's problem is to get to know Caypor well enough to determine his true motives for spying on behalf of the Germans; to assess the likelihood that he could be persuaded to shift his loyalties to the British; and do so without arousing Caypor's suspicions in the process. Establishing a precise motive for his countryman's treachery, however, eludes Ashenden: "He did not think that he had become a spy merely for the money" (1943, 142). Perhaps he preferred deviousness "for some intricate pleasure [such men] get in fooling their fellows." Perhaps he was impelled by vanity. Whatever the case, one thing became clear to Ashenden as he came to know his man: "Caypor was disturbed by no gnawing conscience; he did his mean and despicable work with gusto. He was a traitor who enjoyed his treachery" (1943, 143).

Ashenden concludes the man could not be trusted as a double agent: "His [German] wife's influence was too strong" (1943, 143). Having reached this conclusion, Ashenden must devise a way to persuade Caypor to leave the sanctuary of Switzerland. Ashenden becomes patiently watchful, "his eyes open to seize the opportunity that might present itself" (1943, 144). When a remark of Mrs. Caypor's makes him suspect that she is lying to him ("he hardly knew why") about her husband's whereabouts one day, Ashenden quickly confirms the feeling as well as his surmise that Caypor has been to Berne to see his German controller. When he returns to Lucerne, Caypor appears troubled and distracted. Ashenden guesses that he has been ordered to return to England to be a more active spy: "Guesswork? Of course it was guesswork, but in that trade it mostly was; you had to deduce the animal from its jawbone" (1943, 145).

Ashenden's guesses are confirmed when Caypor approaches him for a letter of recommendation to the Censorship Department, the very department affording Ashenden his cover story. Ashenden, too, is a pawn in the game being played out between R., his controller, and the German spy master in Berne: Ashenden "saw that he had been put in Lucerne, told how to describe himself and given the proper information, so that what actually had occurred should occur. . . . It was a trap . . . and the grim major at Berne had fallen into it" (1943, 146). Knowing how desirable it would seem to the German secret service to have an agent in the Censorship Department, and with reason to think that Major von P. was becoming impatient with Caypor, Ashenden's controller had equipped him with the appropriate cover story and told him to get to know Caypor, who would duly report to his German contact that he had chanced to meet an employee of the Censorship Department. In that event, if the major is as impatient with Caypor as R. has been led to believe, he will act as R. predicts and order Caypor to England, an outcome due less to Ashenden's cleverness, he comes to realize, than to his playing his cover role so well, so "innocently," that Caypor's suspicions are not aroused. Ashenden does not need to know why R. chose the particular details of his cover story. As it is, Ashenden is engaged in that difficult task identified by Erving Goffman of having simultaneously to conceal the fact of the matter (that he is a secret agent posing as a government clerk) and to manage the normal appearances required by that false identity. To have known the point of his particular cover story would have made the management of normal appearances more complicated for Ashenden, thus running the greater risk of his inadvertently betraying something to Caypor, whose own safety depends on penetrating just the sort of deception Ashenden is practicing on him. Put differently, Ashenden's ignorance about the point of his cover story permits him to behave more "naturally" toward Caypor, but at the cost of his being a pawn of R's. In this instance that is not cause for alarm; but it can and does become so when one's "controller" ought not to be trusted.

Between 1936 and 1940, Eric Ambler published six novels employing the convention of the innocent person drawn into intrigue that had served Buchan and Erskine Childers so well: *The Dark Frontier* (1936); *Background to Danger* (1937); *Epitaph for a Spy* (1938); *Cause for Alarm* and *A Coffin for Dimitrios* (1939); and *Journey into Fear* (1940). A failure successively as an engineering apprentice, songwriter, and playwright, Ambler took a job as a copywriter with a London advertising agency in 1934, and rose to a directorship within three years. In the meantime, he had begun to write thrillers, intent on reshaping the politics of the genre. "I was a *very* far left socialist," he said years later in an interview. "I set out to change the genre. I remember reading the accepted masters . . . Sapper and the rest—and deciding they wouldn't do" (Eames 1978, 151). When his initial efforts proved successful with readers, Ambler left the world of advertising in 1938 in order to write full time (Ambler 1985; Lewis 1990, chapter 3; Wolfe 1993, chapter 4; Oram 1974).

The power over others that comes from understanding them better than they understand you is central to the concept of Ambler's *A Coffin for Dimitrios*. The story blends elements of the traditional detective story and the formula success story with the convention of the innocent person caught up in intrigue. Ambler's innocent in this case is Charles Latimer, a former British university lecturer turned detective fiction writer.

In Istanbul, Latimer chances to meet Colonel Haki, the head of the Turkish secret police, who happens to be a fan of Latimer's detective stories. Haki invites Latimer to visit him at his office. Their visit is interrupted when Haki is informed that the body of a man called Dimitrios, in whom Haki has a long-standing interest, has been found floating in the Bosporus. Haki asks Latimer whether he is interested in *real* murderers and proceeds to outline the dead man's career. Latimer asks to see the body—he has never seen a corpse or visited a mortuary, and it would be good background for his writing. Pondering the body, Latimer considers trying to fill in the gaps in Dimitrios's career as Haki has outlined it: "It would be an experiment in detection really. . . . All the routine inquiries over which one skated so easily in one's novels one would have to make oneself" (1939, 28).

Bored, between books, still recuperating from the illness that had prompted his remove to a warmer climate, and unwilling to return to England in autumn, Latimer decides to attempt reconstructing Dimitrios's career. "If you could find [the people who had known Dimitrios] and get the answers you would have the material for what would surely be the strangest of biographies" (1939, 28). He sets out to make the attempt, but it is soon apparent to the reader that Latimer is out of his depth. If anyone is fit for the world Latimer encounters in reconstructing Dimitrios's career, it is Dimitrios, not Latimer. Ambler announces Latimer's ineptness at the outset: "The fact that a man like Latimer should *so much as learn of the existence of a man like Dimitrios* is alone grotesque . . . and that he should ultimately find himself in the position of owing his life to a criminal's odd taste in interior decoration are breath-taking in their absurdity" (1939, 9; emphasis added). In this early passage, Ambler hints at a central element in his conception of Dimitrios—his extraordinary skill at maintaining normal appearances.

Latimer's investigation into Dimitrios's past leads him from Istanbul to Smyrna and then on to Athens, Sofia, Geneva, and Paris as he reconstructs the man's rise to power and wealth from his impoverished origins as a fig packer in Turkey. From documents, but especially from interviews with former associates who survived their dealings with Dimitrios, Latimer discovers Dimitrios to have been a gifted and utterly ruthless manipulator of others for his own purposes. Dimitrios's singular talent, Latimer quickly discovers, is for knowing others better than he permits them to understand him, thus rendering himself opaque and hence proof against their efforts to manipulate him.

Latimer discovers that Dimitrios had begun his career by murdering a Jewish money lender, leaving an accomplice to hang for the crime. From the court transcript, Latimer concludes, "Dimitrios had used the [man's] dull wits, had played upon his religious fanaticism, his simplicity, his cupidity with a skill that was terrifying . . . [Dimitrios's] brown, tired-looking eyes had watched Dhris Mohammed and understood him perfectly" (1939, 41). As he made his way west from Turkey, seeking his fortune, Dimitrios would employ the same skill on others, some of whom were far more difficult to read than his dull-witted accomplice, Dhris Mohammed.

In Sofia, Latimer searches out Madame Preveza, who had taken Dimitrios for her lover years before. "One deceives oneself," she muses to Latimer, recalling her time with Dimitrios. "One thinks that one wants to be understood when one wants only to be half-understood. If a person really understands you, you fear him. . . . Dimitrios understood me better than I understood myself. . . . It was because I feared him and could not understand him as he understood me that I hated him' " (1939, 78–79). Later, in Geneva, Latimer interviews a retired spy master, Wladyslaw Grodek, who had once employed Dimitrios and been bested in the encounter. Concluding his account of what had happened, Grodek anticipates one likely assessment of his handling of Dimitrios to ensure that Latimer gets the point, which turns on a crucial distinction: "You may say that I was careless in my handling of Dimitrios. That would be unjust. It was a small error in judgment on my part. . . . I counted on his being like all the other fools in the world, on his being too greedy. I thought he would wait until he had from me the forty thousand dinar due to him before he tried to take the photograph as well. He took me by surprise. That error in judgment cost me a lot of money' " (1939, 129). Grodek's distinction between an act of carelessness and an error in calculation reveals a by now familiar pattern in mystery fiction: of anticipating the other's most likely course of action in a situation on the basis of one's best guess about their true nature. In this case, Grodek's best guess—that Dimitrios fit a general, predictable pattern of motivation—failed the test. Dimitrios surprises him, which is to say that he proves to be unpredictable, from Grodek's point of view, and the wily spy is fortunate to escape the encounter with his life.

In Paris, Latimer learns a great deal more about Dimitrios from Petersen, a former associate of his, and about the heroin-smuggling operation Dimitrios had organized and managed in the late 1920s. The small group he had gathered included a woman, Lydia, chosen because she possessed a singularly valuable skill: "Her capacity for weighing up complete strangers was extraordinary. She could, I think, tell the most cleverly disguised detective just by looking at him across a room. It was her business to examine the person who wanted to buy and decide whether he or she should be supplied or not" (1939, 154). After becoming addicted to heroin himself, Dimitrios had betrayed his associates to the police, and Petersen admits to Latimer that "Even Lydia, who understood so much about people, was defeated by him" (1939, 160).

In the end, Petersen too is defeated by Dimitrios: "You were always too ingenious," Dimitrios taunts him in the novel's final scene, shortly before shooting him. "Ingenuity is never a substitute for intelligence, you know. Did you really think that I should not see through you?" (1939, 211). Latimer escapes Petersen's fate, as it happens, by behaving unpredictably—jumping *at* Dimitrios just as Dimitrios turns the pistol on him. "Why [Latimer] chose that particular moment to jump he never knew. He never even knew what had prompted him to jump at all" (1939, 211). Latimer's action is inexplicable, after the fact, even to himself. It has no rational or cognitive basis, is part of no strategy. Although the jump saves Latimer's life, it is a matter of chance, in the final analysis, rather than the kind of calculated unpredictability—that deliberate effort to unsettle and disconfirm his adversary's expectations—that defines Sam Spade's self-conscious stance in a world of risk, uncertainty, and danger and which served Dimitrios so well in his encounter with Wladyslaw Grodek.

Latimer, then, is spared by chance, just as Dimitrios dies by chance, or, as he puts it, by "stupidity. If it is not one's own it is the stupidity of others" (1939, 214). Latimer learns nothing from his efforts to trace and understand Dimitrios's rise in the world. He has seen and reported a good deal but grasped little.[2] Through Latimer's encounters with the Bulgarian journalist Marukakis, the retired spy Grodek, and Petersen, Ambler offers his mordant observations on a world sliding into chaos. Latimer, however, remains impervious to their testimony about the realities of power, how it is obtained, how it is exercised, and to what ends. The cleverness required to create successful detective novels fails to prepare Latimer for the world of Dimitrios. By implication, Ambler's assessment of the English country house mystery, Latimer's metier, anticipates that made by Raymond Chandler five years later (1995): the puzzle mystery was out of touch with reality and had little to teach about a world populated by men like Dimitrios or Caspar Gutman.

Few writers have appropriated the Buchanesque formula—the convention of the innocent caught up by chance in intrigue and espionage—with greater commercial success than Helen MacInnes, who published her first thriller, *Above Suspicion*, in 1941. Each of her 20 books rose predictably to the top of the *New York Times* bestseller list, typically remaining there for months. *The Double Image* (1966) exemplifies the uses to which she put the conventions pioneered by Buchan. It depicts a world where "romance, honor, integrity, and personal courage" not only are regarded as admirable, but prove effectual as well. John Craig, the protagonist of *The Double Image*, exemplifies the self-effacing competence of her decent, civilized heroes. A historian, with a Ph.D. from Columbia University, Craig chances to meet a former professor of his on the streets of Paris. The man appears distraught and tells Craig that he has just seen a Nazi war criminal, Heinrich Berg, long believed to be dead. A little later, Berg appears in the cafe where Craig and Professor Sussman have gone for a drink. Listening to Sussman's story and then having Berg pointed out to him, Craig acquires a bit of dangerous knowledge that he ought never to have had. Moreover, he knows that he possesses it and that Berg suspects he does. The next day, Craig learns that Professor Sussman has been found dead, an apparent suicide. In the meantime, however, Craig has attended a party in honor of his sister and brother-and-law, who are on their way home from a stint at the Moscow embassy. At the party, Craig mentions Sussman's story and is overheard by an American intelligence agent and by an American working secretly for the KGB. Both the CIA and the KGB have an interest in Berg, as it happens, and Craig finds himself drawn into the world of cold war espionage. As *The Double Image* unfolds, MacInnes depicts Craig as maturing politically, losing his dangerous illusions about the struggle between East and West and coming to understand, through personal experience, the true nature of that confrontation.

Throughout *The Double Image*, MacInnes challenges the notion that there are no profound differences between East and West. Craig's brother-in-law tells him, for example, of an incident when an American was detained, without reason, for several days by Soviet authorities in Moscow. " 'That's one thing you've got to remember, John,' " he continues; " 'When we detain a Russian or satellite citizen in the United States, we have an honest case against him. We have real evidence. The Russians invent evidence. So that is a big difference between them and us. . . . there are some very big differences indeed between us and 2them' " (1967, 27). One of those differences emerges in a calculated pairing of chapters that follows. The first represents a hastily convened meeting of Western intelligence agents to discuss Craig's conversation with Professor Sussman. Four agents attend the meeting, one French, one British, and two American. Their relationships are friendly, cordial, and business-like, marked by evidence of mutual trust and respect. MacInnes carefully avoids making them seem hardened or cynical. When the group is informed of the death of a French agent who was carrying a valuable photograph, Rosenfeld, one of the American agents asks, "What about the camera?" As if to forestall a reader's negative response, MacInnes adds: "A brutal question, but needed" (1967, 45). The four agents end their conference amicably, with promises of mutual cooperation, their national interests subordinated to coping with a common threat.

Three parallel meetings of Soviet agents to discuss Craig's story contrast sharply with the trust and cooperation evident among the Western intelligence officers. The Soviet agents meet in a Parisian nightclub, whose "patrons were a mixture of the restless rich and the pseudo avant-garde," unaware that the nightclub is Soviet-financed. MacInnes decries the ease with which the Soviets seem able to "stimulate the neurotic among their enemies and make them still more incompetent to deal with the real world" (1967, 61). The meetings between the Soviet agents are tense. There is an undercurrent of distrust, and even a high-ranking agent fears that compromising photographs in his file may be used against him. Orders are issued peremptorily. Information is shared out grudgingly, and only as needed. Soviet intelligence displays a rigid hierarchy. It is a world of suspicion and distrust, whose personnel are kept in line by blackmail and fear—a world epitomized by the ruthless cynicism of the agent Insarov, who served Soviet intelligence during the war as "Heinrich Berg." As Berg, MacInnes makes clear, Insarov (and, by extension, Soviet intelligence) played a leading role in managing German concentration camps like Auschwitz, where Professor Sussman first encountered him.

MacInnes develops the contrast between the two intelligence efforts further when a French agent, Duclos, is captured by the Soviets. Dissension among his captors permits Duclos not only to swallow a cyanide pill he carries, but to make his death seem the result of a blow from an impatient, over-zealous interrogator. By acting as he does, Duclos denies the Soviets not just the opportunity to learn what he knew of their plans, but confirmation that he is an agent at all. Later Craig reflects on what he has learned since his chance encounter with Sussman: "Two week ago . . . I'd have been laughing fit to crack my ribs, making bright remarks about what the best-dressed agent is wearing this season; yesterday, I might have produced a grin, felt a touch of embarrassment when I next met [CIA agent] Partridge. But today? Well, I've learned about Duclos; about a lot of things. The more you know, the less you scoff. . . . If I came to Europe to fill in some gaps in my education, I've certainly succeeded" (1967, 210–11).

Earlier, Craig draws a parallel between Berg and Richard Sorge, "the German-born Soviet spy who had been a trusted Nazi in the German Embassy in Tokyo during the Second World War. He had let Moscow know about Pearl Harbor in advance, too. Yes, that was something that needed remembering" (1967, 134). Craig draws the appropriate inferences: more than a record of wars and peace conferences, "history was a long and bitter story of intrigue and grab . . . of men who knew what they wanted manipulating men who hadn't one idea that anything was at stake: the innocent and the ignorant being used according to someone else's plan. But every now and again, the plan would fail. Because people could be surprising, too, in their resistance—once they knew what was actually happening. Once they knew" (1967, 134). There can be little doubt that MacInnes intends *The Double Image*, and her other novels of innocents caught up in international intrigue, to convey such knowledge. Of her work generally, she has said, "They are novels in contemporary history. . . . I am a research historian telling stories." She attended the trial of Soviet agent Rudolph Abel "to study the eyes, expressions. I want hard facts, want to know about what I am writing about" (White 1974, E2)

Craig proves to be a gifted amateur at the sort of counterespionage into which he is drawn. His training as a historian has accustomed him both to making inferences from fragmentary and ambiguous evidence and to maintaining a healthy skepticism about such inferences. He has had enough military training to be useful in the final confrontation with the Soviets, which involves the rescue of an American electronics expert abducted by Berg/Insarov. The key to Craig's survival, however, lies in his capacity to dissemble, to hide his true feelings and intentions when the occasion requires. His conversation with Professor Sussman in the Paris cafe makes Craig the target of a series of encounters staged by the Soviets and intended to manipulate him into betraying the extent to which he may have been taken into Sussman's confidence. In one incident, an American approaches him, claiming to remember him from Columbia and asking about Sussman. When Craig admits to having spoken with Sussman the day before his apparent suicide, the man tries to pump him for information about the conversation. What was on Sussman's mind? "Something must have been troubling him badly. Now you would think, wouldn't you, that he had a fine chance to tell you his problems when he met you . . . ?" (1967, 83). Suspicious, and increasingly angry, Craig successfully deflects the questions, while taking care not to arouse the other's suspicion.

Two days later, however, Craig is subjected to a second and more serious encounter designed to trap him into betraying what his adversaries think he may know. In a secondhand bookstore, a man strikes up a conversation with Craig and invites him for a drink. As they pass up two likely cafes for no apparent reason, Craig realizes his companion is steering him to the same cafe, and even the same table, where he had sat with Professor Sussman several days before. Barely controlling his rage, Craig sits down. Moments later the man Sussman had identified as Heinrich Berg comes into the cafe. Resisting the impulse to have his companion call the police, Craig betrays no hint that he recognizes

Berg, and the incident is quickly over. Reflecting on the encounter, Craig considers leaving Paris and getting on with the research that brought him to Europe. "Get back to your own world, Craig, and stay where you belong," he tells himself. "But can there be any separate worlds? he wondered as he thought of Sussman" (1967, 90). There is only one world, MacInnes argues in *The Double Image*, and in Craig she defines and displays the qualities that make for being at home in that world.

Whether the protagonist is a private detective, a professional agent, or simply a suitably adept "amateur," mystery fiction represents and dramatizes a close fit between the protagonist and his or her world. Each possesses the requisite skills and aptitudes needed to survive the situations of risk and danger in which they find themselves obliged to act. Exceptions to the more or less optimistic view of the amateur expressed in much detective fiction, as well as in the works of such best-selling authors as Helen MacInnes, are rare, but a notable example is John Bingham's *A Fragment of Fear*, coincidentally published in the same year as *The Double Image*, 1966.[3] Bingham's protagonist, James Compton, like Ambler's Charles Latimer, is a British mystery writer. In Italy recuperating from an automobile accident, he becomes interested in the murder of an elderly English woman, Lucy Dawson. Compton's investigation convinces him that although Dawson appeared to be engaged in helping released prisoners to rehabilitate themselves, she was actually blackmailing them. His efforts to inquire into her death subject him first to rebuff, and then, as he persists, to a series of escalating threats against himself and his fiancée—threats meant to scare him off that he attributes to gangsters bent on taking over Dawson's lucrative blackmail operation. In the end, however, Compton discovers that he was half right: he had been up against, and overmatched by, a foreign intelligence service that wanted to convert Dawson's scheme to their own ends.

Like Charles Latimer, Compton is no match, except perhaps in obstinacy, for his adversaries. The knowledge of crime and investigation that enables him to write his popular detective stories proves to be of no help to him in the dangerous world into which he has stumbled, and he demonstrates surprisingly little skill in investigation. Escalating warnings fail to convince him to drop the investigation, and he can neither protect his fiancée nor otherwise cope with the threats against him. His adversaries act with virtual impunity, able to watch his apartment without his detecting them and to enter it at will without his being able to prevent it or even knowing how or precisely when their entry had occurred. So adroit are his adversaries at manipulating appearances that Compton is dismissed as paranoid when he finally seeks help from the police. He is saved, in the end, by the timely intervention of Special Branch agents.

From the beginning, Bingham locates *A Fragment of Fear* in a framework of "predators" and "peasants" reminiscent of the dichotomy (of tramplers and trampled) invoked in the memoirs of George McWatters or in Erving Goffman's analysis of relations in public: "As in the past, so today, the ordinary citizen must keep his eyes skinned if he is not to go under, a victim either of the dangers he recognizes daily, or to other dangers which come upon him suddenly, of which he can have little inkling until, bewildered and off-guard, he is called upon to defend himself as best he can. And a very poor best it can be on occasions" (Bingham 1969, 1). Bingham's Compton is a modern "peasant," who strays from the safety of his writing—his imagined criminal milieu—into the "real world," where he is menaced and outmaneuvered, virtually at will, by his shadowy and ruthless opponents. They manipulate him with ease, while he fails utterly to penetrate their disguises.

Recalling his ordeal, Compton reflects: "the peasant is surrounded by more than he imagines. Behind the eyes which observe him are yet others, which observe those eyes in their turn, and behind the predators slithering in the undergrowth are yet others, stalking the predators. . . . We live in dangerous times. All one can do is to keep the spear ready . . . touch the amulet, and hope for the best, and trust that, as in my case, the tribe can after all protect not only the tribe but the individual" (1969, 155). Bingham's story is anomalous in its reversal of the usual asymmetry of knowing, in which the protagonist has, or obtains, the upper hand; Compton fails completely in that regard. That reversal aside, however, *A Fragment of Fear* reproduces, dramatizes, and reaffirms the "argument" underlying mystery fiction generally—that effective action, under conditions of uncertainty and risk, depends on knowing one's adversary as well as possible so as to be able to predict, with a high probability of success, what they are likely to do in given circumstances, while denying them access to one's own plans, intentions, and capabilities. Three examples from the espionage fiction of the 1970s provide further elaboration of the basic point: Brian Freemantle's *Charlie M* (1977); Anthony Price's *Our Man in Camelot* (1975); and John Le Carré's *Smiley's People* (1980).

Charlie M is the first of several novels by Brian Freemantle featuring the series character Charlie Muffin. A British agent with professional skills honed in twenty-five years of cold war encounters but of dubious (i.e., working-class) social origins, Muffin has much in common with Len Deighton's Bernard Samson and Muffin's counterparts in the novels of Ted Allbeury, John Le Carré, and others: Muffin is "a disposable embarrassment, with his scuffed suede Hush Puppies, the Marks and Spencer shirts he didn't change daily and the flat, Manchester accent" (Freemantle 1977, 4). Despite his pivotal role in breaking up a Soviet spy ring and capturing its resident controller, Berenkov, Muffin is out of favor with the new leadership of the Service—public school graduates who equate class with loyalty and who are determined to restore the Service to "its former, proper level" (1977, 4). Suspicious of the arrangements made for his crossing from East into West Berlin, Charlie sends someone else in his place and has his worst suspicions confirmed when the car is stopped by East German guards expecting to capture him.

Freemantle's story unfolds as a straightforward operation to arrange the defection of a high-ranking Soviet intelligence official, Valerie Kalenin, whose career has been jeopardized, if not destroyed, by the arrest of Berenkov and the destruction of his network. The would-be defector Kalenin demands that the heads of British Intelligence and the CIA be in Vienna to meet him after he crosses into Austria from Czechoslovakia. Freemantle flips the story at the last minute, however. What appears to have been an operation to bring Kalenin to the West turns out to have been an operation planned by Kalenin and Charlie Muffin to deliver the heads of the two Western services into the hands of the Soviets to achieve two ends: to enable Kalenin to trade for his captured agent, Berenkov, and to provide Charlie Muffin with sufficient funds for his retirement, in lieu of the pension he forfeits. Charlie goes into hiding with the $500,000 that was brought to Vienna as the down payment for Kalenin's defection. Muffin attributes the success of Kalenin's (and his) operation to Kalenin's knowledge of his adversaries: "Kalenin is brilliant. . . . It was his idea to bring in the Americans, knowing that Washington's presence would occupy [the head of SIS] so much initially that any flaws we hadn't covered would have more chance of going unnoticed. Kalenin had a personality file on [the CIA director] and guessed exactly how the American would behave. He and [head of SIS] were too worried thinking about each other to properly consider what I was doing" (1977, 180; ellipses in original). But "Why *did* you have to be so scruffy?" his wife asks. " 'Psychology,' avoided Charlie, 'It made them contemptuous of me. People never respect a person of whom they're contemptuous' " (1977, 181–82). His wife asks about the search that must be underway for him. " 'Bound to be,' he said. 'But knowing their minds they [sic] will think of the Mediterranean. Or perhaps the Far East. Certainly not here, in Brighton' " (1977, 183). *Charlie M* raises issues I will take up in later chapters, but in this novel and the others in the series, Freemantle perfectly exemplifies the pattern of asymmetrical understanding that pervades mystery fiction in general and the espionage novel in particular.

Between 1970 and 1990, the English author Anthony Price wrote more than fifteen espionage novels that, taken together, span the career of Dr. David Audley from his recruitment into intelligence work in the closing months of World War II (Bedell 1982; Reynolds 1986). Price levies overtly and extensively on the oft-remarked similarity between historical research and detection by making Audley himself a graduate historian and by giving each of his novels an essential historical dimension. Price's complicated plots are not easily summarized, but nearly all of the Audley stories find their resolution in a plan that hinges on his betting that he and his associates have achieved an understanding of their adversaries sufficient to manipulate and defeat them. *Our Man in Camelot* offers an especially clear instance of this pattern.

At the heart of the novel is a subtle scheme by Soviet intelligence to discredit the CIA in Britain " 'and with it the whole of the American presence here. And that' [Audley continued] 'means in Europe. And that means the North Atlantic Treaty Organization. And *that* means the Strategic Arms Limitation Talks' " (1988, 199–200). The Soviet operation, run by Nikolai Andrievich Panin—an archaeologist, and, like Audley, an accomplished historian—aims to manipulate British public opinion by revealing that the CIA covered up the willful destruction of a significant historic site, the field of the sixth-century battle of Badon, whose location had long eluded historians and archaeologists. The unwitting instrument of the Soviets' scheme is Billy Bullitt, an eccentric British war hero, amateur archaeologist, and Arthurian buff who passionately opposes the presence of American military and intelligence personnel in Britain. Without knowing he is being used by Soviet intelligence for the purpose, Bullitt becomes convinced not only that the Americans have bulldozed away the actual site of the Battle of Badon, but that Badon was of even greater historical significance than had been recognized. A heretofore unknown copy of the Venerable Bede, a so-called "Novogorod" Bede, places the historical King Arthur at the scene of the battle—the first contemporary account to do so.

Convinced that the CIA has covered up a double desecration, Bullitt prepares to denounce the Americans in the press. Efforts to dissuade him fail, and he has arranged for copies of his statement to be released in the event of his death. Audley is convinced that Bullitt will be assassinated by the Soviets at a site once thought to be Badon, where Bullitt is scheduled to be filmed as part of his arrangement with the press to expose the CIA coverup. Bullitt himself anticipates being killed, by the CIA, but intends to go anyway, Audley concludes, " 'to prove honour is worth dying for' " (1988, 219). Hours before the event, Audley and Moses Sheldon, a CIA agent posing as an Air Force dentist, understand fully the outlines of the Soviet plan. They know what is about to happen and why. The crucial problem still facing them is how to effect a different outcome than the one planned by the Soviets. Sheldon discovers a strategy in the concept of honor and the feudal tradition of Ordeal by Battle: " 'I'm challenging Billy Bullitt to his Ordeal by Battle. And he can't refuse me. . . . Because that's the way the game is played. And once I accept his way of playing it then I take precedence over him because it's my honour that's at stake more than his. So if David's right about the way he thinks he has no choice in the matter' " (1988, 221). Sheldon, wearing Bullitt's trademark red shirt and combat hat, will take Bullitt's place for the filming, allowing himself to be a target for the Soviet sniper he and Audley predict will be there to assassinate Bullitt, whose death will be attributed to the CIA. Audley plans to trap the sniper, however, " 'And then Billy Bullitt can see for himself who's really gunning for him, which is going to make him think twice about blowing the whistle on us' " (1988, 221). Before that can happen, however, Sheldon, disguised as Bullitt, must knowingly walk into the sniper's crosshairs.

Being right about how Bullitt thinks is, of course, a well-informed guess about what is stable and predictable in the man's makeup, based on inferences from his past activities. In these there appears to be a marked pattern: " 'How he ticks, you mean? Oh, that's easy—every once in a while he breaks out and rocks the boat some just to satisfy his sense of honour' " (1988, 154). Honor thus appears to be the master key to Bullitt, and for him, as for many of his countrymen, King Arthur represents the noblest historical expression of honor: "*Rex quondam rexque futurus*—that wasn't a dream to Billy Bullitt, it was a promise" (1988, 217). Possessing that understanding of Bullitt, the Soviets successfully manipulate him in the first place. Recognizing the centrality of honor to his identity and his sense of the British past (and the former cannot be understood without the latter), Sheldon and Audley hit on a way to save the situation—and not incidentally, a way to preserve Bullitt's life in the bargain. Sheldon, impersonating Bullitt, bets his life both on his conviction that he and Audley have uncovered the full range and extent of the Soviet plot (and that the CIA are not planning their own assassination attempt) and on a prediction about the professionalism of the Soviet marksman. The professional assassin will have been trained not to risk a shot to the head. He can be expected, with a high degree of probability, to aim instead at Sheldon's body, the larger target. Wearing body armor, Sheldon can survive a shot to the body, but his head cannot be protected. Knowledge of the relevant professional training provides the basis for assessing the degree of risk involved. That training, it should be noted, rests on a calculus of probabilities that is independent of nationality. Audley, in other words, knows about the training of snipers as a class; he does not know, or need to know, about *Soviet* snipers. There is the possibility, to be sure, that the Soviets will employ an "amateur," but Audley discounts that risk, given what he knows about Nicolai Panin's high standards and careful attention to detail. Sheldon, for his part, anticipating the attack, will do everything he can—by moving slowly, for example—to give the marksman the time needed for a body shot. It goes without saying, moreover, that Sheldon's performance in these circumstances requires iron self-control in order to maintain the requisite normal appearances. Sheldon and Audley turn out to be right on both counts: the sniper is Soviet (not CIA), and he aims for Sheldon's chest; but one can imagine a different outcome, and darker implication, had Price chosen a different ending.

John Le Carré's *Smiley's People* is the final novel in a trilogy devoted to the contest between George Smiley and his Soviet counterpart and longtime adversary, known only as Karla.[4] The contest, played out over more than two decades, is one of wills, of "tradecraft," and of gaining and finally being able to use the knowledge of the other sufficient to defeat him. Round one in their match had gone to Karla, in an incident described in the opening novel, *Tinker, Tailor, Soldier, Spy* (1974). The significance of the incident was not apparent to Smiley until years later, by which time Karla had capitalized on what Smiley had given away about himself on the occasion. Smiley had been flown to Delhi to interview a Soviet agent who had barely escaped the exposure and destruction of his network of agents on the West Coast of the United States. Presumably due to be disciplined, if not executed, upon his return to the Soviet Union, "Gerstmann" seemed to Smiley's Service to be a likely candidate for defection, and Smiley was assigned to make the offer by his masters in British Intelligence, the "Circus." The interview with Gerstmann in a Delhi jail went badly, however. Gerstmann, or Karla as he later came to be identified, refused to consider defecting to the West and returned to the Soviet Union to salvage his career, taking back with him knowledge of Smiley's one vulnerability: his affection for his unfaithful wife, Anne. Karla subsequently used that knowledge to deflect Smiley's suspicions about a "Circus" colleague, Bill Haydon, who is unmasked at the end of *Tinker, Tailor* as a Soviet mole, Karla's agent, and, for a crucial period during Smiley's search for the mole, Anne's lover.

Smiley's People returns Smiley, retired a second time from the Circus, to the decades-old contest with Karla as he follows out the possibility that Karla can be brought down at last by exploiting his affection for his only child, Tatiana, a rebellious and deeply disturbed young woman whom he has smuggled to Switzerland for psychiatric care and treatment unavailable to her in the Soviet Union. Smiley hopes to be able to discover the girl's whereabouts and to use that knowledge, her vulnerability, the evidence of Karla's illegal efforts on her behalf, and especially Karla's affection for his daughter to compel his defection to the West in return for her continued safety. Knowledge of her whereabouts, however, is a necessary but not sufficient condition for the success of Smiley's operation. He must obtain proof of Karla's misappropriation of funds and personnel in support of Tatiana's care. And he must determine that the probability that Karla will defect rather than abandon his daughter is high enough for Smiley to risk the operation on Swiss territory with a British Labour government in power, determined to rein in the Circus for past excesses and well-publicized failures.

Karla, Smiley discovers, pays for Tatiana's care, using as his agent a

Soviet embassy employee, Anton Grigoriev. Having identified Grigoriev as Karla's agent in Berne, Smiley must devise a way to persuade him to betray Karla's trust. Smiley's operatives surreptitiously photograph Grigoriev using a false identity in a Swiss bank and fondling an embassy secretary, and plan to use the photos to blackmail him.

> "Do you think we have enough on him?" Smiley asked [his colleague Tony Esterhase].
>
> "Technically no problem. The bank, the false identity, little Natasha even: technically we got a hand of aces."
>
> "And you think he'll burn," said Smiley. . . .
>
> "Burning, George, that's always a hazard, know what I mean? Some guys get heroic and want to die for their countries suddenly. Other guys roll over and lie still the moment you put the arm on them. Burning, that touches the stubbornness in certain people." (1980, 296)

In short, it's unpredictable.

With evidence sufficient to compromise Grigoriev, Smiley faces two practical problems. He must isolate Grigoriev from the Soviet embassy, his wife, and colleagues long enough to demonstrate the hold he has over him. Second, Smiley must choose the best approach to persuade Grigoriev to do what Smiley requires in order to bring pressure to bear on Karla. Both problems are formidable and involve severe time constraints. If Smiley succeeds in abducting Grigoriev without incident, he can hold him for only a short time before his absence is likely to be noted by his jealous wife or his embassy colleagues. Persuading Grigoriev to betray Karla, of whom he is rightly terrified, involves an irreducible element of unpredictability. Smiley will have only one chance, one approach among the several open to him, to trump Karla's hold over Grigoriev and to induce his complicity in Smiley's plan for Karla's downfall.

On a quiet Sunday afternoon, Smiley's team successfully abducts Grigoriev and brings him to a room where Smiley waits to question him: "Only George will ask questions, Toby had told his team. Only George will answer them" (1980, 324). Entering the room, Grigoriev "was rubbing his shoulder, seemingly unaware of anything but the pain. Studying him, Smiley took comfort from this gesture of self-concern: subconsciously, Grigoriev was declaring himself to be one of life's losers. . . . He looked at Grigoriev and read the same incurable mediocrity in everything he saw" (1980, 323). Smiley temporizes while Grigoriev makes a show of outrage at being abducted and manhandled, but

"Grigoriev was a hooked fish. Smiley had only moments in which to decide how best to land him" (1980, 324). His decision, from which there is no going back, is to adopt a role of dull officiousness: "Smiley, with an air of official regret, opened a notebook on his lap . . . and gave a small, very official sigh: 'You are Counsellor Grigoriev of the Soviet Embassy in Berne?' he asked in the dullest possible voice," inviting Grigoriev to look at photographs documenting his indiscreet behavior (1980, 325). "Smiley had arranged the layout of the pictures himself; he had imagined, in Grigoriev's mind, an orchestrated succession of disasters" that would reveal the hopelessness of his situation (1980, 325).

Grigoriev makes one halfhearted attempt to escape, which is easily thwarted, and then capitulates to the strategy Smiley has chosen for the interrogation. "In every successful interrogation . . . there is one slip which cannot be recovered, one gesture, tacit or direct, even if it is only a half smile, or the acceptance of a cigarette, which marks the shift away from resistance, towards collaboration. Grigoriev . . . now made his crucial slip" (1980, 329). Having done so, his resistance to Smiley's questions evaporates. "George had turned the trick, and Grigoriev's confession had begun. . . . [Smiley's] faceless style, his manner of regretful bureaucratic necessity, were by now not merely established . . . they were perfected: Grigoriev had adopted them wholesale, with philosophic, very Russian pessimism. As to the rest of those present, they could hardly believe, afterwards, that he had not been brought to the flat already in a mood to talk" (1980, 330–31). Le Carré underscores Smiley's mastery of the situation and its demands when Grigoriev begins to talk about meeting Karla himself:

> It was the strongest proof yet of Smiley's tradecraft . . . as well as of his command of Grigoriev altogether—that throughout Grigoriev's protracted narrative, he never once, whether by an over-hasty follow-up question or the smallest false inflection of his voice, departed from the faceless role he had assumed for the interrogation. By his self-effacement . . . George held the whole scene 'like a thrush's egg in his hand.' The slightest careless movement on his part could have destroyed everything, but he never made it. (1980, 336)

Smiley gets Grigoriev to give up every relevant detail of Karla's clandestine scheme to aid his daughter, but with the interrogation winding down and Grigoriev due back at the embassy, he must still secure Grigoriev's continued cooperation and complicity: "Perhaps there was no greater test of Smiley's role as the responsible functionary in charge, than the way in which he now almost casually transformed Grigoriev the one-time source into Grigoriev the defector-in-place" (1980, 350). Through Grigoriev, Smiley communicates with Karla, threatening him and his daughter with exposure and offering "the same carrot he had offered him more than twenty years before, in Delhi: save your skin, come to us, tell us what you know, and we will make a home for you" (1980, 363).

Smiley possesses the familiar constitutive attributes that define protagonists generally in mystery fiction. In dealing with Grigoriev, Smiley is both a skillful psychologist and a consummate actor. His chosen role represents a strategic response to his assessment, made under severe time constraints, of his adversary, whose vulnerabilities he must quickly and accurately identify from a variety of behavioral clues that include minutiae of dress, posture, mannerism, and facial expression. Smiley's preliminary reading of Grigoriev is acute, and he selects the role of bored officialdom, calculating that it will elicit from Grigoriev a predictable response of sullen but ultimately compliant cooperation. Having adopted a strategic role, Smiley's improvisations within it, Le Carré makes clear, are deft and sure and consistent. Grigoriev's revelations test Smiley's emotional control at several points in the interview, but Smiley never betrays what he may be thinking or what may be at stake in a given question. In short, Smiley denies Grigoriev even the smallest opportunity to read him or to penetrate his virtuoso performance of the role he has chosen to play. In addition to being the consummate actor, Smiley is also represented as especially adept in the questions he puts to Grigoriev.

If the capacity to read others is constitutive of espionage fiction generally, the interpretive or inferential process on which it rests typically receives little if any explicit attention. Nor need it, whether from the point of view of readers or writers. Dimitrios's capacity to see through others, for example, is simply a given in Ambler's novel, just as it is in Hammett's *The Maltese Falcon* or in Le Carré's *Smiley's People*. None is concerned to show how that capacity is acquired. One of the few works to make the interpretive process central to the novel of espionage is Robert Littell's *The Defection of A. J. Lewinter*, published in 1973. In it, Littell looks closely at the process of achieving understanding, of rendering the other transparent, and subjects the process, as embodied in rival American and Soviet intelligence services, to a thoroughly skeptical treatment.

The premise of Littell's novel, for which he won an Edgar, is deceptively simple. An American scientist, the A. J. Lewinter of the title, has defected to the Soviet Union.[5] There is some evidence that he has taken with him top-secret information about ballistic missile trajectories. American intelligence is faced initially with the problem of determining whether Lewinter took invaluable secrets with him or not. If he did, the trick will then be to act in such a way as to convince the Soviets that he did not. If what he took was of no value, however, it would be worth acting so as to make the Soviets conclude that the material was genuine. In either case the objective is the same: act so as to insure that the Soviets don't grasp the true fact of the matter—or, more accurately: so the Soviets don't grasp whatever the Americans conclude, on the basis of the evidence available, is the fact of the matter.

Whatever the outcome of the investigation on the all-important question of whether Lewinter took the missile secrets with him, though, the practical problem then confronting the Americans is the same in either case: to anticipate how their Soviet counterparts are likely to interpret a particular "signal" or set of signals. To anticipate their adversaries' response with a high degree of probability requires building up reliable psychological portraits of Soviet intelligence personnel through a painstaking process of inference and interpretation extending over many years. The process differs only in degree of complexity from the process of assessment outlined by Poe in "The Murders in the Rue Morgue" in describing how to excel at the schoolboy game of odds and evens. Confronted by an opponent who is acting to disguise his real intentions, the person seeking to understand the other attempts to infer from behavioral clues what the true state of affairs is. In Poe's example, the contest takes place face to face. In *Lewinter*, the contest is carried on at a distance and in a context of secrecy, mutual distrust, and systematic and mutual efforts at deception and manipulation. The interpretive problem is thus enormously more complex, but in structure it is no different from the situation of Poe's boy trying to determine what manner of simpleton he faces and laying his bets accordingly.

Littell's Americans conclude that Lewinter probably did take the details of the missile trajectories with him when he defected, although the evidence is fragmentary, circumstantial, and ambiguous. Reprogramming the missiles is a complex and costly task. A far less expensive alternative involves casting doubt on Lewinter's authenticity by acting in a way calculated to lead their Soviet counterparts to conclude that Lewinter is a fake and that his missile data cannot be trusted. The Americans' effort, and the success of their strategy, depends crucially on their being able to anticipate, with a high degree of probability, how a given signal will be interpreted in Moscow.

Soviet intelligence has the mirror image of the American problem. They must decide whether to believe Lewinter. The defector may be a plant, after all, part of a disinformation operation. Alternatively, he may genuinely believe he possesses valuable secrets when in fact he doesn't. Or he may be a genuine defector with genuine secrets to reveal. If the Soviets conclude that Lewinter's material is genuine, they must then devise signals calculated to convince their American counterparts otherwise so as to preserve the strategic value of the material. The missile trajectories will have no value to them if the Americans, con- cluding they have been compromised by Lewinter's defection, decide to change them. One of Littell's Russians sums up their problem in this way: " 'Everything depends, in the end, on [our determining] what the Americans *want* us to believe. If they want us to believe [Lewinter] is real, he must be a fake. If they want us to believe he is a fake, he must be real. Here is where it gets complicated. I will raise the possibility that the Americans are signaling us that Lewinter is real *in the expecta- tion that we will discover they are signalling us that he is real and conclude that he is a fraud.* Ergo, they want us to believe he is a fraud. Ergo, he must be real. Do you follow me?' " (1973, 168; emphasis in original).⌈This is the problem of other minds with a vengeance.⌉

The Americans, convinced that Lewinter took with him valuable intelligence, must weigh various "gambits" in light of their best guess as to how their Soviet counterparts will interpret very specific signals: an item placed in the "Periscope" section of *Newsweek*, for example. The interpretive stakes are very high, involving issues of national secur- ity. The pressure is enormous to send the right signals, ones the Soviets will construe "correctly"—i.e., as the Americans want them construed in order to thereby mislead the Soviets.

In the end, Littell has the Soviets conclude that Lewinter is genuine because the Americans appear to them to be reacting to a genuine de- fection (a reading the Americans are trying very hard to avoid). The Soviets, in fact, "misread" the American signals, which were designed to make the Soviets think that the Americans *wanted* them to regard Lewinter's defection as genuine and hence were intended to make them conclude the contrary. Thus, ironically, the Soviets arrive at the truth (although they cannot be said to know it) for the wrong reasons. Having concluded that Lewinter is genuine, however, the Soviets face the problem of acting so as to make the Americans think they have rejected him. Littell ends his story with the Soviets proposing and debating various "signals" of their own intended to convince the Americans that they have not found Lewinter credible, in an effort to insure the continuing value of Lewinter's intelligence. Littell is thoroughly skeptical about how successfully the interpretive enterprise can proceed in the world of espionage, a world riven by bureaucratic rivalries and personal careerism and conducted in the shadow of mutually assured destruction.

Standing back from the foregoing examples, and the body of work of which they are representative, we can discern two broad sets of skills possessed by fictional investigators. One set consists of those skills that create and sustain the detective's "opacity." Put differently, these skills sever the link between the visible and the invisible, between the observable and the unobservable, between appearance and reality. George Smiley's performance in the role of officious bureaucrat, which Le Carré renders in great detail, exemplifies the achievement of opacity and the requisite skills required. The other set consists of the skills that permit the detective or investigator to make connections between the observable and the unobservable, especially in the face of an adversary's determined efforts to conceal such connections. In a given situation, such as Smiley's interrogation of Grigoriev, both sets of skills are in play simultaneously. Smiley must elicit information Grigoriev has sworn to keep secret and fears to divulge. Simultaneously, Smiley must act in such a way as to deny Grigoriev any clues as to the true point of the interrogation and any hint as to what Smiley knows or suspects.

The two categories overlap, however, in substantial and important ways. Underlying both, for example, is knowledge, particularly knowledge of people in general—an understanding of "human nature"—and of people as categorized and typified by their social roles. Secondly, both sets of skills involve and require a highly developed capacity for emotional management, for remaining cool and unflappable, especially in situations that combine a measure of uncertainty and high risk with the need for quick and decisive action.[6] These terms figure prominently in the discourse of detection and investigation stretching from the memoirs of George McWatters and Allan Pinkerton, cited earlier, to contemporary handbooks on the conduct of interrogations (e.g., Aubrey and Caputo 1980).

McWatters virtually defines the detective in terms of his capacity to dissemble, and many of the cases he recounts in *Knots Untied* turn on his ability to adopt a physical disguise and to assume convincingly a particular social role. Additionally, he emphasizes the knowledge the detective must possess: of human nature generally, of the criminal classes more particularly, and of business practices, since many of his cases involved fraud, forgery, and embezzlement, all of which involve manipulating appearances. Similarly, Pinkerton considered knowledge of "human nature," together with a thorough understanding of criminal ways, to be essential to investigative success, along with several capabilities that rest finally on the agent's capacity for emotional management. The ideal Pinkerton agent, for example, would be ever alert and wary, quick to respond appropriately in emergencies, but should appear to be the "careless ordinary" individual, maintaining an outward demeanor calculated to dispel suspicion. Knowledge of human nature—what individuals possess in common—together with knowledge of the characteristics of individuals by virtue of their belonging to various categories form the basis for understanding the other. Poe's prototypical Dupin understands Minister D—— as mathematician, poet, and bold *intriguant*, and plans his moves accordingly.

If we ask, then, how fictional investigators succeed in understanding the other, we are asking how writers pose and solve, in circumstantial particularity, an imagined instance of the general problem of correctly interpreting actions, especially actions undertaken to deceive or mislead—i.e., a type of action that exacerbates the inherently problematic process of correctly construing the meaning of action. A necessary component of any writer's "solution" is knowledge about the social categories that locate and define a given character. That knowledge forms the basis for predicting how such a person would likely respond in specific circumstances. Knowing the other is one thing; acting effectively on that knowledge is something else, requiring the investigator to possess a set of skills on which there appears to be a very broad consensus indeed. Crucial among those skills is a fine-tuned control of emotionality that permits the investigator both to deny the adversary access to the true nature of the investigator's acts and to penetrate the adversary's own efforts at deception and disguise.

The essential characteristics of the detective are effectively summarized and condensed in "The Whirlpool," a short story by Robb White published in the Scouting magazine *Boys' Life* and subsequently reprinted in *The Boys' Life Book of Mystery Stories* (1963). Fiction intended for children and "young adults" typically crystallizes cultural knowledge, connecting action and consequences with notable clarity, simplicity, and moral seriousness (Kelly 1974; Nixon 1977). "The Whirlpool" takes place on a remote, isolated stretch of riverbank in Brazil. There Barry Benton, confined to a makeshift wheelchair after having injured his ankles, waits alone to be rescued. Benton is an Eagle scout, scouting's highest rank and mark of achievement. After a fitful night's sleep, he awakens and settles in to wait for his companions to return. He becomes increasingly uneasy as he hears a rustling sound grow louder in the nearby jungle. His uneasiness becomes alarm and threatens to become panic when he realizes that a column of army ants is flowing out of the jungle, "a shimmering mass—like a snake, but too large to be one" (1963, 28). When the column overwhelms a small tapir, quickly reducing it to a skeleton, Benton realizes his own life is in danger and that he has very little time in which to act and nowhere to go, given his injuries. Piranha infest the river behind him, a steep cliff forms the second side of the triangular clearing, and the jungle the third side. Under the press of time, he faces three distinct challenges. He must maintain his mental poise and capacity for rational thought and resist the temptation to panic as he imagines being devoured alive by the ants. He must try to discover the key to the ants' behavior in the face of the view of some naturalists that the numberless insects possess a superordinate intelligence by virtue of their sheer numbers. Lastly, even if he comes up with an alternative hypothesis about the ants' behavior, he must devise an appropriate strategy based on a better account of their behavior.

Benton begins by confronting the "horrid, sick fear" that threatens to immobilize him. If he continues to indulge it, he will remain helpless and will almost certainly die. Damping down his incipient panic with an act of will, he reviews his observations of the ants, concluding that he has only one "fact" about their behavior—the mass of ants moved forward in a straight line regardless of obstacles. "Why? Did they *know* where they were going?" (1963, 33). Devising a simple experiment, he discovers that the ants can be induced to follow a circular path that would afford him more time for his rescuers to reach him. "He had a weapon now. Whether it was great enough, he did not know, but he was ready now to pit his mind against the quivering mass of ants. . . . He was staking his life on his belief that their line of march was determined, not by intelligence, but by one blind ant following another, multiplied a hundred thousand times" (36–37). Acting on his belief, Benton successfully deflects the march of the ants, confirming his hypothesis about their true nature and his prediction as to how they will respond to specific stimuli and circumstances. Amidst his "experiment," he continues to resist the urge to panic. At the last possible moment, with his strategy beginning to fail as more and more ants pile into the clearing, Benton's companions return and snatch him to safety.

"The Whirlpool" perfectly illustrates the way the control of emotionality and correctly understanding the nature of the other form an effective basis for action. The story models a method that involves deriving from careful observation guesses about what another is most likely to do in specific circumstances and then testing those guesses. Benton's adversary turns out to be "dumb insects," without purpose or intelligence, rather than some superordinate, malevolent intelligence, but that conclusion is something he must achieve through a process of hypothesis formulation and testing. It is a correct interpretation, achieved in the face of alternative hypotheses held by some naturalists, and Benton literally bets his life on having formulated a truer account of the ants' real nature. As such, it permits the prediction, and hence the manipulation, of the other. It follows that the more complete the knowledge of the other, the greater the potential for manipulation. The power gained by rendering the other transparent makes the detective or investigator a figure of intrinsic moral ambiguity: "To have knowledge of other persons is potentially to have power over them. . . . To know something about them that they do not know or do not know that you know, is a distinct tactical advantage because you can anticipate their reactions and movements, while they do not know that you have this capacity" (Bailey 1991, 33). It is to a discussion of the issue of the moral ambiguity inherent in knowing the other that we now turn.

5

Costs and Benefits

Don't be too sure I'm as crooked as I'm supposed to be. That kind of reputation might be good business—bringing in high-priced jobs and making it easier to deal with the enemy.

Dashiell Hammett, *The Maltese Falcon*

Nice guys finish last.

Attributed to professional football coach Vince Lombardi

Detection, as represented in mystery fiction generally, has an intrinsic moral dimension. "As the strong man exults in his physical ability . . . so glories the analyst in that moral activity that *disentangles*," Poe wrote in the opening paragraph of "The Murders in the Rue Morgue" (1938, 141; emphasis in original). In the long discursive passage that follows, he develops his concept of "analysis," or detection, in terms that are both personal and social. The analyst "derives pleasure from even the most trivial occupations bringing his talents into play" (1938, 141). From "The Murders in the Rue Morgue" to the most recent work of such representative contemporary mystery writers as Patricia Cornwell, Jeremiah Healy, or Sara Paretsky, the "occupations" that bring the talents of the investigator into play are anything but trivial. By convention, and admitting of relatively few exceptions, mystery fiction is about murder—that illegitimate exercise of power by one individual over another that deprives victims of life against their will and assaults social order at its root by calling into question society's capacity to protect its members. "Why murder and not some other crime? It's the ultimate crime. It's the ultimate crime in a secular society, and the mystery novel is essentially the expression of a secular society. But it's really symbolic. Murder stands for various other kinds of crime" (Macdonald 1976, 191). Fictional detection, occasioned by murder, is thus an inherently moral activity and profoundly consequential. Moreover, the convention of the successful conclusion sets the writer the unavoidable task of showing the fictional investigator's skills to be commensurate with the perversion of functional rationality expressed in the murder itself. The writer of mystery fiction links action and consequence in the pursuit of "truth" (the facts of the matter) and "justice." In form, mystery fiction proceeds typically from investigation to the identification, apprehension, and disposition of the person (or persons) responsible for the initiating crime. The moral implications of investigation—the pursuit of "truth," leading to the identification of the responsible party—form the basis for this chapter. The issue of "justice"—the disposition of the person or persons whose identification is the outcome or product of investigation—is discussed in chapter 6.

Writers of mystery fiction represent actions conjoined with consequences. They depict actions performed by actors with specific qualities, attributes, and skills, who do what they do out of a combination of belief and desire—the general model of action. By representing the consequences of action, the writer connects specific qualities, attributes, skills, beliefs, and desires to the consequences described. In this sense we can speak of a work of mystery fiction as displaying or being an "argument." Moreover, the consequences of action are subject to evaluation, both "internally" in the work itself, and "externally," from the standpoint of variously situated readers. The concern voiced over the extraordinary popularity of Mickey Spillane's work in the 1950s, the attack on Ian Fleming's James Bond novels in the 1960s, and the skepticism about the political implications of detective fiction expressed by the historian William Aydelotte (1976) illustrate the reaction of readers to the "arguments" embodied in works of mystery fiction (Bennett and Woollacott 1987; Cawelti 1969; Weibel 1976).

Investigative success confers power on the detective—typically, the power of knowing others well enough to anticipate their behavior, and so be in a position to manipulate and thereby harm them. Detection, exercised as the pursuit of truth and justice, is intrinsically moral by virtue of the ends pursued. But to the extent that success confers on the detective power over others, detection is also morally ambiguous—

inherently and profoundly so. Acknowledging, and accounting for, the somber quality of the espionage novels of the English author Ted Allbeury, Robin Winks writes: "His books tend to be sad in tone, for spying and betraying and manipulating weak people into becoming even weaker is rather sad work" (1988b, 1).

In taking up the matter of the moral ambiguity of detection, I want to consider two distinct issues of trust associated with mystery fiction. The first, implied but not addressed directly throughout the preceding chapters, is internal to a given work of fiction. It has to do with whom, and on what basis, the fictional investigator trusts, or can trust, among the various persons he or she encounters in the course of the investigation.

The second issue, I will argue, is "external" to the fiction, in the sense that it necessarily involves the reader. It has to do with the way the writer handles the issue of the investigator's power, which in the conventional hard-boiled detective story, as well as in much secret agent fiction, extends to the use of "deadly force"—the investigator's ability and willingness, when the occasion demands it, to kill. Just how to represent those "demands" in a given instance requires the writer to make choices about what reasonably legitimates or justifies the investigator's resort to deadly force, for example, where "reasonably" involves consideration of audience expectations and broadly shared standards of acceptability. The same considerations extend, *mutatis mutandi*, to the treatment of other manifestations of the investigator's power.

This concern with the trustworthiness of the detective has been present from the beginning in mystery fiction. Poe's prototypical investigator, Dupin, and his adversary in "The Purloined Letter," the Minister D——, are indistinguishable as far as their cunning, their capacity for artful dissembling is concerned. Both are skilled at putting themselves in the place of another and thereby discovering the key to outwitting their adversary. Both are men of "genius," but the minister is "that *monstrum horrendum*, an unprincipled man of genius"—bold, ambitious, unscrupulous, acknowledging no constraint save his own self-interest (1938, 222). What distinguishes Dupin from D—— is a motive: loyalty on the one hand, and on the other the absence of the excessive ambition and desire for self-aggrandizement that drives the minister. Put differently, their acts appear identical without a consideration of motive and desire; that alone permits the meaning of their acts to be distinguished and evaluated.

Closely related to the potential for misuse inherent in the successful exercise of the investigator's skills is another threat: the possibly deleterious effects on the investigator himself of the exercise of those skills and, by extension, the accompanying potential for tainting the investigator's "worthy" ends through the employment of dubious means. John Le Carré raises this question explicitly throughout his work, a point to which I return below in looking once again at *Smiley's People*. George McWatters, the New York police detective whose memoirs I cited in chapter 1, was acutely conscious of the moral dilemma inherent in the activity of the private investigator or police detective in mid-nineteenth-century America. McWatters divided society into two classes, the Tramplers and the Trampled. The detective, whether employed privately or serving in one of the nation's metropolitan police forces, belonged to the former class, in whose service he resorted to the "black lie" when necessary while relying on the "white lie" as his stock in trade. The skillful practice of dissembling, over time, is likely to prompt reflections on the relationship of means and ends (e.g., Thompson 1989, 140).

Writers of mystery fiction address the issue of the detective's power, and the closely related issue of the detective's trustworthiness, in various ways. Occasionally, writers will choose to reassure their readers directly. John Carroll Daly, a popular pulp magazine author during the formative years of the hard-boiled detective story, included the following exchange, between his private detective Clay Holt and a client, in "Ticket to Murder": " 'I want you to work for me, Mr. Holt. Then things will be confidential between us and I can trust you.' 'Sure!' . . . 'Then you can trust me.' He hesitated. 'Everything up to the obstruction of justice! The murderer's got to burn, Mrs. Purdy. Surely you don't mean you want me to protect anyone' " (1934, 19). When Holt later withholds evidence in the case, Daly risks creating doubts in the minds of his more alert readers, but he permits no ambiguity about Holt's motives or trustworthiness to become a thematic element in the story. A more recent example of the direct approach occurs in Sharon Gwyn Short's *Past Pretense*:

> "Jessica's game was blackmail. She had this talent for learning the truth about people, ugly truths."

Patricia [Delaney, who styles herself an "investigative consultant" rather than a private investigator] paused and studied [her informant]. . . . "It's a talent we share," [Delaney] said. "Difference is, I wait until people ask me to get information for them, then I get paid for doing so, and I try to safeguard what I learn and be ethical about it. Not Jessica. She went out and learned what she could and then used her information as a personal tool for getting what she wanted." (1994, 163)

In an oft-quoted passage at the conclusion of *The Maltese Falcon*, Hammett—perhaps anticipating readers' questions about Spade's decision to turn Brigid O'Shaughnessy over to the police for the murder of his partner, Miles Archer—has Spade uncharacteristically justify his action at some length. His reasons range from acknowledging the general obligation one has to "do something" when one's partner is murdered to Spade's intensely personal unwillingness even to think "that there might be one chance in a hundred that you'd played me for a sucker" (1964, 194). Brigid's final appeal to Spade is the question "Would you have done this to me if the falcon had been real and you had been paid your money?" to which he replies: "What difference does that make now? Don't be too sure I'm as crooked as I'm supposed to be. That kind of reputation might be good business—bringing in high-priced jobs and making it easier to deal with the enemy" (1964, 195).

Robert Campbell's Chicago precinct captain cum detective, Jimmy Flannery, acknowledges that he will lie at the drop of a hat if doing so doesn't harm anyone or "cuts through the crap" (1986, 14); but "There's not a soul in the city who knows me who doesn't know I wouldn't steal a pin" (1986, 54). Raymond Chandler, in his critical essay on mystery fiction, "The Simple Art of Murder," defined the detective as the best man in his (fictional) world, adding for good measure that his own improvement on Hammett's practice lay in adding a redemptive dimension to the detective story—a dimension clearly associated with, and owed to, the incorruptible character of Philip Marlowe in Chandler's work. Direct statements about the trustworthiness of the investigator, whether made in the fiction or in self-interested commentary such as Chandler's, occur relatively infrequently, however. Writers typically address the moral ambiguity inherent in the successful exercise of the detective's skills with various forms of indirect reassurance. These strategies, including especially reckonings of the "costs" associated with engaging in investigation, are the subject of the remainder of this chapter.

The process of investigation rests to a greater or lesser extent on interviewing persons thought to have information relevant to the detective's case. This gives the writer enormous flexibility in terms of the range of social types the investigator will encounter, for example, or in the duration of a given interview. In addition to all the other things that get done in these scenes—demonstrating the investigator's ability to deal with denizens of divergent social strata or to maintain rational control or to respond quickly and appropriately to a particularly tricky situation, for example—some of the persons the detective encounters serve to vouch for him or her and thus to offer a measure of reassurance about the investigator's character. Consider an example from Ross Macdonald's *The Galton Case*, a passage in which Macdonald defines Lew Archer's values at the same time that Archer himself is assessed favorably by a character intended to be taken by readers as a shrewd and experienced judge of people.

Early in *The Galton Case*, Archer talks with a retired physician, George Dineen. Archer thinks Dineen may have delivered the young man who, years later, has returned to claim his paternity and his identity. Macdonald describes Dr. Dineen as possessing an old-fashioned integrity, genuineness, and capacity for enduring relationships. Meeting Mrs. Dineen, Archer notes "a look on her face you don't see too often any more, the look of a woman who hasn't been disappointed" (1960, 53). That Macdonald is using Dineen to assess Archer is clear from the outset: "He looked at me intently, as if he was getting ready to make a diagnosis" (1960, 54). When Archer refuses to divulge his client's name, Dineen challenges him directly: "Tell me about yourself. Why would a man of your sort spend his life doing the kind of work you do? Do you make much money?" Archer admits that he doesn't, that he is an investigator because he wants to be, not for the money involved. But "Isn't it dirty work, Mr. Archer?" Dineen continues, to which Archer replies, "It depends on who's doing it. . . . I try to keep it clean," admitting that he's not always successful: "I've made some bad mistakes about people. Some of them assume that a private detective is automatically crooked, and they act accordingly, as you're doing now" (1960, 55). After a show of residual reluctance, Dineen finally agrees to tell Archer what he knows, persuaded that the detective can be trusted with what is at stake in the case from Dineen's point of view: "human lives . . . a boy's love for his parents" (1960, 56). Other characters of transparent moral worth, notably Ada Reichler, a former girlfriend of John Galton, respond trustingly to Archer and so further define and validate his moral character and trustworthiness, both within the novel and, by extension, for the reader.

The Galton Case was a crucial work for Macdonald, permitting him to retain his "investment" in the California crime novel while allowing him to write from and about the "inner shape" of his life. That he had an interest in creating a more acceptable version of the private eye can hardly be doubted, given the personal significance of the hard-boiled convention for Macdonald and the clamorous criticism of Mickey Spillane's brutal investigator Mike Hammer during the heyday of Spillane's extraordinary sales in the late 1950s. Spillane's popularity seemed to his critics to constitute an endorsement of Hammer acting not only as investigator but as judge, jury, and executioner as well in ← such works as *I, the Jury* (1947) and *Vengeance Is Mine* (1950), with its transparent allusion to a familiar Biblical passage. As late as the mid-1960s, Macdonald's publisher, Bantam Books, continued to market Macdonald's works, including *The Galton Case*, with covers that characterized Lew Archer as "the hardest of the hard-boiled dicks," a characterization far more fitting for Mike Hammer than for Lew Archer. Macdonald's conception of the private investigator bears little resemblance to Spillane's, however. One's protagonist, he believed, invariably represented the writer and "carried his values into action in society." The conventions of the mystery novel were sufficiently mature, by the mid-1950s, to "support a full-scale philosophical assault ← on the problem of evil" (Walbridge 1954, 334). In short, Macdonald held a view of the hard-boiled detective formula notable for its moral seriousness, hence his concern to make Lew Archer, especially in *The Galton Case* and subsequent novels, a figure whose motives and desires would command trust—for example, in the eyes of characters whose own trustworthiness would be clearly represented to Macdonald's readers in and through unambiguous cultural symbols such as the retired general practitioner, Dr. Dineen.

What holds for Macdonald holds for other writers of mystery fiction, varying, presumably, with the degree to which a given writer recognizes the moral ambiguity intrinsic to the investigator's vocation and then acts on that recognition, drawing on the extensive stock of cultural resources available to define moral worth. The question "Who vouches for the investigator?" gets answered over and over in mystery fiction as a general formula for offering up reassurance about the investigator's moral fitness. In *The Junkyard Dog*, Robert Campbell's first Jimmy Flannery novel, Flannery and a nurse, Mary Ellen Dunne, meet and fall in love. Quick with a lie when it serves his purpose and continually trading "favor for favor," Flannery is both the product of, and by virtue of his skills a successful player in, a game whose cardinal rule is: To get along you have to go along. Campbell uses the character of Mary Ellen Dunne to vouch for Flannery's essential trustworthiness, his skills at dissembling notwithstanding. "[That's] like getting a seal of approval on your forehead, so far as I'm concerned, if Mary Ellen Dunne trusts you. She reads people's hearts," Flannery hears from a man he is questioning about the story's inciting incident—the bombing of an abortion clinic, in which two women died (1986, 84). Other representative examples of this strategy can be found in Sara Paretsky's popular series featuring V(ictoria). I. Warshawski and in John D. MacDonald's Travis McGee series. Warshawski's circle of devoted friends and admirers includes Lotty Herschel, a Viennese-trained physician who operates a clinic in one of Chicago's poorest neighborhoods, and Mr. Contreras, a retired machinist and widower who lives in the apartment below Warshawski's. Both possess conspicuous integrity, and their faith and trust in Warshawski offer credible reassurance as to her essential trustworthiness, despite the dubious means she adopts on occasion to solve a particular problem.

In his essay "How to Live with a Hero," discussed in my Introduction in a different context, John D. MacDonald notes that he drew deliberately on the "Robin Hood motif" for the concept of his series character, Travis McGee. That characterization, allying McGee with an especially notable and reassuring folk hero, is at least disingenuous, however. McGee is a self-styled "salvage" expert, a specialist in a demanding, tricky, and invariably dangerous trade (Geherin 1982; Moore 1994; Keefer 1985). For a flat fee of fifty percent of what he salvages, he will attempt to recover valuables stolen or swindled from individuals in ways that have left the victims no recourse to legal means of redress. By definition, McGee operates at or beyond the margins of legality from the outset. As a consequence, McGee poses the question of the investigator's means in a particularly direct and insistent way. MacDonald draws on the same resources noted above in the examples from Ross Macdonald and Sara Paretsky. Characters with recognizable probity vouch for McGee: for example, through the character of Meyer, a retired economist, McGee's neighbor, friend, confidant, and sometime accomplice, MacDonald can offer a running commentary on McGee's actions, when needed, that simultaneously questions and legitimates those actions. Meyer is a reassuring model of thoughtful rationality, balance, good will, and moral seriousness. An eminently likable individual, he knows the real McGee and likes (and, more importantly, trusts) him.

From book to book in the McGee series, other characters fulfill the same function by virtue of the markers of cultural authority MacDonald ascribes to them. Winning the trust of shrewd, skeptical, tough-minded, and conventionally successful individuals such as Connie Alverez and Judge Rufus Wellington in *Pale Gray for Guilt* (1968) shows the investigator's capacity to move easily throughout society, and reveals MacDonald's use of markers of class to vouch for the investigator's trustworthiness. Connie Alverez, for example, capably and single-handedly manages a large Florida orange grove. Judge Wellington is a version of that familiar figure, the elderly small-town lawyer whose legal skills, honed during a long career of courtroom victories, are exceeded only by his encyclopedic understanding of human nature. In McGee, both the accomplished businesswoman and the seasoned lawyer recognize and acknowledge an equal. The investigator is known, and can be judged, not only by what he or she does—but by the company each keeps. The representation of *that* depends in turn on the cultural resources available to the writer, resources the writer shares with potential readers. These resources have both a cognitive and an evaluative dimension. Judge Wellington can "vouch" for McGee if, in addition to knowing what a small-town lawyer is, the reader shares with MacDonald the same positive view of his character's imputed shrewdness, knowledge of people, and legal skills.

Fictional investigation manifests a moral dimension and thus raises questions about the fitness of the investigator to possess the power over others achieved in the course of establishing the fact(s) of the matter. In addition to the direct and indirect forms of reassurance adduced above, I wish to turn the matter in a different direction and argue that investigation, represented in mystery fiction both as a process and as an achievement (of understanding and knowledge), typically involves substantial "costs," and that these are best understood as compensatory checks on the investigator arising from the inherent moral ambiguity of investigation. Put differently, the fictional investigator usually pays a price for his or her skill in pursuing truth. These costs are deeply "social" in nature, being reckoned up in the form of cultural goods that tend to occur as opposite or mutually exclusive pairings: head/heart, reason/emotion, work/family, public/private, and opacity/transparency. Moreover, the order in which I have put each pair—that is, head/heart; reason/emotion—is neither accidental nor idiosyncratic; it is both the way we conventionally order them in discourse (not heart/head, for example) and the basis for a master list of what goes with what, consisting of oppositional pairs. Head, in everyday discourse, "goes with" reason, work, the public sphere, and, I would argue, "opacity," an achievement that has survival value in the public world of work and reason. Opacity, however, is incompatible with intimacy, spontaneity, and authenticity—the hallmarks of the private sphere of family, heart, emotion, and "transparency," the opposite of opacity. Historically, modernity has witnessed a rigid and exaggerated separation of the public and private spheres. The modern individual lives in both, but in alternation rather than simultaneously, and what fits one for the demands of the former tends to unfit one for those of the latter. Not only is success in the public sphere no guarantee of felicity in the private; the skills that underwrite conventional success in the public sphere are dysfunctional in the private. Hence the "cost" of success in the public sphere may be reckoned in terms of the sacrifice or loss of the satisfactions afforded only, or best, in the private sphere, since important cultural goods are associated with both, but the separation of public and private makes it difficult to achieve them simultaneously. Successful investigation, as represented in mystery fiction, requires subordinating spontaneous emotionality to rational control, for example, and privileges the skills that culminate in the achievement of an asymmetrical relationship—one in which the investigator knows the other better than the other is permitted to know the investigator. Such an asymmetry, however, is incompatible with the condition of mutual trust Giddens (1990) contends is both essential to the development of the self and attainable only in the private sphere. Whether or not one finds the normative dimension of Giddens's argument persuasive, trust in another does seem to be inextricably tied to knowledge of the other. Conversely, trust, and any action undertaken on its basis, is at some risk if what one takes to be true about another, with whom one must interact in some consequential matter, is inaccurate in important respects.

Investigative skills, as figured in mystery fiction, entail "costs" of

various sorts. These costs include moral corruption (or at least the risk ✳
of it); physical harm; marginal social status; and a perpetual tension
experienced by the investigator between the demands of the case and
the needs of intimates, a tension that may threaten the investigator's
capacity to create or sustain close personal relationships, on the one
hand, or threaten the investigator's effectiveness, on the other. I conclude the chapter by attempting to tie the patterns of costs first to the
issue of trust raised by the moral ambiguity of the detective, and second
to the larger issue of a "moral economy" constituted in mystery fiction.

In creating the character of Sherlock Holmes, Conan Doyle repro-
duced the distinction, everywhere sharpened by the demands of modernity, between the rational and the emotional.[1] Holmes is conceived
entirely in terms of the former, as this characteristic declaration from
the opening paragraph of "A Scandal in Bohemia" makes clear:

> All emotions, and that one [love] particularly, were abhorrent to his cold,
> precise, but admirably balanced mind. He was . . . the most perfect reasoning
> and observing machine that the world has seen; but, as a lover, he would have
> placed himself in a false position. He never spoke of the softer passions, save
> with a gibe and a sneer. They were admirable things for the observer—
> excellent for drawing the veil from men's motives and actions. But for the
> trained reasoner to admit such intrusions into his own delicate and finely ad-
> justed temperament was to introduce a distracting factor which might throw
> a doubt upon all his mental results. (1927, 161)

Doyle here renders the opposition between reason and emotion in utterly conventional terms—familiar because they continue to be useful
in carving up the world conceptually. In contrast with the softness of
the emotions, rationality is cold and machine-like in its precise and
delicate balance. "Grit in a sensitive instrument . . . would not be more
disturbing than a strong emotion in a nature such as his" (1927, 161).

So sharply did Doyle distinguish between reason and emotion, for
the purposes of his detective fiction, that Sherlock Holmes is unimaginable as a lover. That restriction has long since disappeared from the
ratiocinative tradition of mystery writing and was never a convention
of the hard-boiled form of detective fiction, whose protagonists are
invariably sexually attractive, whether exemplified by male private investigators like Sam Spade, Philip Marlowe, Lew Archer, Richard
Prather's Shell Scott, and John D. MacDonald's Travis McGee, who
are typical of the form through the 1970s, or by more recent female
versions of the private investigator such as Marcia Muller's Sharon

McCone, Sara Paretsky's V. I. Warshawski, or Sue Grafton's Kinsey Millhone, who began appearing in the early 1980s. Imagining the investigator in the role of lover, however, requires working within cultural constraints: it does nothing to alter entrenched distinctions and oppositions pitting head and heart, reason and emotion. Quite the contrary: love feigned is a potent trap for the unwary, while the spontaneous expression of emotionality typically threatens the self-control that underlies creating and sustaining opacity, on which rests the investigator's success and, frequently, his or her very survival.

Conversely, the ability to act a role without betraying that fact creates a barrier to intimacy, as do other aspects of the detective's craft that can be implicated, finally, in the opposition between the rational and the emotional. To the extent that survival depends on the possession and exercise of <u>rational</u> <u>self-control</u>, and intimacy requires reciprocal trust and openness as a precondition, the two ends—survival and intimate personal relations—may be figured as mutually exclusive. Sacrificed to the former, intimacy thus becomes the high but necessary cost of survival. The converse is rare, of course; but sacrificing survival can be figured as the price to be paid for love. In the conclusion of John Le Carré's *The Spy Who Came in from the Cold* (1963), the novel that established his reputation and popularity, the British agent Alec Leamas declines escape from East Germany after the woman he has fallen in love with is shot dead as they scale the Berlin Wall. Rather than be rescued, Leamas climbs back down the ladder, where he is shot and killed standing beside her body.

Survival is also very much the issue in the final scene between Sam Spade and Brigid O'Shaughnessy in *The Maltese Falcon*. Spade has every reason to turn Brigid over to the authorities for the murder of Miles Archer, yet he is pulled in conflicting directions, as Hammett's description of his overwrought state is doubtless intended to signal: "His wet yellow face was set hard and deeply lined. His eyes burned madly" (1964, 193). Weighing against the reasons for turning her in, "we've got what?" Spade asks. "All we've got is the fact that maybe you love me and maybe I love you"—not enough, in Hammett's conception of Spade, for such a character plausibly to risk the possibility that Brigid has played him for a "sap"—i.e., that she understands him well enough to anticipate his reaction and hence to manipulate him to her advantage (1964, 194).

Raymond Chandler, in "The Simple Art of Murder," sharply distinguished Hammett's approach to the murder mystery from that of practitioners of the British country house, or ratiocinative, tradition; but he insisted on the conventional separation of investigation and romance characteristic of that tradition until after World War II. In his ten rules for writing mystery fiction, Chandler asserted that some approaches were mutually exclusive. If the mystery novel is a puzzle, it cannot simultaneously be a violent adventure or a passionate romance. In a diary entry, Chandler drew an absolute distinction between the love story and the detective story, contending: "The peculiar appropriateness of the detective or mystery story in our time is that it is incapable of love. The love story and the detective story cannot exist, not only in the same book—one might almost say in the same culture." Chandler laid the problem at the door of "modern outspokenness" that "has utterly destroyed the romantic dream on which love feeds. There is nothing left to write about but death, and the detective story is a tragedy with a happy ending" (Durham 1963, 3). Despite his attractiveness to women, Chandler's Philip Marlowe is isolated, not by some habitual pragmatic skepticism about trusting others too much, but for reasons best summarized in "The Simple Art of Murder." There Chandler defines the detective as "a man of honor" and the best man in his world. As a consequence, "he is a lonely man" and relatively poor. His principal problem, as Chandler conceived it, lay in preserving his moral integrity. The principal threat to Marlowe's integrity is not the appeal of money or sex but physical intimidation.

Ross Macdonald, by contrast, alludes frequently to the costs associated with investigation. Questioning an informant in *The Zebra-Striped Hearse*, for example, Archer reflects on the turn the interview has taken: "[It] was beginning to depress me. Stacy's eyes had a feeding look, as if he lived on these morsels and scraps of other people's lives. Perhaps I feared a similar fate for myself" (1964, 84). Later in the same work, he is challenged by a woman who has overheard him on the telephone, discussing the case with another private detective: "Do you doubt everything and everyone?" to which Archer replies, "Practically everything. Almost everyone" (1964, 190). Investigation—the nature of the work, the hours, the people with whom he comes in contact in the course of a case—had cost Archer his marriage. Although he meets women to whom he is attracted in the course of his work, Archer rarely allows himself to become involved with them. "I wanted to comfort her," he thinks of a woman he meets in *The Zebra-Striped Hearse*,

"But I kept my hands off. She had more memories than she could use, and so had I" (1964, 75). He turns down another in *The Underground Man*, thinking, "I liked the woman. I almost trusted her. But I was already working deep in her life. I didn't want to buy a piece of it or commit myself to her until I knew what the consequences would be" (1972, 207). Archer's characteristic stance of detachment and cool assessment is overridden in a revealing incident in *The Galton Case*, when he locates and interviews John Galton's former girlfriend, Ada Reichler. Responding to her trust and unsparing frankness about the reasons for her failed relationship with Galton, Archer loses his customary self-control and becomes uncharacteristically angry when she blames herself for breaking up with Galton:

> "I betrayed him. Nobody could love me. *Nobody* could.
> "I told you to be quiet."
> I'd never been angrier in my life. . . . She ran blind to the end of the garden, knelt at the edge of the grass, and buried her face in flowers. Her back was long and beautiful. I waited until she was still, and lifted her to her feet. She turned toward me. The last light faded from the flowers and from the lake. Night came on warm and moist. The grass was wet. (1960, 147–48)

Skillful dissembling, as we have seen, is often crucial to investigative success. It creates the mask or cover that screens from others the investigator's intentions or the state of his knowledge about the case, obfuscating the links between intention and action and reducing the possibility of another interpreting correctly what is going on. Skillful dissembling, by definition, blocks knowledge of another. Recognizing that another is capable of assuming a different persona, perhaps instantly, can be unsettling, since trust and intimacy presuppose knowledge of another. A passage from John D. MacDonald's *Pale Gray for Guilt* illustrates the point. Investigating the apparent suicide of an old friend, Travis McGee is accompanied by Puss Killian, who confronts McGee early in the story with a laundry list of discrepancies she has observed between his easygoing manner, on the one hand, and evidence of an underlying wariness and a startling capacity for quick and decisive action on the other, raising the question for her of who and what McGee is. "How about the lightning change of personality," she asks, "for the benefit of the phone man with the old-timey glasses, the way you turned into a touristy goof so completely I didn't even feel as if I knew you? . . . So I have this eccentricity, maybe . . . I started [*sic*] sleeping with somebody and I get this terrible curiosity about them" (1968, 47–48). In response, McGee offers a description of what he does, justifying his vocation, the need for it in modern society, and its special requirements in terms of how the world (really) is: "It's a tricky, complex, indifferent society, Puss. It's a loophole world," in which there are a "thousand perfectly legal" but immoral or amoral ways to fleece the "unsuspecting." In those instances, "law officers have no basis of action. Attorney's [sic] can't help" (1968, 48). McGee's explanation of what he does and why and how he does it merits an approving hug from Killian, suggesting that McGee's justification of his skills at dissembling, as strategic responses to a loophole world, makes sense to her.

Ross Thomas touches on the tension between investigative skills and romantic attachment in *The Briar Patch* (1984), for which he won his second Edgar award. Benjamin Dill, an investigator for a Senate subcommittee, has gone home to the Midwest to look into the murder of his sister, a homicide detective. He and his sister's attorney, Anna Maude Singe, are attracted to one another from their first meeting. She accompanies Dill when he searches his sister's apartment, where they discover, and Dill interrogates, an electronics expert, Harold Snow, who had secreted a tape recorder there, and when Dill questions an aging newspaper reporter about a story concerning his sister. His handling of both situations raises questions for her about Dill and about the wisdom of falling in love with him.

Dill gets Harold Snow to answer his questions by threatening to shoot him in the knee—or, more precisely, by convincing Snow that he is capable of carrying out that threat. When they are alone, Singe asks, " 'Where'd you learn to do what you did to Harold this afternoon?' 'I don't know,' Dill said. 'I think I've always been that way.' 'But it's an act, isn't it?' 'Sure,' Dill said, 'it's an act,' and wondered if it really was" (1985, 233–34). Before their meeting with the elderly reporter, Dill warns Singe, "I'm going to get nasty with [Laffter]." Confronting him in his favorite restaurant, Dill gets the information he wants, but Laffter becomes overwrought, suffers a heart attack, and survives only because Dill and a waiter administer CPR. Later, Anna Maude asks Dill to drop her off at her apartment, saying she no longer wants to be his friend: " 'If I went on being your friend, and not just your lawyer, I'm afraid two things might happen. . . . I might fall in love with you— and I'd probably get into some kind of trouble I don't want to get into.

. . . I was involved with that old man. I helped make it happen. And that got to me because I finally realized it's not just let's pretend, is it?' 'No,' Dill said. 'You remember my asking if you weren't just all act?' [she replies]; 'You're no act. . . . It makes me afraid and I don't want to be afraid. And I don't want to be in love with you either' " (1985, 246–47).

Anthony Price offers a similar take on the tension between investigation and intimacy in the first of his novels featuring Dr. David Audley, *The Labyrinth Makers*. When the novel opens, Audley has been removed from his position as a Middle East intelligence analyst and reassigned to field work, to which he initially feels unsuited. Audley's first assignment is to determine why Soviet intelligence is interested in the remains of a Royal Air Force cargo plane that had been lost in 1945 and recently come to light when a pond was drained. Tracing and interviewing the surviving members of the air crew and accompanied by the dead pilot's daughter, Faith Steerforth, Audley adopts a pose of sinister ruthlessness and intimidates one of the crewmen into telling him about the plane's last flight and the smuggled boxes that had been on it but were not found in the wreckage twenty-five years later. Reflecting on the encounter, Audley doubts his suitability for "this kind of work; not because he was too soft-hearted, as he had cretinously believed, but because with a little practice he could grow to like it too much" (1986, 135). Faith Steerforth, with whom he shares a mutual attraction, expresses doubts of her own: "I just don't know what sort of man you are! I've seen a gentle side. . . . And a diffident side. . . . And that nice man Roskill thinks the world of you—and so does Richardson, and he'd never even met you! But I think there could be a dark side I wouldn't like" (1986, 135). A bit later, Audley admits, "as to that dark side of mine—the answer is 'yes' to that too. I think there's a KGB man inside me trying to get out. And maybe that's another reason why you should stick around; we can both try to keep him in check now we've spotted him. At least until I can get back to my old [desk] job where he doesn't have any chances!" (1986, 137). Audley does not get his job back, but he does marry Faith, although her role in subsequent novels is minimal at best. For Anthony Price, the cost of Audley's effectiveness is not the loss of intimacy but the danger of becoming indistinguishable from one's adversaries—in this case Audley's opposite numbers in the KGB, especially Nicolai Panin, who, like Audley, is an accomplished historian. But more than that, the danger, for Price, seems to lie in coming to enjoy the power bestowed by the capacity to intimidate others, a power that comes back finally to the ability to read others successfully.

For Marcia Muller, who first successfully adapted the hard-boiled conventions to a female protagonist, estrangement is the price her series character, Sharon McCone, must pay for resorting to deadly force when the occasion demands it. In *Trophies and Dead Things*, for example, McCone chases down and physically subdues a sniper, after first shooting and wounding him. Afterwards, she notices a marked change in her colleagues at All Souls Legal Cooperative. "To them I was not the same person they thought they'd known before last night. . . . I doubted any of them would ever fully reconcile their prior conception of me with the near-murderous stranger they'd seen. And while time would somewhat dull the memory, it would always be there, always set me a little apart from them. The realization filled me with sadness" (1991, 219). Later, a man she had been dating leaves a message on her answering machine about the incident: "I always thought you were a gentle person like me, but this thing with the sniper . . . what you did was like police brutality. Sharon, you're just too violent for me. Violent women are unnatural—" (1991, 264).

That earlier incident weighs on her mind as she is deciding whether to use deadly force at the conclusion of *Wolf in the Shadows*, discussed in chapter 3. McCone worries that killing her adversary would estrange her from her brother, who has disapproved of the nature of her work in the past and whom she has involved in her current case, reluctantly violating one of her "cardinal rules" in doing so: "when there's a possibility of danger, never involve, even in the smallest degree, family members or other people you care about" (1994, 124). In this instance, her fears of alienating her brother prove groundless: "he'd seen [the man she killed], seen the evil I was up against; taking him along while I investigated had allowed him a glimpse of the realities of my world that he would never forget and created a stronger bond between John and me" (1994, 360).

The dangers associated with investigation create similar problems for V. I. Warshawski, Sara Paretsky's version of the female private detective. In *Tunnel Vision*, Warshawski's longtime friend Lotty Herschel rebukes her for her handling of a homeless mother and her children: " 'I worry, Vic, when you decide to intervene in other people's lives. Someone usually suffers. It's often you, which is hard enough to watch, but last year it was me, which was even harder.' . . . A year ago [Warshawski recalls] some thugs mistook Lotty for me and broke her arm. Her anger and my remorse had cut a channel between us that we rebridged after months of hard work" (1995, 15–16). Despite her best friend's rebuke, however, Warshawski involves various other friends in dangerous situations in the course of this complicated case, including her neighbor, Mr. Contreras, who is hospitalized for the third time in six years with injuries sustained on her behalf, and her lover, police lieutenant Conrad Rawlings, who is nearly killed coming to her aid. Explaining his decision to "cool things off" between them, Rawlings tells her from his hospital bed,

> my life would never have been in danger if you hadn't gone headlong out to Morris [Illinois] without talking to me about what you planned to do. . . . The last month has taken a real toll on my love for you. You don't have enough room in your breast for compromise. . . . I can't go through another episode like this, Vic. It isn't that I resent you for being right. It's not even the bullet in my shoulder. It's watching you plunge ahead without regard for anything or anyone except your private version of justice. (1995, 446–47)

The nature and demands of investigation thus jeopardize personal relationships in various ways, threatening to alienate or isolate the investigator from others. In the hands of some writers, investigation runs the risk of leading to spiritual corruption, self-alienation, or both. That risk is clear in the passage quoted earlier from Anthony's Price's *The Labyrinth Makers*, in which David Audley discovers, with misgivings, his capacity to enjoy intimidating and manipulating others and thereby his risk of becoming virtually indistinguishable from his adversaries in Soviet intelligence.

Becoming indistinguishable from one's adversary may be the final, inevitable cost of successful investigation—a worry implicit in the very notion of identifying with one adversary, a crucial notion for successful investigation, beginning with Poe's prototypical stories. At the conclusion of John Le Carré's *Smiley's People*, Smiley watches as his nemesis Karla makes his crossing into West Berlin, compelled to defect to protect his only daughter, whose safety Smiley has credibly threatened. Smiley

> looked across the river into darkness again, and an unholy vertigo seized him as the very evil he had fought against seemed to reach out and possess him and claim him despite his striving, calling him a traitor also; mocking him, yet

at the same time applauding his betrayal. . . . I have destroyed him with the weapons I abhorred, and they are his. We have crossed each other's frontiers, we are the no-men of this no-man's land. . . . he did not want these spoils, won by these methods. (1980, 370–71)

With Karla finally and securely in British hands, one of Smiley's protegés congratulates him: "George, you won." His reply is the last line of the work: " 'Did I?' said Smiley. 'Yes, Yes, well I suppose I did' " (1980, 374). Sacrificing compassion to fanaticism calls into question Smiley's moral status, which in turn calls into question the meaning and worth of the achievement effected by an agent using such means. "Peel away the claptrap of espionage and the spy's job is to betray trust. The only justification . . . a spy can have is the moral worth of the cause he represents" (Hood 1982, 11).

John D. MacDonald touches on the same issue in *Pale Gray for Guilt*, in which Travis McGee and his friend Meyer use fraudulent securities transactions in a scheme to avenge the murder of a friend of McGee's. Confronted by Preston LaFrance, one of the individuals taken in and ruined by McGee's scheme, the normally mild-mannered Meyer offers him a way out of his difficulties: "Do yourself a favor. Go kill yourself" (1968, 184). Later, Meyer reflects on his remark, which had goaded LaFrance into a murderous rage:

> "Me! Did you hear me? On the sidewalk if there is a bug, I change my step and miss him. For me the business of the hooks almost spoils fishing. Me! I don't understand it. Such a rotten anger I had, Travis! . . . I am ashamed of that kind of anger. I am ashamed of being able to do something like that. I said to myself when I first got into your line of . . . endeavor, I said—forgive me for saying this to you—I said I will go only so far into it. There are things that McGee does that somehow hurt McGee, hurt him in the way he thinks of himself. . . . Now I find myself a little bit less in my own eyes. Maybe this is a bad business you're in, Travis. . . . Is this the little demonstration of how half the evil in the world is done in the name of honor?" He wanted help I couldn't give him. . . . He had overturned one of the personal stones in my garden too, and I could watch leggedy things scuttling away into comforting darkness. (1968, 184–85)

Habitual wariness becomes second nature to the investigator. Skepticism about others' motives; assuming, as a general rule, that things are seldom really as they appear to be; and identifying with one's (by definition deviant) adversary all have survival value for the investigator—but carry the risk of jeopardizing intimacy with others, or one's sense of moral selfhood, or both. A passage in Doyle's "The Adventure of the Copper Beeches" illustrates the danger. Traveling into the countryside to visit a client, Holmes remarks to Watson " 'that it is one of the curses of a mind with a turn like mine that I must look at everything with reference to my own special subject. You look at these scattered houses, and you are impressed by their beauty. I look at them, and the only thought which comes to me is a feeling of their isolation and of the impunity with which crime may be committed there.' 'Good heavens, [Watson] cried. 'Who would associate crime with these dear old homesteads?' " (Doyle 1927, 323).

Suspicion as a way of life underpins espionage fiction generally and John Le Carré's work in particular: "Survival, as Jim Prideaux liked to recall, is an infinite capacity for suspicion. By that purist standard, Mackelvore should have suspected that in the middle of a particularly vile rush-hour, on a particularly vile evening, in one of those blaring side streets that feed into the lower end of the Elysees, Ricki Tarr would unlock the passenger door and hold him up at gunpoint" (1974, 315). More succinctly, Sara Paretsky's Vic Warshawski, annoyed with herself for failing to notice someone following her, remarks, "That's how you get killed in this business" (1995, 215). Not paying attention increases the risk of a possibly fatal surprise attack. Being overly suspicious, however, amounts to pathology. Marcia Muller's Sharon McCone is repelled by Gage Renshaw, who heads an international security firm: "the world that people like Renshaw operated in was a strange one—full of paranoia, suspicion, distrust. I'd come up against a fair amount of duplicity in my own world, but in his it seemed the accepted norm. . . . Was he ever able to let down his guard and confide in anyone?" (1994, 97).

Allan Pinkerton emphasized the need for the modern detective to be ever "upon his guard, ever ready to take advantage of the most trifling circumstances, and yet, with an outward demeanor that dispels suspicion and invites the fullest confidence" (1886, 18–19). The psychological demands on the detective entailed by the requirement to be ever alert and wary—without appearing to be so—are isolated by Erving Goffman in a passage cited earlier: "those who conceal matters under what is normal appearances for another will have two different things to conceal: the facts of the matter and the fact that they are making an effort to conceal them" (1971, 261–62). Put differently, mystery writers ask where the line is to be drawn between a prudent, pragmatic skepticism on the one hand, and a corrosive, isolating paranoia on the other. To distrust falsely is (merely) alienating. Failure to distrust, when the situation requires it, is dangerous, perhaps even fatal.

To the moral risks inherent in investigation must be added the ever present physical risk, particularly in the case of the private investigator and the intelligence agent. Espionage, as chronicled in fiction from John Buchan to John Le Carré, Charles McCarry, Len Deighton, Ted Allbeury, and a host of others, typically involves mortal danger as a matter of course; the investigation of murder—the conventional inciting cause for the overwhelming majority of mystery stories—very often involves the investigator in conflict with powerful others, if not in mortal danger. As the detective comes ever closer to establishing the facts of the matter, he or she thereby becomes a greater and greater threat to the subject of the investigation. The world of the mystery story is thus inherently dangerous, and protagonists fit for that world must be capable of handling risk, as a psychological threat, and dangerous situations, involving physical threat. The risk of physical injury or death can thus be used to define and test the qualities essential to pursuing the facts of the matter: perseverance in the face of intimidation and discouragement; the ability to subordinate emotionality to rational processes, to resist distraction, and to think clearly under stress; and the trained capacity to maintain an assumed role despite surprise or provocation.

Examples abound. The final scene of *The Maltese Falcon* is prototypical. Returning to his apartment late at night, Spade is surprised by his adversaries, who threaten him at gunpoint for information about the mysterious falcon. Spade gains control of the situation by playing one off against another, beginning with Caspar Gutman and his bodyguard Wilmer Cook, in a virtuoso performance of unpredictability and presence of mind in exceptionally dangerous circumstances. In *Farewell, My Lovely*, Chandler's Philip Marlowe is variously beaten, choked, and confined and kept drugged in a private sanitarium for pursuing his inquiries. Lew Archer, in *The Galton Case*, has paint sprayed in his eyes and suffers a serious beating when his investigation takes him to Reno to look into the possible involvement of "the mob" in John Galton's pursuit of his alleged patrimony: "The fear of blindness is the worst fear there is. It crawled on my face and entered my mouth. I wanted to beg them to save my eyes. A persistent bright speck behind my eyes stared me down and shamed me into continued silence" (1960, 102). Efforts to intimidate Robert Campbell's Jimmy Flannery in *Junkyard Dog* include beating Flannery, leaving him to be attacked by a ferocious watchdog, and making an attempt on his fiancée's life. Vic Warshawski, in Sara Paretsky's *Bitter Medicine*, receives a warning, in the form of a superficial facial cut from eye to jaw line, at the hands of a former client to whom she had gone for information, unaware of the grudge he had been nursing for years. Jeremiah Healey's John Cuddy worries, in *Act of God*, that he may not be up to the physical demands of being a private investigator, after injuring his knee and shoulder.

Espionage, like diplomacy, amounts to warfare conducted by other means and as such is intrinsically dangerous to field agents. John Le Carré illustrates the vigilance born of recognizing the intrinsic dangers associated with intelligence work in depicting George Smiley's return to his London flat in the early pages of *Tinker, Tailor, Soldier, Spy*. Retired from the intelligence service, Smiley nonetheless maintains his habitual watchfulness, systematically noting the cars parked on his street,

> checking which were familiar, which were not; of the unfamiliar, which had aerials and extra mirrors, which were the closed vans that watchers liked. Partly he did this as a test of memory to preserve his mind from the atrophy of retirement. . . . But Smiley had a second reason, which was fear, the secret fear that follows every professional to his grave. Namely, that one day, out of a past so complex he himself could not remember all the enemies he might have made, one of them would find him and demand the reckoning. (1980, 26)

If the fictional investigator typically cannot be intimidated by force, including the threat of death, he (or she) is also typically immune to the corrupting influence of money. The detective's pursuit of truth is not motivated by a desire for personal gain, just as it is not driven by the power that might be gained. Power—often the power of life and death—is the inevitable consequence of a successful investigation, however; money is not. Hence the writer has little choice but to address the moral implications arising from the power that necessarily accrues in the course of successful investigation. Money may not be as intrinsic to successful investigation as I have insisted power is, but greed is a pervasive motive for fictional murder, and many writers make a point of insisting that their investigators are indifferent to money and do not possess material tastes that require money. Conan Doyle, for example, reassures his readers in several stories that Holmes works "rather for the love of his art than for the acquirement of wealth" (1927, 257). In "The Simple Art of Murder," Raymond Chandler insisted that the detective "is a relatively poor man, or he would not be a detective at all." By nature, he will "take no man's money dishonestly" (1995, 992). Philip Marlowe is, in part, Chandler's rebuke to the rationalization voiced by a corrupt police officer in *Farewell, My Lovely*: "You know what's the matter with this country, [Marlowe]? . . . A guy can't stay honest if he wants to. . . . You gotta play the game dirty or you don't eat" (1964, 182). Ross Macdonald's Lew Archer, questioned in *The Galton Case* about his motives for doing the work he does and specifically about whether the work pays well, replies that it pays "enough to live on. I don't do it for the money, though. I do it because I want to'" (1960, 55). Robert Campbell attributes no interest whatever in money to Jimmy Flannery, whose position as a Democratic precinct captain in Chicago offers ample opportunity to enrich himself should he so choose; and his barter of "favor for favor," the currency with which he manages and transacts his political affairs, is shown to have clear limits. Flannery refuses, for example, to accept a "marker" from Carmine DiBella, drawing the line at entering into a contract with the head of Chicago's crime syndicate (1986, 180–81) even though he knows "everybody in Chicago politics has got mob connections" (1986, 93) and recognizes the addictive nature of power: "power's a hard drug to kick. The hardest" (1986, 93).

In adapting the conventions of the hard-boiled private eye story, Sara Paretsky retains those elements that define the detective as socially and economically marginal. Vic Warshawski maintains an office in a run-down building on the edge of Chicago's loop, drives an aging car that lacks air conditioning, and, in *Bitter Medicine* (1987), implies that her annual income is between twenty and thirty thousand dollars— without health insurance. Invited to a dinner in honor of a favorite law school professor, she finds herself seated not at the head table but "decanted with the dregs to a table near the kitchen door. I had to laugh at myself—all my professional choices have consciously led me away from wealth and power. It was absurd to resent denial from their ranks" (1995, 51). Later, Warshawski curtly rebukes a client who challenges her handling of the case, saying "You paid for my professional help. You did not buy me" (1995, 181). At the conclusion of Marcia

Muller's *Wolf in the Shadows*, Sharon McCone remains undecided whether to accept a promotion at All Souls Legal Cooperative, where she has worked happily for years, or to accept an offer from an international security consulting firm. Both involve more money than she currently makes, but the former would tie her to a desk, while the latter would immerse her in a world saturated with distrust and suspicion. Either choice would unacceptably curtail the freedom she prizes above all else: "Sometimes, I thought, the worth of freedom can be measured only by the cost of what you give up to achieve it. If I chose a free path when I returned to the city, it would be valuable beyond reckoning" (1994, 370).

Successfully discovering the facts of the matter raises two troublesome issues, one having to do with the means employed, the other with the use of the knowledge uncovered. Both aspects of detection or investigation possess an intrinsic moral dimension; both raise questions of trust. Allan Pinkerton, in his introduction to *Thirty Years a Detective* (1886), contended that the detective's "calling has become a profession, and himself an intelligent, keen sighted and accomplished gentleman, relying upon his own high moral character, his superior intelligence and his indefatigable energy for the success which he has attained," thus insuring the trustworthiness of the detective by anchoring it rhetorically in some of the period's preeminent cultural categories of moral virtue and responsibility: the code of the gentleman, the standards of professionalism, and the concept of character (1886, 16–17). Much the same view informs Jacob Fisher's handbook *The Art of Detection*, which emphasizes the probity and professionalism required of investigators, public or private.

> The good investigator should develop a reputation for squareness. It is axiomatic that he is expected to be honest. . . . He should meet all his commitments, and above all, he should protect his informants. If the information he receives is of such a nature that the informant requests that the source not be disclosed, the investigator should never fail to respect this request, regardless of any pressure or inducements offered to him. An investigator is often the confidant and repository of family secrets, and he should never gossip about what he knows. (1948, 24)

Contrasting with these injunctions is George McWatters's unsparing description, cited earlier, of the personal qualities and practical means entailed in successful detection—the routine and necessary reliance, for example, on dissembling, impersonation, and lying as aids in getting at the facts of the matter. Reliance on these means raised the issue of trust in the creation of the role of police detectives in the nineteenth century, as Carl Klockars has demonstrated (1985, 63–91). The same issue, and for the same reasons, pervades mystery fiction, where the pursuit of truth rests, to a degree that varies from writer to writer, on the detective's skills at dissembling and deception. Compensating for, and qualifying, the terms of the detective's investigative success and prowess are the sorts of "costs" identified in this chapter.

Investigators are experts of a sort. If, as Peter Berger suggests, bureaucracies (and by extension "expert systems" generally) have a tendency to make their clients nervous, it is equally true that every client is a potential challenge both to the competence of the expert in question and to the expert system the expert both represents and embodies. Throughout the analysis in this and preceding chapters, I have emphasized the crucial importance of the expert's demeanor at those "access points" where clients interact with them. The professional's air of composure and confident expertise are an expression, in part, of a trained capacity to remain outwardly cool, especially in situations of high stress. One wants one's surgeon, or one's lawyer, to remain composed when the unexpected occurs. Such composure is a necessary but hardly sufficient condition for effective action. Expertise—the professional's mastery of his specialty—is essential. Composure in stressful circumstances permits the application of expertise; it is no substitute, however, for knowing what to do in the situation.

Ideally, experts are equal to the challenges presented by their clients. Being "equal to" involves both the degree of expertise possessed by a particular expert and the adequacy and scope of the knowledge and techniques constituting the expert system on which the practitioner draws. In some instances, clients rarely, if ever, present a significant challenge either to the expert or to the expert system to which they have turned for service. Someone with a particularly unusual driving history, for example, may tax the knowledge of a given clerk in a state motor vehicle administration facility, but the case is unlikely to present any challenge to the system of automobile licensing and registration. The situation is arguably different in medicine, however, where a patient may exhaust the expertise of a given specialist or present a condition that defies diagnosis by all the relevant specialists, whatever their professional accomplishments. In that case, it is not simply the skill of a given specialist that is at issue, but the capacity of the system to respond effectively to the client's needs.

Fictional investigators are <u>specialists</u>. The very concept of the detective, beginning with Poe's Dupin, involves expert knowledge on the one hand, and highly developed skills of emotional management and self-presentation on the other. The problems brought to fictional investigators by their clients are both a challenge to the ability of Sherlock Holmes or Sam Spade or Sharon McCone to cope with the situation, and a challenge to the expert system they represent and express— namely, practical rationality in one guise or another. Some fictional investigators are imagined by their creators as courts of last resort after other experts, and their systems, have failed: Dupin and Sherlock Holmes, obviously; but also investigators as varied as Philip St. Ives (created by Ross Thomas writing as Oliver Bleek); Travis McGee; George Smiley; and William Haggard's Colonel Charles Russell, to name only a representative handful. Thus the stakes involved in their cases are very high indeed, since those cases, by definition, present exceptionally difficult challenges to the investigator and, by extension, to the imaginable capacity of practical rationality to cope with a class of problems: namely, those in which an acceptable resolution hinges finally on the ability of the investigator to unmask the other while remaining opaque to the other's probing.

The convention of the successful solution means that mystery fiction can assess the relationship between the investigator's means and ends, with results such as those discussed throughout this chapter. The convention precludes challenging the efficacy of the constellation of traits, skills, and trained capacities that constitute the successful fictional investigator. To be sure, Irene Adler defeats Holmes in "A Scandal in Bohemia," but she does so by being better than he is at dissembling and anticipating her opponent. Holmes's method is upheld rather than challenged, just as the principle of knowing the other better is upheld in *A Coffin for Dimitrios*, despite the protagonist Latimer's ineptitude. Even Robert Littell's skepticism about achieving a correct interpretation in the context of cold war tensions seems more aimed at the factors, both institutional and personal, that jeopardize understanding what others are truly up to than it seems intended to call into question the very possibility of interpretation. Arguably, what frustrates correct interpretation in *The Defection of A. J. Lewinter* is inadequate expertise on the one hand, and lack of decisive evidence on the other. Neither, however, constitutes any challenge to the claims of mystery fiction that practical rationality is, in principle, equal to the demands made on it for explanation. Having said that, however, we might recall Poe's response to the acclaim engendered by his first detective story: "where is the ingenuity of unravelling a web which you yourself . . . have woven for the express purpose of unravelling?" Mystery novels—or, rather, those who write them—model a way of being in the world. In the next chapter, I turn to the question of other things writers do with mystery fiction, subject to various enabling and constraining factors—of which the character of the real world is surely the most important and the most problematical.

6

Doing Things with Mystery Fiction

Tales are tools . . . .
Clifford Geertz, *New York Review of Books,* 10 April 1997

Patricia Cornwell has won an enviable reputation for mystery writing with half a dozen works devoted to a female investigative character, Dr. Kay Scarpetta, chief medical examiner for the state of Virginia. Cornwell's first novel, *Postmortem* (1990), garnered the Edgar, Creasy, Anthony, and Macavity awards and the French Prix du Roman d'Aventure in one year—an unprecedented achievement. *From Potter's Field* (1995) has Scarpetta joining in the hunt for a serial killer, Temple Brooks Gault, a young man whose ability to anticipate the moves of his pursuers seems, for a time, to be terrifyingly complete, in large measure because he has successfully penetrated and compromised CAIN, described by Cornwell as "a centralized computer system linking police departments and other investigative agencies to one massive database maintained by the FBI's Violent Criminal Apprehension Program, or VICAP" (1995, 111).

In the final pages of *From Potter's Field*, Scarpetta confronts Gault in a New York City subway tunnel. Against all odds, he has evaded the elaborate trap set for him and holds a knife at the throat of Scarpetta's niece Lucy, the only child of Scarpetta's only sister. When Gault drops the knife and suddenly shoves Lucy toward the third rail, Scarpetta manages to pull her away from certain death, but drops the shotgun she was carrying. Gault's attempt to kill Lucy with the pistol he has taken from her fails when the unfamiliar weapon jams, and at Scarpetta's urging she escapes, leaving her aunt to face Gault alone. Having failed to clear the jammed pistol, Gault is poised to kill Scarpetta with a karate kick; Scarpetta spots Gault's knife "close to the third rail, and I groped for it as a rat ran over my legs and I cut myself on broken glass. My head was dangerously close to Gault's boots. . . . I saw him tense as he looked at me. I could feel his thoughts as I tightened my grip on the cold steel handle. I knew what he could do with his feet" (1995, 410). Before Gault can deliver the kick, however, Scarpetta snatches up the knife and stabs him in the thigh, severing the femoral artery and immobilizing him long enough for FBI sharpshooters posted farther away in the tunnel to bring him down.

The final confrontation between Cornwell's investigator and her deadly, implacable adversary represents in especially dramatic terms (or "melodramatic" terms, depending on your view) that trained capacity for decisive action in circumstances of consequential risk that underlies mystery fiction generally. Cornwell "models" a way of being in the world by demonstrating the fit between the characteristic challenges posed by that world and the qualities required to meet those challenges, which mystery fiction conventionally figures as matters of life and death. To model a way of being in the world is <u>to undertake or perform a certain type</u> of (symbolic) action, but that is only one of the things writers do in and through mystery fiction. In this chapter I explore a range of actions attributable to writers who adopt the conventions of mystery fiction, and address four questions: (1) What have writers done with mystery fiction? (2) What are some of the chief constraints on "doing" mystery fiction? (3) Given that action, including symbolic action, involves belief, does it make sense to attribute an ideology to mystery fiction? (4) In what sense, if any, can mystery fiction fairly be characterized as doing "cultural work"?

What can one do with mystery fiction—or, rather, what can one do by choosing to work with, and within, the resources and constraints of mystery fiction? I hope the meaning of the question will become clear, if it is not already, through my choice of examples, but at least two caveats are in order. First, the discussion is meant to suggest—it can hardly exhaust—the range of actions attributable to writers of mystery fiction. I hope my readers will, from their own acquaintance with this fiction, extend the range of actions attributable to mystery writers as well as recognize in works not selected for analysis further examples of the specific intentions discussed below. Second, my characterization of a given work as being an instance of defending, celebrating, warning, condemning, informing, assessing, or whatever is never offered as an exhaustive characterization of the author's intentions in that work or meant in a spirit of reductionism (cf. Thornton 1992).

We can begin to answer the question about what writers do with mystery fiction by noting that some writers, from Poe to authors currently active, have used mystery fiction as a form to think with as well as a vehicle for social commentary. Poe, for example, in "The Purloined Letter," rethinks a distinction between mathematics and poetry common at the time and defines Dupin's approach to problem solving as combining the rigor and precision of mathematics with the constructive, meaning-making power of the Imagination, the mark and endowment of the true poet. Ross Macdonald likened the conventions of the hard-boiled novel to a "disguise, a kind of welder's mask enabling [writers] to handle dangerously hot material," and thought that by the mid-1950s those conventions were sufficiently developed to "support a full-scale philosophical assault on the problem of evil" (Walbridge 1954, 334). Recently, Jeremiah Healy, a trial attorney and law professor as well as the creator of the novels featuring Boston private investigator John Cuddy, has said, "I think a number of P[rivate] I[investigator] writers, myself included, use the genre to explore those problems that one branch of government (the judiciary) doesn't deal with very well through formal operation," including "the problem of the battered spouse in divorce cases, reporters with confidential sources, the right to assisted suicide, and so on" (Healy 1996).

In creating a fictional investigator, every writer necessarily defines a "stance," a way of being in a fictional world, the features of which are also of the author's choosing and creating. There is therefore a close and necessary fit between the demands of that world and the characteristics and qualities of the investigator, given the convention of the successful ending. More or less consciously, writers defend or celebrate their investigator's stance, as a consequence of defining it. Sam Spade's stance of self-conscious, calculated unpredictability is a case in point. Spade epitomized the capability prized by the Pinkerton operatives with whom Dashiell Hammett worked: the ability to be equal to any situation, however unanticipated, that might arise in the course of an investigation. And the Flitcraft episode, as noted earlier, serves the same function in *The Maltese Falcon* as the discursive passages on method do in the stories of Poe and Conan Doyle: the story-within-a-story defines the key elements of Spade's stance and justifies that stance in terms of beliefs about the true nature of the world in which Spade must act and try to survive.

Writers have used the conventions of mystery fiction, especially in the form of the spy novel, to issue warnings. Erskine Childers's *The Riddle of the Sands* (1903) remains one of the best examples of this use of the spy novel, cautioning an unprepared and complacent Britain of the risk of Germany mounting a surprise invasion from its North Sea coast. Amidst talk of East-West *detente* in the 1960s, Helen Mac-Innes used her platform as a best-selling novelist in the tradition of Childers and John Buchan to warn of the dangers of Soviet manipulation of ignorance and complacency in the Western democracies. As a Book-of-the-Month Club alternate selection and subsequently a Reader's Digest Condensed Book selection, *The Double Image* (1966) reached a large audience. MacInnes made plain her intentions in the book's dedication: "To the men who don't get medals," referring to the CIA's policy not to acknowledge publicly, or permit its agents to display, medals earned in the course of duty. In passages such as the following, MacInnes spelled out her views:

> [H]istory was a long and bitter story of intrigue and grab, of hidden movements and determined leaders, of men who knew what they wanted manipulating men who hadn't one idea that anything was at stake: the innocent and the ignorant being used according to someone else's plan. But every now and again, the plan would fail. Because people could be surprising, too, in their resistance—*once they knew what was actually happening*. . . . But before they knew? Then we have men like Partridge [a CIA agent] . . . or else we could lose. (1967, 134; emphasis added)

More recently, Arnaud de Borchgrave and Robert Moss (*Monimbo*, *The Spike*) have appropriated the conventions of the spy novel to issue, from a conservative political perspective, thinly veiled warnings about dangers from abroad. A warning is an act, a serious utterance, and rests on a claim to knowledge—about the nature and magnitude of a particular threat, for example. Fiction used as a vehicle to issue a warning may be said to convey knowledge if the writer's treatment of the threat is accurate. Erskine Childers believed that the warning embodied in *The Riddle of the Sands* accurately depicted the manner in which a German invasion of Britain might be organized and launched in secrecy.

In the wake of Tony Hillerman's commercial success with mystery novels set in the Southwest featuring Navajo Tribal policemen Joe Leaphorn and Jim Chee, one of the most notable recent trends in mystery publishing has been the proliferation of ethnic detectives, together with reliable—i.e., true—information about the groups to which they belong. "Mystery novels provide a satisfying way to learn about other ways of life," but only, it must be added, if the ways of life are accurately depicted (Anthony 1994, 43). Hillerman's works have been used as teaching materials in Navajo high schools and community colleges, and he has been quoted as saying "I know more about the Navajo religion than most Navajos know" (Gorney 1987). The claim that mystery fiction offers "a satisfying way to learn about other ways of life" raises several questions I take up later in this chapter. Readers of romance novels offer the same argument in defense of their reading, as Janice Radway reports in *Reading the Romance*. The issue of factual accuracy has obvious relevance to historical fiction.

Writers have also used the spy novel to assess or reckon the costs and benefits of, for example, the West's intelligence efforts during the cold war, as the contrasting positions taken by Helen MacInnes and John Le Carré illustrate. MacInnes's *The Double Image* draws an invidious distinction between the Soviet intelligence service and the services of Britain, France, and the United States, whose representatives (in this novel) are models of professional cooperation in responding to a common threat that renders irrelevant and petty both personal ambition and national rivalries. John Le Carré presents a different picture, depicting the British Secret Intelligence Service, the "Circus," as riven by personal ambition and incompetence, and indistinguishable, in terms of the means it will employ, from its Soviet adversaries, thus negating any easy claims to moral superiority.[1] In his introduction to *The Philby Conspiracy*, Le Carré suggested that "a considerable and original virtue of this book [is] that it treats the British secret services for what they surely are: microcosms of the British condition, of our social attitudes and vanities" (Le Carré 1968, 7). The statement serves equally well to characterize a central element in Le Carré's own work. George Smiley's ambivalence at having successfully induced the defection of his Soviet nemesis Karla, in the final scene of *Smiley's People*, could hardly be farther from the assessment of allied intelligence activities MacInnes offers in and through her portrayal of "the men who don't get medals" and in her account of what John Craig learns in the course of *The Double Image*.

On occasion, writers may act to exact revenge or to offer a more satisfactory conclusion to events than actually occurred. Manning O'Brine's *No Earth for Foxes* (1974) may serve to exemplify the former, while the conclusion of Le Carré's *Tinker, Tailor, Soldier, Spy* illustrates the latter. O'Brine's book was marketed with the following information about its author on the back cover of the paperback edition: "Manning O'Brine is a former British secret agent. He killed his first Nazi in Heidelberg in 1937 and his last in Madagascar in 1950." *No Earth for Foxes* recounts an unsanctioned operation, undertaken years after World War II, to avenge atrocities inflicted on villagers in the mountains of northern Italy by German SS troops in late 1944, and ends with the death and symbolic castration of the former SS commander who had ordered the *"rastrellamento."* Le Carré's account of George Smiley's efforts to root out a Soviet mole in the top echelon of Circus personnel concludes with the seizure of his long-time colleague Bill Haydon, whose resemblance to the Soviets' actual double agent "Kim" Philby can hardly be coincidental. After being apprehended, in a trap devised by Smiley, Haydon is sequestered for questioning by Circus "inquisitors," but security is lax and Haydon is killed—by a colleague he had betrayed into Soviet hands. However satisfying such a symmetrical *quid pro quo* might be to imagine, Philby, as is well known, escaped (or was permitted to escape?) from Beirut to Moscow in 1963, where he lived until his death in 1987.

Celebrating (e.g., an investigative stance), condemning (e.g., the corruption of investigation by political considerations), informing (e.g., about Navajo ways), assessing (e.g., the moral claims of rival intelligence services), remembering and avenging (e.g., past atrocities) admittedly capture only partially and in a very crude way the range of acts undertaken in and through the writing of mystery fiction. Moreover, some acts—revenge, for example—are rare; works like Manning O'Brine's *No Earth for Foxes* are uncommon. Every work of mystery fiction, however, constitutes an argument, implicitly if not explicitly, and typically involves some "disposition" of the culprit(s) unmasked in the investigative process. More controversially, perhaps, mystery writers may be said to "reproduce" cultural categories, and in doing so define and maintain the "boundaries" of these categories.

Mystery fiction as argument is clearest and most explicit in those works purporting to solve real mysteries (e.g., Carr 1936; de la Torre 1945). "The Mystery of Marie Roget," noted earlier, presents Edgar Allan Poe's solution to the actual case of Mary Cecilia Rogers, whose murder, unsolved for months, was the subject of extensive coverage in the New York press in 1842. Equally explicit as argument is Josephine Tey's *The Daughter of Time*, which rehearses the case for Richard III's innocence in the murder of his two young nephews (Talburt 1981), and Malcolm Reybold's *The Inspector's Opinion* (1976), which reviews evidence in the case of Mary Jo Kopechne, who drowned when a car in which she was riding, allegedly driven by Senator Ted Kennedy, went off a bridge on Cape Cod in July 1969. (Reybold concludes that Kennedy was not, in fact, driving at the time of the accident.) Less detailed and circumstantial, Charles McCarry's *The Tears of Autumn* (1975) suggests that the family of Vietnamese president Ngo Dinh Diem, blaming the United States for Diem's death in the aftermath of the coup that deposed him, possessed motive, means, and opportunity to assassinate President Kennedy (Means 1991). Ted Allbeury's *The Other Side of Silence* (1981) explores "Kim" Philby's career in Britain's SIS and his defection to the Soviet Union in 1963, using as a premise Philby's (imagined) request to return to England to die. An investigation ensues aimed at making a recommendation, a process Allbeury uses to raise a number of still unanswered questions (e.g., "Why did SIS, after all that was known and suspected [of Philby's treachery], still get him on to the *Economist* and *Observer*, use him themselves, and keep contact with him in Beirut?" 1981, 289) and to present a more balanced portrait of Philby, the circumstances leading to his recruitment by Soviet intelligence, and the nature and extent of the damage he inflicted. Allbeury suggests that Donald Maclean was a far more damaging spy than Philby, for example, because, for a time, Maclean's access to American nuclear facilities was virtually unlimited.

More generally, a writer's work in novel after novel may embody a broad argument, as Ross Macdonald's work after *The Galton Case* urges the therapeutic value—initially personal, ultimately social—of facing up to the truth, however unpleasant or threatening it may seem for the individuals concerned. Anthony Price, in the nearly twenty novels he devotes to the career of David Audley, argues that past and present are inextricably intertwined in small ways and large, asking by implication in his first novel, *The Labyrinth Makers*, what could be so valuable to Soviet intelligence twenty-five years after the end of World War II that would justify undertaking an operation on British soil and be worth several deaths. The answer: the files (i.e., the documentary sources with which to establish the truth) regarding Stalin's purge of the Red Army's officer corps in the 1930s. In *Other Paths to Glory*, members of Audley's team defend themselves with World War I munitions, which they discover stored in tunnels dug and provisioned a half-century earlier. *Our Man in Camelot*, as I noted earlier, turns equally on recognizing that centuries-old chivalric values and beliefs still motivate the eccentric Billy Bullitt and on knowing—being able to recover—the content of the chivalric code well enough to think within its categories and use them to fashion a plan of action to trump the Soviets, whose manipulation of Bullitt rests on *their* understanding of that code and the beliefs embodied in it.

Finally, whether explicitly, as in this handful of representative examples, or implicitly by virtue of its depiction of successful action, mystery fiction constitutes an argument for the efficacy and indispensability of a set of traits and skills that enable the fictional investigator to discover, in virtually every case, the true facts of the matter. Foundational to that endeavor is (1) the familiar distinction between reason and emotion; (2) the priority assigned to the former over the latter in circumstances requiring decisive and effective action in defense of the self and others; and (3) the enormous value placed on the mastery of spontaneous emotionality in the face of dire threat. Consider again the situation facing Patricia Cornwell's Kay Scarpetta at the conclusion of *From Potter's Field*, as an assemblage of elements constituting a threat to Scarpetta's capacity for decisive, rational action: alone, within reach of a merciless killer, she gropes for a weapon amid broken glass, in close proximity to the subway's third rail, as a rat suddenly runs over her legs.

Dismissing such moments as melodramatic may be acceptable (if predictable) criticism, but it risks missing the point. Considered structurally, as the solution to a technical problem and a generic imperative, Cornwell's scene is no different from the climactic scene in *The Maltese Falcon*, when Spade faces the remorseless threat of Gutman and his bodyguard, or the life-threatening situation depicted in the Scouting story "The Whirlpool," or the scene in *The Thirty-nine Steps* in which Hannay's life depends on his ability to play the role of a rough Scottish road mender sufficiently well to allay the aroused suspicions of men who have been pursuing him. All these scenes are solutions to the same technical problem and the same imperative: namely, how to represent a degree of threat sufficient to jeopardize the protagonist's resolve, resourcefulness, and ability to retain rational control, which constitute the very basis and precondition (so the implicit argument runs) for effective action.

Mystery fiction may be said to describe or model the pursuit of "truth," so long as we mean by that term not Truth with a capital T, but truth in the unimposing sense of "the facts of the matter" as these are invented by the writer. But writers of mystery fiction seldom settle for simply resolving the mystery at the heart of the narrative in terms of sorting out who did what, to whom, in what order, and so on. Actions have consequences, in mystery fiction as in life; typically there is some comeuppance for the malefactors whose identity is discovered and revealed. The process of investigation does not culminate simply with the identification of those found to be responsible; by convention, it must be rounded out with their apprehension and with some sort of "disposition," for want of a better term. Readers sometimes report that they like reading mystery fiction for its depiction of justice done. "Justice" is thus a characterization, doubtless highly variable in its sense, that readers themselves make about the relationship of act and consequence. What writers of mystery fiction *do*, however, is associate specific acts with specific consequences—consequences that, in their circumstantiality, constitute a given writer's solution to what is both a technical and a moral problem set by the terms of the story itself. The specific consequences—or disposition—in a given instance offer clues to what a writer considers fitting or appropriate, what he or she thinks goes best with the nature of the crime committed. "Fitting consequences" are to be understood not as "justice," but as a function of a given writer's beliefs, including his or her beliefs about the nature of "justice" in the abstract as well as about what readers will accept or tolerate as appropriate in the circumstances portrayed in the story. Many a murder mystery, leaving aside for the moment the resolution of spy novels, couples the identification of the murderer with apprehending and remanding that person into the custody of law enforcement officers as the first step toward the formalities of trial, conviction, and imprisonment: murder will out and justice be done. In this familiar sense, "justice" is simply shorthand for both the established judicial process and the anticipated outcome of that process—namely, conviction on the basis of the body of evidence uncovered by the investigator. Evidence, in this sense, is a judicial concept and widely accepted as an appropriate constraint by writers, at least since Conan Doyle, who has Sherlock Holmes remark on more than one occasion, "It is not what we know but what we can prove [in a court of law], Watson" (Doyle 1927, 744).

Generic convention as well as moral imperatives demand of mystery writers that they do something, at the end, with the accused. Remanding the accused into the custody of the authorities is one solution. Killing off the accused is another. Letting the accused go is yet another. Occasionally, a writer will use both of these latter solutions, as in Jeremiah Healy's *Act of God*, discussed below. Instances of these modes of "disposition" suggest, at the least, that mystery fiction resists any simple or straightforward characterization as the pursuit of justice, however aptly it may be characterized as the pursuit of truth (i.e., the facts of the matter). Agatha Christie, in *Murder in the Calais Coach*, lets her murderers go. Patricia Cornwell concludes *From Potter's Field* (1995), as noted earlier, by killing off the serial murderer whose apprehension has been sought throughout the narrative. In *Act of God* (1994), John Cuddy kills one murderer and assures a second that he will not turn her in to the police. Whether any of these resolutions are just—and in what sense—is a matter, finally, for readers to decide; but each writer offers some justification, implicitly or explicitly, for the choice of disposition, and the terms in which those justifications are offered tell us something about the writer in question and about their sense of their audience.

In *Murder in the Calais Coach*, Hercule Poirot concludes that twelve people were involved in the murder of Ratchett, who is discovered dead of multiple stab wounds in a railroad sleeping car. Each of the twelve in turn had stabbed the sleeping man once. Combined, the wounds were fatal, but it was impossible to determine who caused any particular wound or whether, by itself, any given wound would have been fatal. Rather than have all twelve arrested and charged with conspiracy and murder, Poirot lets them go for reasons that seem carefully crafted by Christie to offer maximum mitigation. The victim Ratchett turns out to be a Chicago gangster—an "animal," Poirot calls him at one point—who had kidnapped and killed the child of a wealthy couple. Charged with the crime and brought to trial, he had escaped conviction on a legal technicality (there are hints that his successful challenge owed more to bribery and intimidation than to a point of law). The twelve who subsequently conspire to bring about his death served in the household of the couple whose child Ratchett murdered. In the face of the state's failure to secure a conviction in the case, they constitute themselves a jury of his peers, hear testimony, duly convict him, and carry out their sentence of death after drugging him into insensibility to insure that each will have a hand in his execution. Multiple suspects, all of whom turn out to be guilty, is a clever variation on the classical ratiocinative detective story and a solution to one of its key technical challenges—whodunit (they all did it). Letting the twelve go posed a further technical problem for Christie—choosing terms sufficient to justify their exoneration. Christie solved that problem, as we have seen, by invoking the decisive failure of the judicial process to convict Ratchett and (via the allusion to the Lindbergh kidnapping case) invoking, by extension, the universal revulsion attendant on that crime for which Bruno Hauptmann had not yet been arrested when the novel was published in February 1934.

In *Act of God*, John Cuddy's investigation into the bludgeoning death of Abe Rivkind, an elderly furniture store owner, and the disappearance of one of his secretaries leads to the identification of two murderers: Beverly Swindell, Rivkind's secretary and mistress for years, who killed Rivkind; and Roger Houle, who was having an affair with Rivkind's missing secretary and murdered his wife for her life insurance, then murdered again to cover his tracks. Cuddy refrains from turning Swindell over to the police to protect his client, Rivkind's widow, from the suffering and humiliation of learning of her dead husband's infidelities (Healy 1994, 283). Convinced of Houle's guilt in two killings, Cuddy later confronts him as noted in chapter 3; goads him into a murderous attack; and shoots him three times, killing him (1994, 310). Questioned by the police after the incident, Cuddy agrees it was " 'stupid coming out here alone, what you suspected and all,' " replying disengenously, " 'That's just it, though. I only suspected. There wasn't any solid evidence of Houle being the killer except for suspicion and what I hope you find under that shed. . . . Even if he'd given himself up peacefully, a lawyer would have told him to take the Fifth when you questioned him and to stay off the stand come trial.' . . . The townie coughed, stubbing out his smoke on the lawn. 'Par for the course' " (1994, 312).

How seriously Healy wants his reader to accept this view as partial justification for Cuddy's action is an open question. Prosecuting Houle, who was himself having an affair with Rivkind's other secretary, might well have revealed Rivkind's own liaison, thus resulting in the suffering and humiliation to Cuddy's client he had sought to avoid by not turning Beverly Swindell over to the authorities for Rivkind's murder. Cuddy's calculated killing of Houle eliminates that possibility, and with it the risk that Pearl Rivkind will have to bear not only the loss of her husband but the destruction of her image of him. Through his disposition of the case, Healy invites his reader to agree that sparing Pearl Rivkind the truth about her husband constitutes sufficient justification for circumventing entirely the formal judicial processes of indictment, trial, and verdict. Put differently, Healy invites his reader to consider that mercy and a due regard for the feelings of an innocent victim may, on occasion, require such circumvention if justice is truly to be served. Healy is careful to make clear that Swindell and Houle are guilty—both, in effect, confess as much to Cuddy, thus removing one possible source of concern at Cuddy's assuming the role of jury and (Houle's) executioner by meeting the terms of the Holmesian dictum quoted earlier: "It's not what we know but what we can prove." The two confessions confirm Cuddy's reconstructions of what must have happened with each of the three murders. There is no residual ambiguity about who did what to whom. Thus the reader's assessment of Cuddy's actions is not further complicated by any doubts about the guilt of Swindell and Houle.

Finally, as noted earlier, Patricia Cornwell concludes *From Potter's Field* by killing off rather than remanding to custody the serial killer who is the object of the intensive manhunt that gives the narrative its structure. If Agatha Christie's *Murder in the Calais Coach* may be said to answer a question about the circumstances in which murderers may be permitted to go free, Cornwell may be said to offer a set of terms calculated to justify ending the book as she does. Temple Gault is a horrific example of the "unprincipled man of genius," a conscienceless killer capable of murdering his twin sister on Christmas Eve and leaving her naked body propped in the snow in Central Park. Scarpetta's job has made her familiar with the gamut of motives leading to homicide, but Gault is an inexplicable, hence terrifying enigma: "It is not difficult to comprehend people being so enraged, drugged, frightened or crazy that they kill. Even psychopaths have their own twisted logic.

But Temple Brooks Gault seemed beyond description or deciphering" (Cornwell 1995, 76). Nevertheless, Scarpetta mortally wounds him only after it becomes clear that he will stop at nothing to try to kill her if she does not act quickly and decisively to defend herself; she has no choice but to use deadly force.

Mysteries that conclude with dispositions other than remanding the accused into the custody of the authorities can be arrayed along a continuum. At one pole are works like Christie's *Murder in the Calais Coach* in which the investigator permits the murderer (or in this case murderers) to go free. Such a disposition, however, requires of the writer an argument along the lines offered implicitly by Christie— namely, that the victim deserved to die. The writer's technical problem is to come up with the appropriate terms with which to make this persuasive, and I have suggested that Christie invokes, by implication, the kidnapping of the Lindberghs' infant son and the universal revulsion occasioned by that crime to define Ratchett's villainy. To this she adds the miscarriage of justice that precluded a second trial on the same charges and thereby permitted Ratchett to continue his depredations. In the wake of the court's failure to insure justice in this instance, and given the nature of Ratchett's crimes, individuals are free, perhaps even obligated, to make up the deficiency. So runs Christie's argument, the terms of which constitute her bet as to what her readers will find morally acceptable—or at least will not reject as morally repugnant.

At the opposite pole are works as various as Cornwell's *From Potter's Field*, most of John D. Macdonald's Travis McGee novels, Marcia Muller's *Wolf in the Shadows*, and Jeremiah Healy's *Act of God*, which end with the death of the murderer, typically at the hands of the investigator. This too requires the writer to come up with terms sufficient to justify that outcome. Defining the situation as kill or be killed, as Cornwell does in the final confrontation between Temple Gault and Kay Scarpetta, is virtually self-justifying. In *Wolf in the Shadows*, however, Sharon McCone shoots someone—a villainous someone, to be sure—in the back without warning him. The threat posed in the situation is clear enough: an armed, known killer blocks the escape route open to McCone and her party across the Mexican border. Nevertheless, shooting even the murderous Marty Salazar in the back requires explicit justification, and Muller describes McCone as worrying briefly about the dilemma she faces. After the fact, McCone is too "honest" to spare herself acknowledging the true character of her act—

"murder"—although officially her shooting of Salazar is classified as self-defense. "Sure, Lieutenant Gary Viner had congratulated me on ridding the county of one of its more noxious vermin. But I'd shot a man in cold blood. Taken his life to get my people through" (Muller 1994, 360). McCone's muted *mea culpa* hardly seems calculated, however, to set the reader worrying about the justification for her act—under the circumstances.

The arguments underlying the continuum of dispositions outlined in the foregoing examples—and whatever persuasiveness, plausibility, or acceptability those dispositions may possess for readers—depend on and presuppose a variable but still considerable overlap between the fictional world created by a given author and the real world, such that the elements of the former may be said to be constrained by the nature of the latter. I now turn to the question of the constraints on "doing" mystery fiction, using as examples three sorts of constraints: facts; explicit advisements such as publishers' guidelines or the "rules of the game" promulgated by mystery writers like Ronald Knox, S. S. van Dine, and Raymond Chandler; and cultural rules.

"Fictions would be wholly incomprehensible," Jeffrey Sammons reminds us, "if they did not refer constantly to the phenomena of external experience" (1977, 55). The issue of intelligibility aside, abundant evidence exists to suggest that factual accuracy is implicated in reading pleasure. Readers expect writers to get the details right and are annoyed, or worse, when they catch an author in a factual error. Raymond Chandler condemned A. A. Milne for errors in forensic procedure in *The Red House Mystery* as part of his general attack on the English ratiocinative detective story—an attack premised on the supposition, announced in his opening sentence, that "Fiction in any form has always intended to be realistic" (1995, 977). Ian Fleming reportedly used a London research service to help him insure factual accuracy in the James Bond novels and, former journalist that he was, carried a note pad with him in which to record information that might later prove useful; but when he made the mistake of equipping the Orient express with hydraulic (rather than mechanical) brakes, readers wrote to him pointing out his error (Alpert 1962).

Facts matter in yet another way. The claim that mystery fiction can be genuinely informative—can provide "a satisfying way to learn about other ways of life," for example, as noted earlier in connection with the recent proliferation of ethnic or regionally-based investigators—is unintelligible if references and allusions in fictional works can't reliably hook onto the real world. Unless statements contained in mystery fiction can be assessed as factually accurate, it makes no sense to say that one can learn about horse racing from Dick Francis, the British antique trade from Jonathan Gash, forensic anthropology or the art world from Aaron Elkins, the Navajo Blessing Way from Tony Hillerman, or arcana of British history from Anthony Price, for example. It is impossible to read mystery fiction without encountering instances like the following from Ross Thomas's *The Briar Patch*, when the protagonist is asked about the name of a recently completed regional airport somewhere in the Midwest: " 'Who was [William] Gatty, anyway?' 'He flew around the world with Wiley Post in thirty-one,' Dill said" (Thomas 1985, 313). Or consider this partial list of allusions from Sara Paretsky's *Bitter Medicine*: Ipana, Gervase Fen and Peter Wimsey, Grant Park (summer 1968), *Abbey Road*, "She-Who-Must-Be-Obeyed," Stewart Alsop, Leo Buscaglia, Harry Caray, and "When duty whispers low, *Thou must*, the youth replies *I can*" (1988, 252–53). Intelligibility suffers if the reader fails to connect "Grant Park" with the Democratic convention of 1968 or fails to recognize the excerpt from Emerson's poem "Duty."

Readers who know that Gatty and Post set out to circumnavigate the globe in 1931 expect Ross Thomas to have gotten that fact right; readers who don't know about the flight can learn that it occurred—but only if Thomas has, in fact, correctly attributed the flight to 1931. The paradigmatic example of Gatty and Post's flight can only be pushed so far, but it instances one type of constraint on writers, and it raises in another way the issue of trust between writer and reader. Readers expect—and trust—that writers will be accurate in referring to specific features of the real world, whether those features be the intersection of two streets in Chicago or the characteristic deformation of a hollow point round taken from the body of an assassinated agent: "[Tell them] it's probably a Remington Soft Point Core-Lokt" (Deighton 1995, 332).

Facts matter. Mystery writers increasingly acknowledge the technical assistance of various experts, as Marcia Muller does in *Wolf in the Shadows* or Sara Paretsky does in *Tunnel Vision*: "As always, my work benefitted from the advice of experts," such as one who told her "how to circumvent a phone-linked alarm system" (Paretsky 1995, ix). Helen MacInnes took pride in her attention to realistic detail—airline schedules, geography, clothing—and attended the New York trial of Soviet agent Rudolph Abel, as noted earlier, "to study the eyes, expressions. I want hard facts, want to know about what I am writing about" (White 1974). Writers attend seminars on such topics as forensic science offered by experts like Larry Rayle, who testified for the defense in the O. J. Simpson trial in 1995. Newsletters like *Deadly Serious* cater to writers' factual needs. Two New Jersey detectives collaborate on *Modus Operandi: A Writer's Guide to How Criminals Work*, part of an eight-volume series published by Writers Digest Books (lift a fingerprint from a door knob? Nonsense: "You *never* get a print on a doorknob. Doorknobs and phones are the greasiest surfaces in the world"—Span 1995).

The fact of Gatty and Post's flight in 1931 is a clear but limited example of a real-world feature that constrains writers on the one hand, and structures the expectations of readers on the other. But the clarity of the example comes at the price of oversimplification and limited applicability to the range of references to "the phenomena of external experience" one typically encounters in mystery fiction. The factuality or accuracy of the following statement made by a police officer in Jeremiah Healy's *Act of God* is, arguably, less clear-cut but probably more representative of the form of information in mystery fiction: "FBI says something like thirty percent of all homicides nationwide never get solved. Of the ones we do close, most them are made on eye witnesses, which we don't have [in this case]" (1994, 41). Or consider this thought of Sharon McCone's from Marcia Muller's *Wolf in the Shadows*: "The international security consulting business is an outgrowth of the rise of terrorism against employees and executives of U.S. companies both at home and abroad" (1994, 51).

The accuracy—the truth, if you will—of these statements aside, the issue of the way writers are constrained by features of the real world is complicated by the degree to which writers may, at their option, accept or decline certain specific constraints. In John Le Carré's first novel, *Call for the Dead* (1962), George Smiley suffers a blow to the head that leads to a month's stay in hospital. Writers of the more action-oriented forms of mystery fiction, especially for the pulpier venues of the hard-boiled tradition, are rarely so scrupulous about acknowledging the realities and consequences of serious head injuries. Chandler simultaneously mocks and utilizes the convention of ignoring (or minimizing) the constraints of physical injury in an oft-quoted passage in

Farewell, My Lovely as Marlowe prepares to escape from the sanitarium where he has been confined: "Okey, Marlowe . . . You're a tough guy. Six feet of iron man. One hundred and ninety pounds stripped and with your face washed. Hard muscles and no glass jaw. You can take it. You've been sapped down twice, had your throat choked and been beaten half silly on the jaw with a gun barrel. You've been shot full of hop and kept under it until you're as crazy as two waltzing mice. And what does that amount to? Routine. Now let's see you do something really tough, like putting your pants on" (1964, 133). John D. MacDonald's work, including the Travis McGee series, is notable for its verisimilitude in small details and large, but consider this incident in *A Deadly Shade of Gold* when McGee is shot once in the back while leaving a house carrying two sacks of gold Inca statuettes, each sack weighing "close to a hundred pounds": "I was fire-hot-wet in back, and fire-hot-wet in front, without pain but suddenly weakened. I wavered and stumbled and got the gold into the car with a vast effort" (1965, 262). In this and numerous similar instances, it would seem that generic conventions, and the expectations created by them, loosen the connection, the constraint, between what can be acceptably depicted as cause and effect in mystery fiction and the likely consequences of the "same" causal sequence occurring in the world of "external experience."

If some constraints are to some degree optional (and perhaps more optional in some periods and by some writers than in others), there are also instances of writers accepting as fact, and thereby as a constraint, something that would not now be considered factual at all. An inference Holmes makes in "The Adventure of the Blue Carbuncle" illustrates the point. Examining a hat, Holmes tells Watson that "there are a few inferences which are very distinct, and a few others which represent at least a strong balance of probability. . . . That the man was highly intellectual is of course obvious upon the face of it." Why? " 'It is a question of cubic capacity,' said [Holmes]; 'a man with so large a brain must have something in it' " (1927, 246–47). Whatever Doyle's belief about the degree to which there existed a well-confirmed positive correlation between cranial volume and intelligence in human beings, that correlation is not a matter of fact today in the sense of enjoying either theoretical or empirical support among the relevant experts. Holmes's inference, which would indeed have seemed "obvious upon the face of it" to many of his contemporary readers, has no factual status today, and no contemporary writer would seriously consider hat size as offering a clue to its owner's intelligence.

Finally, it is worth observing briefly that the phenomena of external experience are sometimes insufficiently constraining for the writer's purpose; there are things that happen in real life that writers cannot use in fiction because they seem too improbable or unrealistic. Charles McCarry makes the point in discussing a dramatic revelation in Donald T. Regan's memoir *For the Record*, on which McCarry collaborated—namely, that First Lady Nancy Reagan "had consulted an astrologer on the details of her husband's schedule." As a former CIA officer, McCarry was appalled at the flagrant breach of security; as Donald Regan's collaborator, he thought it would be a "nice surprise" for their publisher, good for business presumably; but "as a writer, what [he] thought was: 'I could never get away with anything as weird as this in a novel' " (1994, 7).

Several efforts to delineate the acceptable boundaries of mystery fiction—what writers could or could not "get away with"—shed additional light on assumptions about the relationship between the worlds of mystery fiction and everyday experience, and so on what I have characterized as the constraints of the one on the other. Raymond Chandler's "Casual Notes on the Mystery Novel," written in 1949, expressed the perspective of the leading practitioner of the hard-boiled private detective novel of the day, but had much in common with the earlier prescriptions for the classical mystery story offered by Father Ronald Knox, S. S. van Dine, Marie Rodell, and Howard Haycraft in the 1920s and 1930s. The mystery novel, Chandler advised, "must be credibly motivated" and "technically sound about methods of murder and detection. . . . It must be realistic as to character, setting and atmosphere" (Gardiner and Walker 1962, 63). Moreover, it "must punish the criminal in one way or another, not necessarily by operation of the law courts"; but Chandler insisted this requirement had nothing to do with "morality"—it was simply entailed by the "logic" of the form (1962, 66).

Chandler, like Father Knox and the others, was concerned especially to guarantee the reader "fair play": "The mystery novel must be reasonably honest with the reader. . . . It is not enough that the facts be stated. They must be fairly stated, and they must be the sort of facts that can be reasoned from. . . . The reader cannot be charged with special and rare knowledge nor with an abnormal memory for insignificant details. . . . If the reader has to know as much as [R. Austin Freeman's] Dr. Thorndyke to solve a mystery, obviously he cannot solve it. If the premise of [E. C. Bentley's] *Trent's Last Case* is plausible, then logic and realism have no meaning" (Gardiner and Walker 1962, 66–67). The principle of fair play, Chandler added, was a "professional and artistic" requirement; it had "no moral significance at all" (1962, 68). The constitutive premise, the "basic theory of all mystery writing," Chandler insisted, is "that at some stage of the proceedings the reader could, given the necessary acuteness, have closed the book and revealed the essence of the denouement" (1962, 66). The very concept of fair play, however, as Chandler's "Casual Notes" reveal at every turn, requires that the world of fiction and the real world overlap to a large degree and that the nature of the latter constrain all manner of content in the former.

A further type of constraint on writing mystery fiction exists in culturally constituted, taken-for-granted categorial relationships of the sort embodied in such familiar and ubiquitous binary oppositions as reason/emotion. With that point in hand, I will revisit the discussion of doing things with mystery fiction, begun earlier in this chapter, and suggest that mystery fiction can be said to be engaged in the larger, ongoing process of reproducing cultural categories and making and sustaining meaning, before going on to assess the claim—made, for example, by the late Ernest Mandel—that mystery fiction may be said to possess an ideology. I conclude the chapter by touching on the notion of "cultural work" and asking in what sense, if any, mystery fiction may be said to perform it.

Mystery fiction participates in the reproduction of cultural meanings by means of repetition—instance after instance of a concept, such as reason or rationality—and consistency, both in the meaning of the concept and in its relationship, whether binary or continuous, with other concepts. An invidious distinction between professional and amateur, for example, has become increasingly common in mystery fiction generally, and especially in the spy fiction of writers such as Le Carré, Deighton, Allbeury, Price, Freemantle, Donald Hamilton, and others. In *Faith*, the first work in Deighton's second trilogy devoted to him, British intelligence agent Bernard Sampson characterizes an operation that ended disastrously with the death of his sister-in-law in East Germany as "a typical London Central balls-up" and lays the blame to "a fumbling amateur" brought in from London (1995, 91). Amateurs can get you killed, one of Desmond Bagley's protagonists suggests: "I'm a professional and I don't like working with amateurs—they're unpredictable, careless and too dangerous for my taste" (1973, 5). We saw earlier that the calculation of risk at the conclusion of Anthony Price's *Our Man in Camelot* turned on the same distinction, with the lower risk assigned to a professional sniper, who could be counted on to act in a predictable fashion consistent with widely-known standards and training. Adherence to professional standards, here and elsewhere, works a measure of predictability into circumstances of uncertainty and offers a limited basis for rational planning, at least within acceptable tolerances of risk, by assigning a probability to an anticipated action; thus it offers some basis for trust. The professional is trustworthy, in part owing to known standards of training and performance and the professional's pride in meeting those standards.

In the foregoing examples, professionalism "means" or connotes a level of specialized training assessable by well-understood standards of performance. As the master of certain skills, the professional can be expected to perform accordingly: Price's fictional sniper, if he is a professional, will aim for the body, which offers a larger target than the head. Additionally, professionalism, in the context of mystery fiction, also refers to certain trained capacities. Composure, the ability to think effectively and act decisively under the twin pressures of high risk and limited time—in a word, "unflappability"—are essential elements of the demeanor associated with professionals per se (fictional intelligence agents such as George Smiley, for example) or with individuals who exhibit the professional's ability to remain cool under stress, including Sherlock Holmes, John Buchan's Richard Hannay, Helen MacInnes's John Craig, and the Eagle Scout, Barry Benton, discussed in an earlier chapter. Smiley's composure, maintained throughout the interview of Grigoriev that alone will determine the possibility of bringing about Karla's defection to the West, exemplifies the professional's demeanor of cool composure under stress. The ultimate test of unflappability, perfectly exemplified in Holmes's lonely vigil in the dark at the conclusion of "The Adventure of the Speckled Band" or Sam Spade's confrontation with Gutman and his armed cronies, occurs in life-threatening situations, where the temptation or instinct to panic threatens the investigator's rational control and hence his or her capacity for effective action.

Under the pressures of mortal risk and limited time in which to complete an assignment, emotion—"stomach think," as Adam Hall's series hero Quiller puts it—threatens to undermine composure and destroy rational self-control and the ability to think clearly and act effectively on the basis of reasoned thought. Reason/emotion and professional/ amateur are binary opposites that in mystery fiction almost invariably co-occur in mutual and reciprocal implication, definition, and reinforcement. The professional exemplifies instrumental rationality and unflappability. Reason is "cool" reason (when it is not "cold") and icy unflappability. By contrast, emotion or blood are hot; to be hot-headed is the opposite of remaining coolly rational. The ordered cultural pairs, professional/amateur and reason/emotion, thus also involve cool/warm and, by extension, head/heart.

Mystery writers have beliefs—about the genre's constitutive conventions, about what-goes-with-what, about what readers want and will accept, for example. I have argued that mystery fiction participates in the general process of cultural reproduction. Can mystery fiction be said to have an "ideology"? Some commentators have asserted that it does (and that it is much the worse for that fact!). The late Ernest Mandel, a Belgian Marxist economist, devotes a chapter in his "social history" of the crime story, *Delightful Murder* (1984), to "the ideology of the detective story." Mandel summarizes that ideology as follows: "Reified death; formalized crime-detection oriented toward proof acceptable in courts of justice operating according to strictly defined rules; the pursuit of the criminal by the hero depicted as a battle between brains; human beings reduced to 'pure' analytical intelligence; partial fragmented rationality elevated to the status of an absolute guiding principle of human behaviour; individual conflicts used as a generalized substitute for conflicts between social groups and layers— all this is bourgeois ideology *par excellence*, a striking synthesis of human alienation in bourgeois society" (1984, 47). Mystery fiction, Mandel goes on to assert, "plays a powerful integrative role among all but extremely critical and sophisticated readers," suggesting on the one hand the legitimacy of bourgeois society "regardless of [its] shortcomings and injustices," while "completely" obscuring on the other hand "the class nature of the state, property, law and justice" (1984, 47).

In a similar vein, Theresa Ebert asserts "that detective narratives are one of the main arenas for the ideological reproduction and legitimation of patriarchal social relations and subjectivities. Ideology . . . compels individuals to occupy the gendered subject positions signaled by their anatomy by harnessing their desire and yoking it to specular, imaginary identifications which it reduplicates on the level of the symbolic (to recall Lacan's orders)" (1992, 9). The detective "is a key ideological apparatus for the representation and reproduction of male gender" (1992, 10). Furthermore, detection, as depicted in mystery fiction, is best understood as "a process of 'discovery' that deflects attention away from the operation of exploitative social relations and accounts for abuses and oppressive practices solely in terms of deviant individuals. Detecting, then, 'uncovers' the 'truth' of a social disorder—finds the 'criminal'—and in the process *obscures* the *actuality* of exploitative social practices" that characterize and constitute bourgeois society (1992, 24).

Ideology, taken as a concept, has a complicated history.[2] As coined by the French philosopher Destutt de Tracy in the late eighteenth century, ideology was a philosophical term that referred to the "science of ideas." That meaning was lost to a large extent as subsequent usage reshaped the word's sense, reference, and appraisive force. Ideology can be a term of neutral description, referring to "a system of beliefs characteristic of a particular class or group" (Williams 1987, 55), but its appraisive force is generally pejorative, as is clearly the case in the passages quoted earlier from Mandel and Ebert. For both critics, ideology is not only a system of beliefs characteristic of the ruling class (bourgeois *and* patriarchal), but a system of illusory or false beliefs—a second important sense in which ideology has long been used and understood. Both Mandel and Ebert charge detective fiction with obscuring the real nature of social relationships under the conditions of (patriarchal) late capitalism. Finally, ideology can refer to a process of meaning making, as Ebert, for example, uses it in pointing to (and castigating) detective fiction as "one of the main arenas for the ideological reproduction and legitimation of patriarchal social relations and subjectivities" (1992, 9).

Leaving aside its common use as a stick with which to beat upon the bourgeoisie and all their works, the concept of ideology picks out a relationship between social circumstances on the one hand, and beliefs on the other. This relationship, which defines the core sense and reference of the concept, has been understood and debated in complex and subtle ways for more than a century. The intricacies of the history of that debate, which has taken place both inside and outside of Marxist discourse, need not detain us. Throughout this study, I have argued for analyzing mystery fiction as a kind of <u>action</u>, as a species of <u>doing-in-saying</u>, undertaken by culturally situated actors possessed of beliefs and cultural resources, including especially the resources of language and generic convention, which enable and constrain their narratives, the materialized, consultable "record" of their expressive activity. If that is the case, why not say, or admit, that this study is an analysis of ideology?

In the hands of Mandel and Ebert (notwithstanding the question of their representativeness), ideology is consistently used in its pejorative sense. It both describes a system of belief and evaluates that system negatively from the point of view of the authors' respective political commitments: Mandel's a doctrinaire version of Marxism, and Ebert's a feminism strained through a neo-Marxist and postmodernist vocabulary. More seriously, both Mandel and Ebert use ideology in a totalizing, reductive, and dismissive sense that flattens or obscures differences among writers and everywhere begs the question of a given writer's relationship to "society," a key term that remains unanalyzed by either writer. Finally, both critics assign to ideology, taken now as a process, a causal potency that ignores any mediating processes that might variably intervene between texts, considered to be historical agents in their own right, and variously situated readers—or, as the jargon would have it, "positioned subjectivities." In this way, their work begs the question of what readers make of their reading. Moreover, both questions—the one having to do with the writer's relationship to society and the other having to do with the reader's relationship to the text—are foreclosed by the "theory," of which the concept of ideology is one element. Ebert's assertion that "the detective does the *work* of patriarchy" has no evident empirical basis and in no way derives from the "sustained ideology critique" she promises; the assertion simply announces one strand of the theory with which she begins and ends. Similarly, Mandel's claim for the "powerful integrative role" of crime fiction derives exclusively from his theoretical commitments, his political "faith," rather than from his analysis, which focuses almost exclusively on works of mystery fiction. Works of fiction are evidence of authorial (and editorial) activity; they are not evidence of what readers make of their reading. As a consequence, fiction provides no secure basis for inferring how readers construct meaning in the act of reading. Evidence of the reading process must be sought elsewhere.

The notion that literature (and, by extension, the arts more generally) performs "cultural work" has much in common with the process-ual view of ideology that permits both Mandel and Ebert to attribute causal significance to detective fiction. The concept of cultural work figures prominently in Jane Tompkins's influential rereading of antebel-lum American literature, *Sensational Designs* (1985). Her subtitle, "The Cultural Work of American Fiction 1790–1860," announces the centrality of the concept to her study and also provides the title for her introduction. In quick succession, Tompkins moves from characteriz-ing literary texts as "attempts to redefine the social order" to claiming that such works reveal "the way a culture thinks about itself" to justi-fying the inclusion of some texts for analysis because they were works of "obvious impact on their readers" (1985, xi).

The notion of cultural work is well suited to express the conflation of intention and effect: the word *work* is ambiguous between effort and achievement. To engage in work, in the sense of some productive endeavor, is one thing; for that productive endeavor to result in the desired achievement is something else. Nowhere is this more obviously the case than in the work of writing. My intention to write so as to "redefine the social order" (assuming I realize that intention *in* my writing as opposed to merely announcing it as my plan or purpose) may or may not have the effect of reorienting the social order. Texts do not predictably compel particular responses, and the "power" attrib-uted to texts in Tompkins's formulation simply redescribes a given text's "popularity," its sales relative to other books. The sharp separa-tion between intention and effect is especially clear in the metaphor of the "blueprint," which Tompkins invokes to distinguish her critical approach from modernist critical orthodoxy: "a text offers a blueprint for survival under a specific set of political, economic, social or reli-gious conditions" (1985, xvii). No one would think to attribute power to a blueprint *qua* blueprint or to claim that one compels a particular response or effect. To create a blueprint is one thing; to follow a blue-print with the intention of realizing its provisions in some material form is something else. Following a blueprint closely will, all else being equal, materialize the planner's intention. Works of fiction cannot be analogized to blueprints in any meaningful sense.

Conflating intention and effect in the notion of cultural work has an evident payoff, hence a clear appeal, to the student of texts. It permits the text to be taken as evidence of both the writer's activity (the work of writing and the "work" as finished product) and the reader's response. This move is less easily made if the equation text = blueprint is substituted for the notion of text as cultural work, as my readers can judge by making the appropriate substitution in the following, final characterization Tompkins offers for her approach: "It is the notion of literary texts [read blueprints] as *doing work, expressing and shaping* the social context that produced them, that I wish to substitute for the [modernist] critical perspective . . ." (1985, 200; emphasis added). This passage also implies an acceptance of the supposition that literary texts can be treated as historical agents in their own right—"doing work, expressing and shaping"; that is, that literary texts act in the world, in addition to, or instead of, the writers who "express" and the readers, suitably motivated, who undertake to "shape."

If "ideology" is understood and used in the limited (and limiting) sense employed by Mandel or Ebert, then detective fiction does not have an ideology. And if "cultural work," collapsing the distinction between writers writing, on the one hand, and the consequences of readers reading, on the other, permits texts to be taken as evidence of both activities, rather than evidence of the former only, then ideology does not perform cultural work.

None of this, however, is meant to deny the residue of truth and value in "ideology" or "cultural work." Belief is always situated, always "interested." Writing, like any productive activity, is simultaneously and reciprocally enabled and constrained by a range of contextual elements, some of which are texts themselves: writers are readers before they are writers. Reading may affect belief and action and therefore enter into the explanation of both. Commentators like Mandel, relying on "ideology" to connote false belief, insinuate that some beliefs—the ideology of the bourgeoisie—are suspect simply by virtue of being the beliefs of a particular social class. That move, however politically or rhetorically inviting it may be when preaching to the converted, amounts to an *ad hominem* argument. True beliefs, one wants to insist, can be held independent of one's socioeconomic status. More to the point, however, our task is first to understand a writer's beliefs, not to pronounce on their truth or falsity, and to pay close attention to what a given writer is *doing* with the available resources.

In addition to confusing truth with class affiliation, both Mandel and Ebert confuse capitalism and modernity, ascribing to the former what are more properly understood as features of the latter. The investigative process, as dramatized in mystery fiction, demands of the investigator certain skills and qualities that are not, finally, bourgeois or middle-class traits; rather, they are the skills and qualities demanded under the conditions of modernity. Whether the means of production are organized under capitalism or communism, the core requirements of technological production and bureaucratic organization remain the same. Regardless of the form of ownership of the airliner in which I travel, I expect the pilot to possess the skills to fly it, and the trained capacity to remain composed in the event of a sudden emergency. Put differently, I care far less about the pilot's location in the class structure than I do about his ability to make the right decision in a high risk situation with little time in which to consider the available options.

7

Some Readers Reading

Through fiction we broaden our knowledge of people and places. . . .
Ultimately, I believe we read to connect with another mind, satisfying
one of life's most powerful needs. Reading may well be the second-best
intimacy.

Posted to DorothyL, 28/29 April 1996

The main question raised by the thriller is not what kind of world we live
in, or what reality is like, but what it has done to us.

Ralph Harper, *The World of the Thriller*

Until now, I have dealt almost exclusively with what might be called the context of production—that is, with questions about authorial activity and writing as a form of action, and about the relationship between mystery fiction and modernity. In this chapter, I turn to the context of reception and look at what some actual readers do with their reading of mystery fiction.[1]

The relatively widespread appeal of detective fiction, like the appeal of "popular culture" more generally, has raised two sorts of questions. One has to do with the appeal of the genre: why do people read it? how is its popularity to be explained? why has it remained popular for so long with only minor modification of its generic conventions? A second, equally broad question has to do with the effects of reading mystery fiction: does such reading influence behavior? or, more tendentiously, to what extent is the reading of mystery fiction a socially conservative activity, helping to sustain existing (by definition, inequitable) divisions of power, for example? The two questions are not unrelated, since an explanation of the appeal of mystery fiction implies some consequence of reading. A psychoanalytic explanation such as the one formulated by Geraldine Pederson-Krag, for example, locates the appeal of mystery fiction in the child's intense curiosity about the "primal scene" (i.e., parental sexual behavior). Reading detective stories allows the reader to "gratify his infantile curiosity with impunity, redressing completely the helpless inadequacy and anxious guilt remembered from childhood" (1983, 20).

Efforts to explain the appeal of mystery fiction fall into two categories: explanations that are ultimately psychological in nature and those that emphasize social factors of varying sorts and in varying combination. Richard Raskin divides psychological explanations into three categories: "*ludic*, involving one or another form of play for the reader; *wish-fulfillment*, when compensatory or vicarious gratifications are central; and *tension-reducing*, referring to the detective story's capacity to dispel feelings of guilt or anxiety" (1992, 70). Ludic theories frequently invoke an analogy between reading detective fiction and solving puzzles. Such theories locate the appeal of the fiction in the battle of wits, conducted within rules of fair play, between author and reader. Solving the puzzle before the author resolves the mystery in the denouement is held to be pleasurable in itself. Other commentators locate the pleasure of mystery reading in the enhanced self-esteem said to attend successful puzzle solving, or in the temporary escape it provides from the problems of the real world. Others find a darker pleasure associated with puzzle solving, "an unconscious masochistic satisfaction" deriving variously from the state of "helpless confusion" in which the reader is held during reading or from the reader's unconscious identification with the victim (Raskin 1992, 73–75). Still other theories explain the popularity of detective fiction in terms of *vicarious* ludic pleasure, the enjoyment derived not from puzzle solving per se but from recognizing and appreciating "the writer's virtuosity in playing with and against the conventions of the genre," such as "finding a novel blend of idiosyncratic and admirable qualities in composing the character of the detective" (1992, 76).

The second category in Raskin's "functional typology" consists of theories that explain the genre's appeal in terms of its capacity to provide various sorts of wish-fulfillment, both conscious and unconscious, ranging from the vicarious experience of adventure to the vicarious fulfillment of the reader's ego ideal or inhibited aggressive or masochistic impulses, depending on whether the reader identifies with, respectively, the investigator, the murderer, or the victim (1992, 80–88).

Raskin's third category gathers together theories that locate the appeal of mystery fiction in its capacity to relieve the reader's feelings of guilt or anxiety. These feelings are rooted in readers' perceptions: the "diffuse feelings of anxiety produced by ominous social developments," for example, or the "feelings of guilt and anxiety resulting from the individual's resignation to facelessness and mediocrity," for another (1992, 90–95).

From categorizing explanations of the appeal of mystery fiction, Raskin moves to the question of effect—"the ways in which detective novels can influence the reader's perception of the social world as well as the reader's values and patterns of thought" (1992, 96)—and identifies five "orienting" functions attributable to reading detective fiction. Reading mystery novels can reinforce "social myth," a socially conservative function generally imputed to the classical or ratiocinative tradition; or it can subvert social myth, as alleged with regard to the American hard-boiled tradition. Second, the detective novel can arguably heighten the reader's "awareness of the process and possibilities of sign-interpretation" (1992, 103), providing information and techniques for connecting appearances with "reality." Detective fiction can impart "stray bits" of information and teach the reader about role-specific behavior "appropriate for persons occupying particular roles or statuses in crime-related situations." Finally, detective fiction can have an evaluative function, affirming or challenging the legitimacy "of the particular behaviors, attitudes and practices depicted" (1992, 107). It is clear, Raskin concludes, "that detective stories have a potential for influencing the attitudes of a vast reading and viewing public—not only with regard to specific police practices, but also concerning deeper problems of privilege and power" (1992, 108). How that potential is realized among actual readers, however, remains largely unknown.

In addition to Raskin's primarily psychological explanations of the appeal of mystery fiction, there are arguments that emphasize social factors. Howard Haycraft, writing in 1941, traced the emergence and ensuing popularity of the detective story to the development of democracy and to Anglo-American judicial procedure, especially the right of fair trial and the standard "that no man shall be convicted of a crime in the absence of reasonable proof, safe-guarded by known, just, and logical rules [of evidence]" (1941, 313). Arguing against this benign view, the historian William Aydelotte, in the aftermath of World War II, contended that detective fiction reflected not order and the rule of law, but disorder: "The detective story does not reflect order, but expresses on the fantasy level a yearning for order; it suggests, then, a disordered world, and its roots are to be sought in social disintegration rather than in social cohesion" (1976, 324). In the detective and the criminal, Aydelotte sees "the two principal political figures of totalitarianism," the dictator and the scapegoat. Reading mystery fiction permits the gratification of fantasies of dependence and aggression deeply inimical to the democratic ethos (1976, 322). Seen in this light, detective fiction reveals "disturbing evidence of psychological tensions, and of the prevalence in our modern western culture of elements of character-structure which do not provide adequate support for democratic institutions" (1976, 324).

The contrasting views of Haycraft and Aydelotte define the two poles that organize much subsequent commentary about the function of reading mystery fiction. But what is at issue between the two is less the relationship presumed to exist between popular literature and society—both men regard underlying social factors as conditioning and determinative—than with their divergent attitudes toward the trends and tendencies of modern society, to which both attribute primacy in their otherwise similar, and equally implicit, models of the relationship between the fiction and its social context. Moreover—and to bring the discussion back to the point at which it began, namely readers and explaining the popularity of mystery fiction—none of the foregoing efforts to account for the emergence and popularity of the genre or to describe the functions of reading it rest on empirical evidence about readers. "When these studies speak of audiences," Heta Pyrhonen summarizes, in her valuable *tour d'horizon* of mystery fiction commentary, "they mainly allude to hypothetical constructs formed on the basis of analyzing the textual, implied roles of the reader and only occasionally on whatever evidence the scholar has gathered about actual reading audiences" (1994, 85). If anything, this assessment is too generous. The studies to which Pyrhonen refers contain virtually no data on actual readers or reading, and certainly none that is systematic. Existing commentary on the functions of mystery fiction reading rests exclusively on the fiction itself, but as I have argued throughout this study, works of fiction are evidence of the processes of creation and production; they are not evidence of the processes of consumption and use. That evidence can only come from readers themselves, and from "texts of reception" that embody their responses. It is to the nature of the audiences for detective fiction, and then to selected texts of reception, that I now turn to suggest the uses to which real readers put their reading of mystery novels.

Obviously, there is no such thing as "the" audience for detective fiction. From the perspective of a given body of work—say, the stories of Conan Doyle—there is a finite but empirically undeterminable number of readers, distinguishable, in principle, by familiar categories of analysis—age, gender, education, prior reading of mystery fiction, for example, and temporal and geographical situation. We are, however, unlikely ever to know the precise size of that historical audience, or very much about its composition. (These variables may not be decisive. If the argument of this book is correct, what we want are measures related to the experience of modernity.) Nor are we likely ever to know many of the identities, let alone anything about the responses, of the overwhelming majority of those readers, who are scattered temporally over more than a century and geographically over the English-speaking world and the countries into whose languages Doyle's corpus has been translated. The texts of reception that do exist may be few and unrepresentative, but they are better than nothing.

One of these readers of Conan Doyle is Edward J. Perkins, who served as United States ambassador to the Union of South Africa in the late 1980s. When he first joined the Foreign Service as a staff assistant, Perkins systematically reread the Holmes stories, studying the character of Holmes for his use of logic and cunning in defeating his adversaries. " 'Arthur Conan Doyle's writings have helped me to hone my analytical skills and appreciation for detail,' " he told *Washington Post* reporter Juan Williams (1987, 37). Much the same claim is made by a reader posting to the Internet discussion list DorothyL, who denied taking fictional detectives as potential role models, with the single exception of Sherlock Holmes: [His] "powers of observation and deductive reasoning are worth serious consideration by the average person" (21/22 February 1996).

As a process, reading does not typically create a durable, hence consultable, record with which to reconstruct a history of response. Reading is typically a solitary activity in the sense that one reads silently, "to oneself." When the process creates a durable record of some sort, it may take a form that poses daunting problems of interpretation, as in the case of the marginalia and dedications examined by Cathy Davidson in her study of the early American novel (1986, 77–79). In his study of nineteenth-century dime novels and American working-class culture, Michael Denning can muster only a single autobiography with which to explore directly the role of "working girl novels" in "working women's reading and imaginations" (1987b, 197). Dorothy Richardson's *The Long Day: The Story of a New York Working Girl* (1905) is not, Denning acknowledges, "the most unequivocal source: little is known of Dorothy Richardson, of when the experiences related took place, or when the account was actually written. It seems clear that she was of middle class background and did not share the culture of her fellow workers in the box factory" (1987b, 197). Even when the evidence of reading use and response poses fewer interpretive difficulties, as it does in the late-nineteenth-century correspondence between female members of the cultivated upper-middle-class Indiana household analyzed by Barbara Sicherman, the question of the appropriateness of making generalizations to a larger population is as insistent as it is difficult to answer (Sicherman 1989, 201–25). For what subset of the population are the Hamilton sisters of Fort Wayne, Indiana, representative?

It is possible, however, to project what is almost certainly an overly fragmented view of the audiences for detective fiction. To be sure, we need to acknowledge the complexly varying "situatedness" of individual readers by recognizing the host of variables involved—not simply the familiar demographic variables already noted, but such factors as differential access to books, differences in self-acknowledged reasons for reading, in interpretive skills, in relative familiarity with the conventions of the genre, in levels of engagement with the form. For some, reading mystery fiction may be no more than an occasional recreation, an airport diversion slightly (but not predictably) preferable to some other form of reading. For others, a whole social life comes to center on reading and discussing mystery fiction, attending conferences, seeking out favorite authors at book signings, and keeping up with electronic discussion groups such as DorothyL. Nevertheless, there is much that suggests enduring commonalities associated with reading mystery fiction. The defining conventions of the genre have remained stable for more than a century. Readers, as a consequence, come to possess stable, determinate, highly predictable expectations about the experience of reading mystery fiction. Moreover, and not unexpectedly, the experience of reading mystery fiction appears to be tightly constrained (but more on this later).

Polling data consistently suggests that the audience for mystery fiction constitutes a large segment of the adult population and that education, more than any other factor, is a key distinguishing feature of its readership. A survey conducted in 1941 by Columbia University Press among the subscribers to its *Pleasures of Publishing* found that those who replied read an average of 4.5 mysteries per month, with women typically reading more (5.5 per month) than men (3.5 per month). Among this sample, 78 percent reported reading mysteries ("Columbia Surveys" 1941). A national poll, conducted by the Gallup organization in 1950, found that 25 percent of Americans read mystery fiction "more or less" regularly, but among college graduates, the reading rate was just over half (53 percent). Overall, readers were about equally divided between men and women ("Gallup" 1950). A 1986 poll, asking a different question, found an even larger audience: more than 60 percent of the adults interviewed had read a mystery book, with those most likely to have done so being the college educated (74 percent), employed women (69 percent), readers under the age of 50 (67 percent), and people residing on the East or West coasts (65 and 67 percent respectively) rather than the Midwest or South (Wood 1986).

These data, based as they are on the responses of actual readers, represent an advance, however slight, over the wholly fictional reader conjured up by analyzing works of mystery fiction on the basis of a particular theory, whether psychological, as in the case of a Freudian critic like Pederson-Krag, or sociopolitical, as in the case of William Aydelotte, who saw in the totalitarian political movements of the twentieth century convincing evidence of the heavy, perhaps insupportable, burdens placed on the individual by modern society. Construing the reader's experience of detective fiction as one of dependence on the detective and the detective's extralegal methods, Aydelotte saw yet another unwelcome symptom of the dynamic that had underwritten the century's totalitarian regimes in Europe and that threatened democratic institutions in the United States.

A rather different picture emerges, however, from an examination of three other sorts of texts of reception: postings to the electronic discussion list DorothyL; book reviews by Anthony Boucher, the nation's preeminent reviewer of mystery fiction in the 1950s and 1960s; and the account of an academic philosopher turned private investigator, who found much to emulate in the "worldliness" of Dashiell Hammett's Sam Spade. Linking these different forms of reader response is the expectation, amounting to a requirement, that detective fiction, if it is to be pleasurable (let alone "good"), must be "realistic." That is, it must accord or fit with how the world is (allowing always for variations in individual belief about how the world is).[2] The rest of this chapter is devoted to making good on that claim and exploring its implications for the experience of reading detective fiction. In brief, I argue that reading pleasure is bound up in recognizing and responding to the "realistic," especially in character, setting, and detail. "Realistic" also plays a central criterial role in the reviewing of detective fiction in the case of Anthony Boucher. For nearly two decades before his death in 1968, Boucher's columns, appearing in the *New York Times Book Review*, were the most prominent reviews of mystery fiction in the country. Finally, in the unusual case of Josiah Thompson's *Gumshoe* (1988), what is deemed realistic in a work of fiction serves as a trustworthy basis for action in the real world.

"Realistic," it should be noted, is the readers' term of choice and belongs to a family of closely related terms, including accurate, authentic, credible, believable, and plausible. All are terms belonging to our appraisive vocabulary, words that both describe and evaluate (Tully 1988, 119–32). "Realistic" describes a degree of perceived fit between the represented world of the fiction and the experiential world of the reader. It acknowledges phenomenological agreement or coincidence between author and reader on at least some features of a shared world. Accuracy and authenticity are, to a degree, amenable to intersubjective validation. At issue are the facts of the matter. Credibility and plausibility, on the other hand, are judgments deriving from individual, hence variable, experience, including experience with fiction and its conventions (McCarry 1994; Maugham 1928, 5–13).

In its evaluative dimension, "realistic" is uniquely favorable; there is no term of higher praise, and few that come close to matching it for evaluative power. To be realistic is to grasp accurately and represent faithfully what *is*. The application of the term constitutes both an assertion—[I find] this work accords with my sense of how things go— and an invitation to assent to that characterization. To assent to or to acknowledge the aptness of "realistic" in a given instance is for reader(s) and author to share the same world, or so much of the world as is bound up in that to which the term is applied in a given instance. Tom Clancy, whose techno-thrillers have brought him an immense and loyal readership, captures this point when he describes his greatest satisfaction as deriving from having experts acknowledge his accuracy: "I'm proudest when people I write about, in the military or police or intelligence communities, write or call to say, 'This is the way things really are' " (1989, 70). In addition to being a term that describes, evaluates, and invites assent, "realistic" must also be understood as perspectival: it characterizes and invites assent to *a* world, not *the* world. This is to say that in terms of its reference, the meaning of the term must vary somewhat with the variability of readers' experience, even though its evaluative force is univocal and unambiguous. Postings to DorothyL reveal how one knowledgeable group of readers of mystery fiction invokes a conception of realism as both descriptive and normative.

Begun in July 1991 by a group of librarians attending a meeting of the Association of Research Libraries, DorothyL is an electronic discussion list, accessible on the Internet, intended "for the lovers of the mystery genre." The list takes its name from Dorothy L. Sayers, the still highly regarded English mystery writer of the interwar period—for many, the Golden Age of the ratiocinative detective story. At this writing, more than 2,000 mystery readers, authors, and mystery bookstore proprietors subscribe to DorothyL. The large majority of these subscribers are women. A single day's digest can bring anywhere from 40 to 60 or more individual posts, ranging in length from a few lines to four or five hundred words. Postings regularly include announcements of conferences, forthcoming books, author appearances and book signings; book reviews, recommendations for reading, and chat about books and authors; and queries ranging from the location of that "great used book store" on the Welsh border (Hay-on-Wye) to the meaning of an item of English slang (e.g. "berk" or "twee") or an unfamiliar allusion encountered in a mystery novel. A recent query from a reader puzzled by Raymond Chandler's reference (in *The Lady in the Lake*) to a "PBX" resulted in over twenty replies posted to DorothyL, including several from former operators of those telephone switchboards. One of the things subscribers to the list have refused to do, however, is to get into the business of making awards. When the issue came up in 1996, most of those who spoke out on it rejected the idea of establishing awards in the name of the list, fearing that doing so would drastically alter the character of the discussion (e.g., 9/10 April 1996). Despite the resounding rejection of a scheme of formal awards, a central function of the list is critical: "I read DL to learn about good reads" (11/12 April 1996); "I am more likely to read a book that is recommended by someone who has previously recommended a book I like" (23/24 February 1996); "[DorothyL saves me] hours of agonizing over what to read next" (7/8 January 1996).[3] These postings raise several questions: (1) What are the critical criteria employed by the list's subscribers? (2) How do they read mystery fiction? and (3) What is the role of this reading in their lives? Taken together, the answers to these questions shed some light on the appeal mystery fiction has for that subset of its audience represented by those active, contributing subscribers who sustain the discussion on DorothyL.

In their recommendations, subscribers to DorothyL refer almost exclusively to one or another of seven aspects of mystery fiction: character, setting, "writing," plot, puzzle (or mystery), humor, and social commentary (or "issues"). Recommendations invariably offer some evaluation of character, and the vast majority refer to just three other constituent elements: setting, the overall quality of the writing, and the plot. Although the majority of subscribers appear to prefer the subgenre of the "cozy," and although this modernized version of the ratiocinative form is constituted by a puzzle, recommendations do not typically characterize that feature of the fiction. Humor and social commentary receive only occasional attention. The presence of humor is almost invariably a positive factor in evaluating a work, but the matter of social commentary is more complex. If the commentary is judged "intrusive," or if the author's treatment of an issue is substantially at odds with the values of the reader, social commentary will be seen to interfere with reading pleasure and will be marked accordingly: "I like a little social commentary with my mysteries. . . . I do not like it when the issue/s overtake the mystery. I don't want a speech in the middle of the action about the hot topic of the day" (18/19 April 1996). Postings to DorothyL simply do not refer to "themes" or "symbols," let alone to such current arcana of the literary critical trade as "aporia" or "intertextual(ity)."

It is a fair inference, I believe, that these recommendations, with their clear hierarchy and priorities, align closely with how these readers read and what they read for. In a word, they read first for character and then, in varying preference orders, for setting, writing quality, plot, and puzzle. They praise authors for characters who are realistic, believable, recognizable, likable, memorable, interesting, or vivid; who are well-developed or well-drawn; and for settings that are realistic, authentic, memorable, and evocative. Writing may be praised as skilled, excellent, masterful, deft, richly textured, or superb. Especially good writing may "sing." A first-rate plot is gripping, involving, or suspenseful; well-paced or fast-paced; or simply "strong."

Engagement with character is central to the reading experience for these readers. They expect fictional characters to be realistic (or believable, recognizable, individualized), but while realism is a necessary aspect of their reading pleasure, it is not sufficient. Characters must also be likeable. DorothyL readers, like the readers in the reading groups studied by sociologist Elizabeth Long, tend to talk about, and judge, characters as if they were real persons (Long 1986). Realistic, well-developed, well-rounded, interesting, vividly drawn, nonstereotypical characters must also be likeable or sympathetic if the reading experience is to be really pleasurable.

For example, a reader favorably contrasts the protagonist of Noreen Gilpatrick's *Final Design* with other versions of the female private eye "who seem to act like they've had a partial lobotomy and are too tough for human relations." Gilpatrick's "Kate felt like a real person" (DorothyL 14/15 April 1996). Another reader calls Steve Womack's series investigator Harry Denton a "realistic PI, a likable human who happens to investigate . . . [Denton] continues to grow and mature which only adds to the book" (15/16 April 1996). After reading her first Marcia Muller novel, another reader wrote, "I look forward to getting to know her [protagonist Sharon McCone] better" (1/2 January 1996). Of the lead characters in Polly Whitney's *Until Death* and *Until the End of Time*: "I have to say I really like Abby. . . . I'm sorry to say I don't like Ike very much. I want to like her, and sometimes I do, but most of the time she and I don't get along. . . . The only thing that bothers me about Abby is that he doesn't dump Ike and find somebody new. By the end of [*Until the End of*] TIME I was thinking, Abby, don't be such a shmutz" (14/15 April 1996). Another of Whitney's readers replied, "I also liked Abby and thought Ike was the jerk. She was too easily offended for my taste, and needed to lighten up or get a sense of humor or something" (15/16 April 1996).

Defending a female character criticized by a subscriber for making light of the abuse she had suffered at the hands of her ex-husband, a reader offered a different "take" on what the character's actions meant: "that the humor is a coping mechanism, but that Goldy has always taken her ex-husband's abusiveness very seriously" (11/12 April 1996). Of the characters in Sarah Caudwell's *Thus Was Adonis Murdered*, a member of a mystery reading group in New York City wrote: "Many of us felt that we would enjoy living down the hall from the book's characters . . . but even admirers thought that a little of them might go a long way. Even those who loved the book mentioned that they'd probably wait awhile before reading another Hilary Tamar mystery" (21/22 April 1996). Responding to a criticism of Jill Church-ill's investigator Jane Jeffries as a "wuss," a subscriber defended the author as engaged in trying to show an evolution of her character and went on to describe Jeffries's appeal: "The thing I like most about Jane is her appreciation of the absurdity—even the surrealism—of life. In the midst of catastrophe, she is aware of the underlying silliness of it all without minimizing or trivializing the problem" (21/22 February 1996). Looking forward to further works in a series after enjoying the inaugural novel, a reader wrote that she "can't wait for more— especially a book that would *do something* about Theresa's chauvin-istic husband" (10/11 April 1996). Commenting on *Brother Cadfael's Penance*, after the death of author Ellis Peters in 1995, a reader praised it as a fine story, "full of thoughts on aging, belonging to a community, and conflicting duties and choices we all must make in life. . . . It felt so good to have Cadfael meet his son again!" (9/10 January 1996).

Just as the reading experience to which these readers testify involves realism in the rendering of character together with responding to them (or at least talking about them) as real persons, so the evaluation of setting involves both realism, in the sense of accurate depiction, and a response on the part of the reader as if to the experience of a real place: "I loved Nevada Barr's latest book [*Firestorm*]. I thought her word paintings of the bleak post-fire landscape were absolutely amazing. I could feel and smell the ashes" (23/24 April 1996). Or: *The Strange Files of Fremont Jones* is "set in San Francisco around the turn of the century, and [author Dianne] Day made me feel like I could actually smell the fog rolling in at dusk" (17/18 April 1996). Or: "[Francine] Mathews has great skill in evoking the smell, feel and look of [Nan-tucket]—I felt as if the fog were touching my face as I read, and that I could see the marshes and cranberry bogs" (15/16 April 1996). Ac-knowledging the abundant plot twists of J. D. Christilian's period mys-tery *Scarlet Women*, another reader admitted that "it was the atmosphere of the novel that appealed to me most. . . . The author had clearly done a lot of research" (21/22 February 1996). Another undoubtedly voiced the view of many subscribers when she wrote: "I like a complex world for the protagonists to move around in, and Ayres taps into real world texture, smells, and sensibilities" (2/3 January 1996). The following recommendation of Lynda Robinson's *Murder at God's Gate* combines succinctly both the emphasis on setting and character and the two senses of the "realistic" that predominate in these communications: the realism of accurate depiction and realism in the felt sense of valid experience (if I had really been there, I would have felt as I do): "Besides a detailed historical background that gives a real sense of place and the daily life of ancient Egypt, you get to know and like Meren, his son Kysen, and the teenaged Tutankhamum" (18/19 April 1996).

Since the 1920s, literary critics generally have contrasted mystery fiction unfavorably with modernist fiction for the former's continued reliance on traditional modes of plot and character and the conventions of Realism. This persistent invidious distinction, long a factor affecting the writing of mystery fiction as well as its reception, surfaces occasionally in posts to DorothyL that comment on the reading experience. "One of the reasons I read mysteries is the satisfaction I get from having a real ending to a novel. So much of modern fiction is end-less (and reads that way, too)" (17/18 April 1996). Another dismissed "the so-called literary establishment's opinion that mystery fiction is just popular genre fiction" as simply "envious of us who get to read novels with a beginning, middle and end (not to mention a PLOT!)" (18/19 April 1996). Another located the source of her "love" for mysteries (as well as her enjoyment of "a good conspiracy theory") in the experience of <u>closure</u> provided by a traditional ending: "There's that deeply satisfying sense of having all the ends tied up, being 'in the know' " (9/10 January 1996).

In addition to judging mysteries for the realism of characters, the evocation of place, and the satisfaction of narrative and cognitive closure, readers anticipate and value being really engaged by a book: "I read 250 pages in one sitting because the book just grabbed me by the collar and hasn't let go" (2/3 January 1996). "The mark of a good story is one that connects with you emotionally . . . [Steve Womack's] *Chain of Fools* grabbed me by the hand and pulled me into the story" (26/27 April 1996). Mary Willis Walker's *Under the Beetle's Cellar* was "absolutely riveting" from the first word to the last (24/25 February 1996). That phrase pales, however, beside the testimony of another reader, who claimed she delayed the delivery of her child in order to finish the mystery she was reading during labor (9/10 April 1996).

Realistic characters, evocative settings, a high degree of emotional involvement—these are both essential criteria DorothyL readers use to assess books and frame their recommendations, and some of the most important expectations they bring to their reading. Criteria and expectation are closely related to the question of the "effects" of reading: effects, at least in some cases, amount to fulfilled expectations. This is clearest, perhaps, in the case of "distractibility": I expect to be drawn into a work; this book (*The Clue of the Blood-stained Will*) is "absolutely riveting." Clearly, we are entitled to say that one effect of my reading *The Clue of the Blood-stained Will* is bound up in that experience, admittedly transitory, of intense engagement induced by the work in hand. This type of more or less brief but intense engagement is part of what is captured, most often dismissively, in the notion of "escape" as that term is used to describe and evaluate involvement with the manifold forms of popular culture.

Other forms of effect are transitory but hardly qualify as "escape:" "Though [Sara Paretsky's] V. I. [Warshawski] lives in a bleaker world than some of us, she does make you think and challenges the mind" (25/26 February 1996). To make one think is clearly to have brought about an effect, but in this case the effect is probably short-lived and not necessarily consequential. Of far greater interest is the possibility and nature of long-term, especially permanent, effects of reading mystery fiction. Allowing for a bit of rhetorical license, the following posting to DorothyL suggests one form of permanent effect—a decisive shift in the way something is perceived: "*Skin Tight* [is] the best [Carl] Hiassen book so far, you will never see a weedwacker or watch Geraldo in quite the same way again" (9/10 January 1996). Another reader alludes to the same kind of shift in attitude motivated by reading when she asks how chambers of commerce feel about violent mysteries set in their cities (10/11 April 1996).

One form of long-term, even permanent, effect is change in belief: broadening or increasing one's knowledge, for example. There is abundant evidence of this type of effect in the postings to DorothyL. "Although a serious student of the English novel," one reader remarked, "I only learned from Dorothy Sayers and Agatha Christie" about the "extraordinary inequalities" of British life between the world wars (15/

16 April 1996). Another estimated, with some exaggeration perhaps, that "90% of the factoids I know come from the hundreds and hundreds of books I have read. Psychology from Jonathan Kellerman. . . . Australia from 'Bony' [Arthur Upfield's part-Aborigine investigator], spy lore from [Brian Freemantle's] Charlie Muffin. . . . Oxford from [Colin Dexter's Inspector] Morse, forensics from [Patricia] Cornwell. . . . Although every bit of the knowledge gained might not be absolutely perfect or totally factual, a certain amount of curiosity is stimulated . . . which pushes me to learn more and be more tolerant of different ideas" (16/17 April 1996). Another reader, if her hope of visiting Venice materialized, would "skim back over Donna Leon's excellent series" for information about the city (23/24 April 1996). Another subscriber describes spending a "cool, damp and delightful day at Sandown Race course in Esher, Surrey," in honor of a favorite author: "Dick Francis prepared us to make all sorts of decisions," from train tickets to the "occasional pound bet" (7/8 January 1996). The following is representative of the now widespread expectations among readers that have underwritten the diversification of setting in mystery fiction since the 1980s: "I enjoy learning about other parts of the country/world through mystery writers and appreciate the research that has gone into their efforts" (24/25 February 1996; see also King 1997).

Many who subscribe to DorothyL expect not only to be entertained by their reading of mystery fiction, but also to derive accurate information from that reading. In short, they expect their reading of mystery fiction to have a long-term effect, namely to broaden or increase their fund of knowledge. If that is truly the case, we might expect that reading pleasure would be seriously jeopardized when readers encounter (what they believe to be) the inaccurate, the unrealistic, or the implausible in their reading of mystery fiction. There is abundant evidence on this point, and with it we return to the matter of "realism" and its centrality in the reading experience as both a crucial expectation and a privileged criterion of evaluation.

"How important is realism in a fictional story? Very," a subscriber writes before launching into a critique of the television series *Murder One* (shown during the 1995–96 season) for failing to present characters acting "as serious people would"—i.e., realistically or believably (25/26 April 1996). Responses to detecting errors of fact range from mild annoyance to giving up on a book. A software company president writes: "I used to grind my teeth at the inaccuracy and silliness of so much of the computer stuff in mysteries" (14/15 April 1996). Another computer-literate subscriber cautioned the list, "It's a lot harder than people think to hack into computer systems," and went on to recommend a mystery with a "technically plausible scenario," Barbara d'Amato's *Killer.app* (11/12 April 1996). Another, remarking an error in a "much loved book frequently mentioned on DorothyL," reminded the list of the fact that a "loofa sponge is something one GROWS in a GARDEN," adding, "Fortunately the book was so good that this error did not distract me too much" (15/16 April 1996). For a reader knowledgeable about Harley-Davidson motorcycles, however, encountering a reference to an "antique Softail" that required kick-starting, nearly caused her to stop reading the mystery in which this "howler" occurred. "Softails were not manufactured at all until 1985 or so, and never had kickstarts. . . . Now I finally understand the previous posters who almost had to quit reading books because of ongoing howlers. Every time he referred to the bike, and it was often, I had to grit my teeth, unclench my hands, and say 'it's okay, keep reading' " (10/11 April 1996).

Accuracy, then, is not simply important; it is a necessary element of reading pleasure. I noted in the preceding chapter the New Jersey police detectives who were collaborating on a reference work for mystery writers, and who found nearly all fiction about police unreadable, except for the work of Joseph Wambaugh, himself an ex-police officer. Readers with expert knowledge expect authors to get it right. Allan Dulles, by profession a spy and President Eisenhower's choice to head the CIA, was a reader of spy novels and even compiled an anthology of espionage stories. Helen MacInnes won Dulles's praise for employing the convention of the innocent caught up by chance in intrigue: "By this means she—very wisely, I think—avoids cluttering her books with a lot of unauthentic claptrap about contemporary [intelligence] services and methods, which is what puts off the reader who has any acquaintance at all with the real business" (White 1974). Robin Winks, a historian who has written about and reviewed mystery and espionage fiction, has suggested that someone interested in South African society could do no "better, in learning about the meaning of apartheid in South Africa, than to read a James McClure mystery novel" (1993, 221). Conversely, Winks castigates the popular Robert Ludlum for inaccurately describing a Geneva street in one of his novels: "could you not have taken out a map [to verify the setting] . . . or are you writing such a confection, such a concoction, that it did not matter?" If a work is "to be at all convincing as fiction," Winks continues, "it is essential that it be accurate *in all particulars in which it can be accurate*" (1993, 225; emphasis added). In reviewing espionage novels, Winks tends to see quality, to a large degree, as a function of accuracy, and accuracy as grounded in firsthand experience: "of those writers of spy novels who blend fiction with a firm grounding in reality, there are two who stand above the others [including John Le Carré], because both have been there: Charles McCarry, formerly of the CIA, and Ted Allbeury, formerly of SIS" (1988b, 14). Allbeury "pretty much tells it as it is: he was there, and he knows what it feels like to lie to a man, to walk the streets of Addis Ababa in a cold sweat, to be bored in Berlin" (1988b, 1).

Getting the "particulars" right is necessary but not sufficient, however. The reading experience depends crucially on readers' perception of character as well as the author's position on any social issue that may have been worked into a story. A female character who seems to make light of her abuse at the hands of her ex-husband doesn't "ring true" for a reader (10/11 April 1996). Another has difficulty "understanding" a character who fails to learn from experience: "Maybe he's not the introspective kind, but I don't understand how any man cannot [*sic*] look at his father after the father has committed murders and not try to change his own patterns of behavior" (9/10 April 1996). Implausibility creates the "annoyance" expressed by several readers at a character of Dorothy Cannell's: "[*Mum's the Word*] was my last Cannell. I actually like her humor, but Ellie [Haskell] has got to be the most annoying fictional character I have ever discovered. She is always turning on Ben (or turning away from him) for the slightest, most ridiculous and imagined reasons . . . there is only so much of this that the gentle reader can take!" (1/2 January 1996).

Not being able to like a character, with its adverse effects on the reading experience, is not always, or simply, a function of the character's plausibility or believability, however: "[I] found it hard to like the characters [in *Going Nowhere Fast*] as there seemed to be a lot of threats and anger amongst the family members which took away from my ability to concentrate on character development or even the mystery for that matter. [I] Would try one more but certainly hope that the main characters lighten up a bit and treat each other with more respect" (2/3 January 1996). In this instance, and especially in the case of an author's politics or position on a particular social issue, the relevant criterion is not so much accuracy as the degree of fit with the reader's beliefs and moral standards. Agreeing with an earlier post that she too reads for both issues and quality, this subscriber added, "but I also find that sometimes the author's opinions are so drastically opposed to my own that I can't enjoy the story" (26/27 April 1996). Another, responding angrily to Margaret Yorke's *The Hand of Death*, was shocked and "dismayed to find her spouting all sorts of nonsense about women who invite rape and other violence" (7/8 January 1996). A male reader admitted, "I have a hard time identifying with (or enjoying the process of identifying with) a protagonist who, while still married, enters an affair. I know it's the 90's, but it still hurts me to see her do that" (7/8 January 1996).

For those who read primarily for entertainment or escape, social issues are likely to be off-putting. Reacting to the prevalence of stories involving "incest and child abuse," a reader explained, "But then, I don't really read mysteries for social commentary but to visit another world for awhile and I'd rather like most of the people there" (15/16 April 1996). Another seeking "entertainment for escape from [the] workaday world," and picking her authors accordingly, objected to the presence of social issues, which stood in opposition to the "transcendent": "I resent the all-too-frequent intrusion of 'substance'—so-called contemporary issues. . . . Surely there's still such a thing as the transcendent? that which will appeal or 'speak' to all of us, regardless of our creeds, beliefs or political persuasions?" (15/16 April 1996). It is not, finally, the presence or absence of social issues, but the degree to which they are judged "intrusive" by readers, that affects the degree of pleasure derived from a work. It goes without saying that the experience of "intrusiveness" varies. "I don't mind issues in stories and feel that I learn from them but I don't want to be overwhelmed" (27/28 April 1996). No doubt many a subscriber to DorothyL would agree with this sentiment while differing sharply on whether the treatment of social issues in a given work was intrusive and "overwhelming." Put simply, there is widespread agreement on this discussion list about the critical criteria appropriate to reading mystery fiction, and even the ordering of the criteria—the near universal priority afforded character, for example. Disagreements, when they occur, tend to be over the application of a given criterion in a given instance.

*   *   *

These excerpts from DorothyL suggest, on the one hand, how powerfully distracting the experience of reading mystery fiction can be, overriding pain, anxiety, and fear: "Reading has helped me through labor, hundreds of hours in hospital waiting rooms, boring bus trip[s], frightening plane rides, lovely summer afternoons, etc." (27/28 April 1996). On the other hand, these posts suggest with equal insistence the vulnerability of "the willing suspension of disbelief," to invoke the familiar bromide that still serves to define, if not exhaust, a central aspect of the psychology of reading fiction. The reading experience of these readers is closely, indeed essentially, tied to the "realistic" (in character and setting), the "likeable" (in character), the "acceptable" (in social issues and commentary), and to the degree of experiential "involvement" brought about primarily, but not exclusively, through scene, incident, and plot. Inaccuracies of fact, annoying or unrealistic characters, or an author's stand on a social issue that diverges too greatly from the reader's may suddenly disrupt the reading experience. At best, the pleasure and distraction of the reading experience is diminished to some degree; at worst, the reader puts down the book unfinished, or, finishing it, never reads that author again. At the heart of this fragile, inherently vulnerable process is a match or fit, constituted of both perception and evaluation, between the beliefs the reader brings to a work and the fictional world that comes into being in the course of the reading experience. To characterize or designate this fit or match as instancing "realism" or the "realistic" risks carrying into the discussion the unwanted and distracting connotations of a word with a long and complex history. My reasons for doing so should be apparent, however; it is not my term, but the one used by the readers of mystery fiction who sustain the discussion on DorothyL. Moreover, what they mean by the term does not seem to me to be especially complicated.

Readers expect mystery fiction to be true to their experience. Moreover, in matters of which they know little if anything, readers expect mystery fiction to be accurate "in all particulars in which it can be accurate" (Winks 1993). Without the confident expectation that their fiction will be accurate, readers of mystery fiction could not reasonably or coherently hold the belief that they can learn about the world from mystery fiction. And many, perhaps the vast majority of readers, do hold that belief. For some, trusting an author to have presented accurate facts smooths the way for a day's outing at an English race course or sends a "previously kitchen-phobic DorothyLer into the kitchen to learn to bake pastries" (23 January 1996). For others, trusting the knowledgeability of the writer is more consequential, as in the instance of Josiah Thompson, which I take up at the end of this chapter. Before turning to Thompson's apprenticeship as a private investigator, however, I want to argue that the professional reviewing of detective fiction frequently involves assessing its "realism," as the example of Anthony Boucher suggests.

Anthony Boucher (William Anthony Parker White) began writing the "Criminals at Large" column for the *New York Times Book Review* in 1951. He held that visible, and arguably influential, position until his death in 1968. During those years, Boucher was also writing introductions for anthologies of mystery stories and mystery reprints as well as reviewing science fiction for the *New York Herald Tribune* (1961–1968) and for *The Magazine of Fantasy and Science Fiction*, of which he was co-founder. From 1961 to 1968, he conducted a biweekly program of mystery reviews on a California radio station.

As a professional reviewer and critic, Boucher possessed a catholic appreciation for mystery or suspense fiction in its various forms: the traditional whodunit, the hard-boiled private eye story, the spy novel, the thriller, and the police procedural. He was quick to spot emerging writers and generous in his support of them. By and large, the writers against whose achievements he measured newer writers were at the time, and have mostly remained, the writers who figure prominently in such standard histories of the genre as Julian Symons's *Bloody Murder*, especially Agatha Christie (the "mistress of fair deceit"); Dashiell Hammett and Raymond Chandler in the hard-boiled tradition; John Buchan, Graham Greene, and Eric Ambler for the spy novel and thriller; and Ed McBain, whose 87th Precinct novels inaugurated the American police procedural as a popular form in the mid-1950s. These writers best embodied in their work the qualities that Boucher valued, that constitute his essential evaluative criteria.

Boucher's evaluation of traditional whodunits turned principally on his assessment, first, of the author's cleverness in disguising the clues, and second, on the degree to which the author played fair with the reader. Thus Christie's *A Pocket Full of Rye* (1954) made his best-of-the-year list for displaying "the game-of-wits mystery as its most dexterously misleading" (1973, 53). Boucher appreciated warmth, humanity, compassion, and humor wherever he found them. A writer of fiction himself, he prized evidence of craftsmanship and professional skill—nowhere more than in the construction of a fair puzzle, a tight or intricate plot. His "all-out, no reservations rave" for Ira Levin's first novel *A Kiss Before Dying*, for example, emphasized especially its "superlatively enviable sheer professionalism," in addition to its "full-bodied characterization, subtle psychological exploration, vivid evocation of locale" (1973, 46–47).

Fair play and faultless plotting were hallmarks, for Boucher, of first-rate mystery writing, but a writer's skill was equally evident in a work's effects. Boucher employed a wide range of terms to characterize and assess the affective dimension of the reading experience—a dimension that was important to him across the several types of suspense fiction. A good work was chilling, vivid, compelling, immediate, touching or moving, or simply memorable; more intensely, a work might be breath-taking, terrifying, almost unbearably suspenseful. In some instances, affect has unmistakable cognitive overtones: a work is chillingly convincing or credible or believable. Boucher called John D. MacDonald's *The End of the Night* (1960), for example, "terrifyingly believable" (1973, 76).

Boucher was deeply aware of the invidious distinction between works of entertainment and works of art. He was quick to praise works he felt challenged that distinction, often by invoking a notion of "fusion." John Trench's *What Rough Beast* (1957), for example, is both an "admirable formal detective story" and a "novelistically impressive picture of [a] decaying English town" (1973, 66). Margaret Millar, one of his favorite authors, was particularly adept at blending the "novelistic" with the conventions of the classical detective novel. Millar's *The Fiend* (1964), published in the same year that saw Hans Helmut Kirst's *The Night of the Generals*, Eric Ambler's *A Kind of Anger*, Ross Macdonald's *The Chill*, and John Le Carré's *The Spy Who Came In from the Cold* ("*The* spy novel of our time"), nevertheless won Boucher's highest praise as "a perfect combination in which puzzle and serious novel are one" (1973, 93). In an earlier review of Graham Greene's self-styled "entertainment" *The Ministry of Fear* (1943), Boucher reduced to the vanishing point the gap between art and a well-wrought work of genre fiction, saying, "[Greene] is something so close to a great novelist that it is hard to see the difference; perhaps there is none" (1973, 14). The best mysteries, Boucher insisted throughout his tenure as a reviewer for the nation's "newspaper of record," were also good novels, to be judged as such, and he deplored the "influential critics" who maintained "that what is 'entertainment' cannot be 'art' " (1973, 79).

Boucher once wrote that the only common factor he could discern in "this indefinable category of mystery/suspense is <u>story-telling</u>—the narrative vigor that keeps us turning the pages" (1973, 64). Narrative vigor bespoke craftsmanship and skill, just as did the varied effects Boucher endeavored to discriminate so precisely, using the affective vocabulary discussed above. What distinguished the best mysteries— the works Boucher singled out for special praise or included in his best-of-the year columns—was not craftsmanship per se, however, but the "realism" (alternatively the "plausibility" or "credibility" or "authen-ticity") manifest in such works as Meyer Levin's *Compulsion* (1956), a "psychoanalytic adaption of [the] Loeb-Leopold case, superb both in quality as fiction and in fidelity to fact" (1973, 61).

The centrality of realism as a criterion is nowhere clearer than in a tart reply Boucher made to historian Jacques Barzun, himself a notable aficionado of the ratiocinative form, who had ridiculed Boucher for recommending a detective novel, in part, for its capacity to "lead us to an understanding of many aspects of rural Austria in 1945." By implication, according to Barzun, the cases of Sherlock Holmes " 'led us to an understanding of many aspects of British Railways before na-tionalization' " (in Boucher 1973, 66). On this point Boucher remained adamant, however. Wasn't the secret of Holmes's "immortality" that "his cases do lead us to an understanding of the whole late Victorian era?" Doyle's plots weren't very good even by the (presumably more relaxed) standards of his day, Boucher averred; what keeps the stories alive and re-readable "is the keenly observed background details." In-deed, "many a young Englishman owes to the journeys of Holmes his entire knowledge of British Railways before nationalization (And a doctor's thesis on that topic could be written from the novels of Free-man Wills Crofts)." Novels do not take place "*in vacuo*," Boucher lectured Columbia University's eminent scholar: "a good novel has a local and temporal habitation, and a good novelist lends reality to place and time as he does to his characters" (1973, 66–67).

Frequently, however, Boucher invoked realism obliquely, by charac-terizing authorial intention as: examining, studying, analyzing, explor-ing, or providing a picture. Hubert Monteilhet, in *The Road to Hell*, for example, used the detective story "as a penetrating examination of conscience" (1973, 92–93). More indirectly still, Boucher often characterized a work as a "detailedly fascinating study" or a "believable history." Ross Macdonald's *The Far Side of the Dollar*, Boucher's pick for best private-eye novel of 1965, was "a considerable novel of social observation" (1973, 98). Jeffrey Ashford's *The Hands of Innocence* (1966) offered "truly terrifying insight into a psychopathic criminal mind" (1973, 101). In Dick Francis's *Odds Against* (1966), the reader encountered a "substantial study of the making of a detective—probably the year's best crime novel" (1973, 101). John D. MacDonald's *The Last One Left* (1967), considered by Boucher to be one of the major suspense novels of the 1960s, was not only ingeniously plotted, but contained "enough perception of the Texas-Florida-Bahamas scene (in all its aspects . . .)" to justify its unusual length (170,000 words) (1973, 103). The emergence of the police procedural in the 1950s, exemplified by the credible treatment of investigative techniques in Ed McBain's 87th Precinct series, yielded novels that competently "explored" the "technical investigative details of a wide variety of professions" (1973, 59).

Whether indirectly, as when characterizing Nicholas Freeling's *Double Barrel* (1965) as possibly the best of that author's "grand genre studies of modern Holland and its crimes" (1973, 97), or directly, as in the reply to Jacques Barzun quoted above, Boucher's critical criteria bottom out in realism—fidelity to fact, and credibility or believability—effects born of a writer's skill in representing factuality in convincing fashion. Accuracy and believability, in turn, warrant the claim, explicit in Boucher's explanation for the continued appeal of the Holmes stories, for mystery fiction as a source of knowledge. Boucher reiterated that point in his review of *The Annotated Sherlock Holmes* (1967), a year before his death: "Good detective stories are, as I have often quoted Hamlet's phrase about the players, 'the abstracts and brief chronicles of the time,' ever valuable in retrospect as indirect but vivid pictures of the society from which they spring" (1973, 127).

Creating fiction that is "accurate in all particulars in which it can be accurate" admits the possibility that authors can and should get those particulars right. On that possibility, in turn, rests any coherent claim that readers can learn from reading detective fiction. Boucher accepted the validity of that claim. It is equally clear that subscribers to DorothyL expect factual accuracy in their mysteries, believe they gain knowledge from mystery fiction, and are annoyed, or worse, when they encounter inaccuracies in their reading. It is one thing, however, to rely on Dick Francis for help in planning a day at an English race course or to be tempted back into the kitchen to take up baking pastries for one's family on the basis of an author's appealing recipes; it is another to have medical students read mysteries as a way to sharpen their diagnostic skills or to do as Josiah Thompson did and discover in Dashiell Hammett's depiction of Sam Spade a suitable model for fashioning a real professional identity, in effect betting his life on what Hammett both knew and succeeded in representing in the figure of Sam Spade.

Josiah Thompson was a faculty member in Philosophy at Haverford College, a Yale Ph.D. who had won early tenure on the strength of his publishing record and teaching, when he resigned his position in 1978 to become a private investigator after having spent a sabbatical leave in San Francisco getting a taste of the business. In *Gumshoe: Reflections in a Private Eye*, written a decade later, Thompson describes his apprenticeship, spent with David Fechheimer, a notably successful private investigator and devotee of *The Maltese Falcon*: "David probably knew more about Hammett than any of his biographers. . . . More to the point . . . the *Falcon* had something to do with him becoming a detective" (Thompson 1989, 41).

Thompson reports reading the *Falcon* to pass the time on the first case he worked with Fechheimer, but at that time "[I] hadn't been able to make much of the Flitcraft story. Nor, for that matter, of the whole book" (1989, 38, 41). Later, however, after rereading the Flitcraft episode (and having gained more experience in the workaday world of investigation), "*The Maltese Falcon* became a kind of original text against which I kept comparing my own experience" (1989, 110). Thompson began to underline passages in the novel and to write notes in the margins. "After a while I'd come to recognize I was actually *studying* it," finding in it "asides, *aperçus*, and references that connected in some uncanny way with my own experiences of the last year. Some would remind me of a jam I'd gotten into or of a technique Fechheimer had used or suggested to me" (1989, 111). Many of Thompson's notes had to do with what he terms "Spade's worldliness." Reading the novel in light of his experience as a novice investigator, Thompson characterizes the "problem" posed by the *Falcon* as this: "how to survive in a world where there are no general principles to guide action, where one plays the percentages, follows rules of thumb, trusts hunches, and has to act swiftly—all without any sort of rational comprehension. . . . Spade's wisdom consists in knowing that any action is, inherently, partly out of control. . . . In Spade, then, we have a portrait of the detective as fully worldly, as literally awash in the world" (1989, 111–12).

Spade's significance for Thompson is not that Hammett shows Spade capable of taking care of himself. Rather, "the interest is in *how* he does it" (1989, 128). Spade does it, Thompson suggests, remembering a conversation with Fechheimer, by "paying attention," something Fechheimer had emphasized from the beginning. Paying attention "was the only difference between a master detective and a bungler, and also the only insurance policy most of us would ever get" (1989, 37). Failing to pay attention results in Spade's getting taken twice at Caspar Gutman's hands, but Hammett, Thompson notes, "won't let Spade make the lethal mistake . . . to trust Brigid . . . to give in, to 'play the sap' for her" (1989, 129).

Like Anthony Giddens, and for that matter mystery writers from Doyle to Le Carré, Thompson draws on the familiar distinction between public and private—"the world of power and the world of love." Spade is an archetype, an exemplar, of the "cogent actor" who is at home in the world of power: " '*a hard and shifty fellow, able to take care of himself in any situation, able to get the best of anybody he comes in contact with*' " (1989, 141; emphasis in original). To get on in the world of power, "whether one is an Ivan Boesky or a lowly detective," demands that the "cogent actor" be able "to lie effectively, to appear different than one really is." In the world of love, these skills are liabilities, blocking the possibility of intimacy and mutual trust. "Hammett knew all this," Thompson concludes. He represented Spade as the consummate cogent actor (1989, 141).

Thompson's use of *The Maltese Falcon* thus differs in degree, not in kind, from the uses examined earlier in this chapter. "Studying" *The Maltese Falcon* to learn the *how* of Spade's survival in the deceptive and dangerous world of power, where "the ability to lie effectively" is essential, bottoms out finally on the same set of assumptions, the same relationship between text and real world, employed by a reader who uses a Dick Francis novel to plan a day of English racing. Unless there is a world of "particulars," at least some of which writers can and do get right and readers can and do construe correctly in the course of their reading, there is no day at the races and Spade is simply a character in a book, with no possible relevance or conceivable connection to the world in which discontented professors of philosophy abandon the security of the academic life for the uncertainties and real risks of life as a private investigator in a large city. Thompson opens *Gumshoe* by acknowledging those risks specifically, in a bid perhaps to make his reader pay attention from the outset: "Until I saw the bullet hole, it was all playacting" (1989, 1). Moreover, it is in the context of those potentially mortal risks that he reads *The Maltese Falcon* and gradually comes to accept Hammett as a knowledgeable guide to becoming a cogent actor in the world of power. Neither as a philosopher nor as a working detective, then, can Thompson have taken lightly his flat, unqualified assertion: "Hammett knew all this." That statement lays a number of bets—about language, about fiction, about reading, and about the relationship between an author's text, a reader's response, and those features of the world that author and reader, in and through the work of fiction, jointly apprehend.

Conclusion

We live amid surfaces, and the true art of life is to skate well on them.
Ralph Waldo Emerson, "Experience"

Planning is a quintessentially modern activity. It finds application and expression in the most intimate of settings (family planning) as well as in corporate boardrooms. It is impossible to imagine modern society without the projection onto future time entailed by imagining and assessing various possibilities for future action. Fictional investigation requires not only the skills of the historian (or, as Sanders argues, the talents of the sociologist). If mystery fiction is as closely linked to the essential features of modernity as I have argued throughout this work, it is reasonable to expect the typical investigator to be a competent planner and to possess the skills and trained capacities involved in projecting present purposes into an uncertain future with the aim of minimizing danger and enhancing the chances of success. By way of concluding this study, I shall try to make that last point about the relationship of mystery fiction and modernity.

Recently, the state university at which I teach initiated a "strategic planning" process in the face of severe fiscal constraints and intense political pressures for accountability. Reduced to its essentials, the process involved reaffirming the institution's mission; assessing its strengths and weaknesses in order to isolate "competitive advantage"; analyzing the contextual factors affecting the institution, especially in the long run; and formulating realistic goals or objectives consistent with the university's mission, its strengths, and its situation as that came to be understood and defined in the planning process. Strategic planning of this kind is a high-stakes activity, involving significant risk, both to the institution and to those charged with conducting the planning process. The problem of "getting it right" is key at every step—in formulating or revising the institution's mission; in assessing its strengths and competitive advantage; but especially in achieving a suitably robust understanding of its situation, its context for action. Getting that right is crucial, since realistic and achievable goals and objectives depend, for their formulation, on an accurate assessment of the overall environment for action. Strategic planning of this kind is not a skeptic's game—at least not past a certain point. The aim of strategic planning is not simply "getting it right" as an academic exercise, but getting it right as the necessary basis for purposeful action that aims at realizing concrete goals, including sheer survival in a complex, changing, and competitive environment.

As a response to environments characterized by predictably unpredictable change, strategic planning typically faces significant time constraints. As in virtually every modern productive activity, time is a critical factor. Strategic planning is no exception. The process, one outcome of which is a schedule of future actions, is itself subject to a timetable and constrained by the limited time available to those responsible for it. Time is a nonrenewable resource, and its efficient use in the planning process constitutes one important measure of processual effectiveness.

Getting the context right, however, faces formidable obstacles, both epistemological and organizational. The latter, in the final analysis, reduces to the qualities and characteristics of the individuals involved. Planning—conceiving of future states and formulating, implementing, and coordinating the activity necessary to realize them in time and across increasingly great distances—is quintessentially "modern" in the sense in which I have used that term throughout this study.

In this regard, Anthony Giddens's *The Consequences of Modernity* may itself be profitably read as a strategic planning document. Giddens describes both the characteristic and distinctive features of "high" or "radicalized" modernity and the dynamic that underlies modernity and accounts for its distinctiveness. His analysis amounts to a comprehensive description of the context for action under the conditions of modernity, together with an assessment of its strengths and weaknesses and its opportunities and risks. The essential nature of modernity, he argues, can be captured in the image of a "juggernaut," a powerful vehicle whose movement is not fully predictable, hence not fully controllable. The juggernaut defines the context of action that is high modernity. Giddens dismisses the possibility of an individual significantly withdrawing from modernity in the hope, for example, of reducing or evading its effects. The all-encompassing tendencies of modernity include especially the globalization of high-consequence risk—nuclear warfare or ecological disaster—from which there can be no refuge.

With his analysis of modernity as context in hand, Giddens asks: "How far can we—where 'we' means humanity as a whole—harness the juggernaut, or at least direct it in such a way as to minimize the dangers and maximize the opportunities which modernity offers us?" (1990, 151). This is a question with both an epistemological and a political dimension. The latter is parasitic on the former: "harnessing" or "directing" the juggernaut of modernity bottoms out on knowledge claims about its features and processes. It is only with those settled (pragmatically, "until further notice") that the question becomes one of political policy, of setting realistic, achievable goals, given the nature of modernity as an arena for action. For Giddens, the overriding goal must be minimizing "high-consequence risk," in order to "further the possibilities of a fulfilling and satisfying life for all, and in respect of which there are no 'others' " (1990, 156). In characterizing the stance required of those who would guide the juggernaut—to the degree that its nature admits of intervention and limited control—Giddens offers the term "utopian realism." By "realism" he seems to mean a measure of understanding of how things truly go. A realistic assessment of our situation must be in place if we are to realize achievable goals—goals whose formulation depends, in large measure, on recognizing "institutionally immanent possibilities."

Giddens rejects as unrealistic, and hence unusable as a basis for action, the Marxist view that "history has an overall direction and converges upon a revolutionary agent, the proletariat, which is a 'universal class' " (1990, 154). Guiding the juggernaut involves recognizing that it "has no teleology, and there are no privileged agents in the process of transformation geared to the realization of values" (1990, 154–55).

Put differently, appropriate and effective action in the service of worthy and achievable goals depends on achieving as realistic an assessment of the context for action as is possible. That achievement implies a rejection of currently fashionable forms of skepticism and cognitive relativism. Giddens summarily dismisses as unwarranted "the idea that we no longer have viable methods of sustaining knowledge claims in the sense of [Jean-François] Lyotard and others" in explaining either why we live in the "runaway" world symbolized by the juggernaut or how we might improve our situation (1990, 151). The "erratic character of modernity" is to be explained otherwise than by a failure of reason.

The defining qualities of the fictional investigator are just those qualities required by the predictable unpredictability of modernity. These are the trained capacities suited to the features and challenges of modernity, considered as the cultural world brought about by "technologically induced economic growth." The trained capacities constitutive of fictional investigators have remained remarkably stable over the century of the mystery story's popularity because these capacities continue to offer an effective basis for action in the face of uncertainty and risk. Trying to harness or direct a juggernaut, so as to minimize risk and maximize opportunity, is not a bad metaphor, it turns out, both for the process of strategic planning and for the process of investigation, whether the latter is imaginatively embodied in a Sherlock Holmes, a Sam Spade or Sharon McCone, or a George Smiley. Their underlying similarities outweigh their superficial differences. In the final analysis, that is so because the context of action has the same "deep structure" and thus makes relevant the same core qualities. These in turn have broad applicability in the real world. Strategic planning and the representation of investigation in mystery fiction have a world in common—literally. Getting the context right is crucial and often a matter of life and death; and the context is ultimately a matter of other people, particularly those possessed of power to do one harm, whether deliberately or unwittingly by the unintended consequences of their actions: "most important of all [for the individual's easefulness]," Erving Goffman reminds us, "is the individual's acquired understanding of the motives and intents of others around him" (1971, 250). Acquiring that understanding—knowing what others are up to—requires interpretive skills sufficient to counter disguise and deception. This is the problem of other minds, not as a philosophical problem, but as a practical matter of getting on in everyday environments in which interdependence requires knowledge of others in assessing risk as well as creating and sustaining trust.

Riding a juggernaut aptly characterizes the sudden shifts in Ross Macdonald's *The Galton Case*; or the precariousness inherent in George Smiley's interrogation of Anton Grigoriev, on which the entirety of Smiley's plan to trap his Soviet nemesis Karla depends; or the situation of mortal danger faced by Sam Spade in the closing scenes of *The Maltese Falcon*. Unarmed, facing adversaries who have only one reason to spare his life, and that temporarily, Spade must act in a fashion best calculated to insure his survival. In the short run, he must survive the threat posed by Caspar Gutman and his bodyguard Wilmer Cook; in the longer run, he must prevent himself from being charged and perhaps convicted, falsely, of the murder of his partner. In order to survive, Spade needs to be that "hard and shifty fellow, able to take care of himself in any situation, able to get the best of anybody he comes in contact with" (Thompson 1989, 141). To get the best of "anybody" comes down to possessing interpretive skills of a high order; it means being able to read "anybody" correctly, especially in circumstances of high risk when panic predictably threatens the concentration and presence of mind required to assess a shifting situation and respond quickly and appropriately. This "cool efficacy" (the phrase is Erving Goffman's) was the trained capacity Allan Pinkerton especially valued in his operatives. Goffman, in his extended analysis of the anatomy of normal appearances, links it with professionalism and expertise, calling it "the mark of the professional—the *machismo* of the expert classes," born of experience (1971, 243). To say that cool efficacy is the outcome of experience is to say something about how it comes to be possessed by a person, but what that capacity *is* bottoms out in that asymmetrical relationship of knowing someone else better than you permit them to know you.

"Knowing the other" asserts, if not with certainty, then with a high degree of probability, how things really are as a usable, reliable basis for formulating plans for action—strategic plans—in situations of high risk. In mystery and espionage fiction, that challenge often takes the form of having to bet one's reputation or career or freedom, if not one's life, on one's beliefs about what another is up to, as Spade does in needling Wilmer Cook, for example, at the end of *The Maltese Falcon*. Failing the test of "cool efficacy"—failing, in other words, to see where his best interests lay (and those of his employer, Gutman)—and failing, too, to understand his adversary, Wilmer loses out to Spade by reacting heedlessly to Spade's taunts with threats to kill him. With no time to think about the consequences of his own actions, Gutman acts heedlessly himself, without planning or forethought, to protect Spade; and Spade, as we saw earlier, capitalizes on the opportunity by knocking Wilmer out and disarming him. At that point, Spade's calculated unpredictability has solved his short-term problem; however, he remains faced with the need to know more about what has been going on. To learn what he needs to know, he must both act in and pay attention to the unfolding situation, adjusting his actions accordingly as the features of that situation shift in the thrust and parry of his conversational duel with Gutman.

Mystery fiction models a way of being in fictional worlds in which interpretive skills of a high order are required as a basis for effective action when there is much at stake. Authors of mystery fiction create protagonists; they create the worlds in which their protagonists are depicted acting; and in the process of doing both, they create the "fit" between protagonist and fictional world. The convention of the successful ending insures that a high degree of fit exists between the protagonist and his or her world. As a consequence of the writer's control over every element of the story, and given the convention of the successful outcome, mystery fiction models a plausible and persuasive way of being in the fictional worlds represented in works of mystery fiction. To the extent that readers expect, demand, and actually experience mystery fiction to be "accurate in all particulars in which it can be accurate" (recalling Robin Winks's phrase), it becomes possible for readers to move, on occasion, from the world(s) of mystery fiction to the real world, expecting to apply what they have learned from the former to the demands of the latter. The fit perceived to exist between the worlds of mystery fiction and the real world makes it both possible and reasonable for would-be ambassadors, for example, to study the stories of Conan Doyle for strategies "of logic and cunning to foil his adversaries" (Williams 1987, 37), or for medical students to be assigned Holmes stories for the insight they afford into a general process of inference from symptoms (visible signs or "clues") to underlying (hidden) causes (Dorothy L, 2/3 January 1996).

For Josiah Thompson, the apprentice private investigator reading *The Maltese Falcon*, one of the chief lessons Hammett taught was the importance of "paying attention." Paying attention has much in common with that "infinite capacity for suspicion" on which, in the fictional world of George Smiley, an agent's survival finally depends (Le Carré 1974, 315). "Paying attention," moreover, is fundamental to sociologist Peter Berger's phenomenological analysis of modernity: "One of the most important characteristics of technological production is that from the point of view of the individual 'many things are going on at the same time.' This is true both of the production process itself and of the multifold social processes that are connected to it" (Berger, Berger and Kellner 1973, 36). To attend effectively to this aspect of modern experience requires "a particular tension of consciousness characterized by a quick alertness to ever-changing constellations of phenomena" and constitutes, for Berger, an essential and distinctive element of modern consciousness (1973, 37). An important corollary of Berger's analysis is his claim that ways of thinking that have their origins in the requirements of technological production are generalized and applied to other arenas of activity.

In a similar vein, the historian Robert Wiebe, seeking to characterize the shift in values that occurred in response to the emergence of the urban industrial world in the late nineteenth century, concludes that "the [new] rules, resembling orientations much more than laws, stressed techniques of constant watchfulness and mechanisms of continuous management" (1967, 145). Assessing the demands made by modernity on the individual, the psychologist Kenneth Kenniston writes: "Continual social change . . . requires extraordinary flexibility and adaptability to a changing environment" (1970, 318). The ordinary requirements of workaday life require a distinctive personality organization: "a capacity to govern [one's] own behavior, to make [one's] way in a world of strangers, to do a job requiring years of training in the basic skills of literacy, to cope with unexpected situations and unfamiliar people" (1970, 319). The more demanding positions in contemporary society "require . . . specialized training and, with it, high levels of dispassionateness, ability to remain cool under stress, capacity to concentrate, to maintain long-range goals yet to adapt rapidly to new conditions" (1970, 319). These are precisely the distinguishing traits and trained capacities of fictional investigators from C. Auguste Dupin and Sherlock Holmes to Sam Spade, Lew Archer, Sharon McCone, George Smiley, and the rest. And they are arguably the qualities of strategic planners, indeed of anyone who, by taking thought, seeks to act effectively in the midst of predictably unpredictable change "to minimize the dangers and maximize the opportunities which modernity offers to us"—or to survive in those situations of deceptive appearances and substantial risk that typify mystery fiction generally.

Neither strategic planning nor mystery fiction is likely to appeal to the radical skeptic, however. Strategic planning assumes that the context for action can be understood well enough, in principle, to make some courses of action seem preferable, on rational grounds, to others. Mystery fiction, since its inception, has "argued" for the investigator's capacity to discover the facts of the matter in the face of the most formidable obstacles, even obstacles that appear to threaten the very possibility of interpretability. The efficacious stance modeled in mystery fiction amounts to a measure of fit with a world whose features are, in effect, given in the investigator's trained capacities. To the extent that mystery fiction constitutes an argument for a particular stance in the world, it is equally an argument for the knowability of the world, within limits that vary from author to author in their depicted worlds. Reflecting on the conclusion of *The Maltese Falcon*, Josiah Thompson insists, "we're no closer to knowing the true story of Brigid, Thursby, Cairo, Gutman, and the falcon than we were at the beginning" (1989, 113), but this is surely to minimize Spade's achievement and the real, if limited, efficacy of the process of assessment that issues in his calculated unpredictability. To know something, it is not necessary to know everything, and Spade succeeds in learning what he needs to know, with a high enough probability, to defeat his adversaries and to insure his own survival. Gutman has been shown to be knowable, hence manipulable, and Brigid O'Shaughnessy to be resistible.

The capacities of the fictional investigator can be sorted finally into two complementary categories. One involves skills of emotional management—dispassionateness, the ability to concentrate, to resist distraction, to remain self-possessed in the face of stress. The other involves cognitive skills, exemplified in the abductive reasoning of Sherlock Holmes: inferring connections between the observable (cigar ash, smear of mud, or even credible testimony of absence—the dog that *didn't* bark) and an unobservable, uniquely determinative cause. These interpretive skills of observation and inference depend on, and hence legitimate, the capacity for concentration, the resistance to distraction, the cool unflappability required of the expert. Or the novice investigator. Barry Benton, the Eagle scout trapped on the shores of a piranha-infested river, must first control his incipient panic before he can focus on the task of coming to understand the nature of his adversaries, and thereby come to possess the power to manipulate them, all under the relentless press of time. Similarly, Josiah Thompson's apprenticeship revolves around his learning what it means to pay attention in circumstances typically of predictable unpredictability and high risk.

Emerson's essay "Experience," which furnishes the epigraph for this chapter, appeared within a year of the publication of Poe's third detective story, "The Purloined Letter." Conceding to the Sage of Concord that the true art of life is to skate well on the surfaces amidst which we live, we are left with the all-important question of how best to accomplish that. Emerson's pronouncement and Poe's tale may be taken as "*strategic* answers," in Kenneth Burke's phrase, to the cultural situation in which both arose—the onset of "radical modernity." But it is Poe's story that embodies a stance, a strategy for acting in situations of high-consequence risk in which reliable knowledge of others is both essential and difficult to achieve—a situation intrinsic to modernity and hence, with the expansion of modernity, relevant to the experience of ever-increasing numbers of people. Mystery fiction dramatizes the strategic value of the trained capacities demanded by conditions of modernity—making those capacities, in the final analysis, matters of life and death.

Notes

Introduction

1. On the "agency" of writers, see also Burke 1992, Thomas 1992, Giddens 1987, and Skinner 1988.

Chapter 1

1. On the history of emotion in this century, see Stearns 1994. For the emergence of professionalism in the nineteenth century, see Bledstein 1976.

2. Peter Berger argues both that urbanization is the preeminent secondary carrier of modernizing tendencies and that, as a process, urbanization is not limited in its effect to the residents of cities per se (Berger, Berger, and Kellner 1973, 63–68). In the boom towns of the West, for example, the question of whom to trust was often pressing—and for the same reason: the prevalence of strangers (see Marks 1989). Priscilla Brewer notes that during the revivalism of the 1840s, some young Shakers feigned "gifts" (spirit messages) and "discovered that the elders had trouble detecting the difference, thereby eroding the leaders' authority at its most vulnerable point" (1984, 48). In the conditions of urban life, the problem of trust affected every aspect of living, as the following anecdote suggests: "Moses Weinberger, another rabbi who arrived in New York in the mid-1880s, left a scathing indictment of dietary practices in the city. The newcomer, Weinberger noted, did not anticipate the great difference between the new situation and that of the shtetl, where the shoykhet, the ritual slaughterer, knew the condition of his animals exactly, and where 'people knew everything that was done and said, even behind closed doors.' In the old world, 'not even the stupidest butcher' could transgress, because 'every stone had seven eyes,' whereas in New York City, corruption was impossible to check" (Heinze 1990, 175). I am indebted to Shelby Shapiro for this example.

3. See for example Hanson 1993; Barnes 1994; Lewis and Saarni 1993; Kalbfleisch 1992; and Mitchell and Thompson 1986.

4. Cf. William Colby: "The perfect operator in such operations is the traditional gray man, so inconspicuous that he can never catch the waiter's eye in a restaurant" (quoted in Hendrickson 1996, D1).

5. Cf. Charles McCarry's fictional CIA agent, Paul Christopher, writing to his case officer: "there is a certain amount of strain involved in holding conversations with people like Miernik. Two sets of expectations operate at all times. I pretend to like him for your purposes. I *do* like him for reasons that have nothing to do with your requirements. I lie to him for your reasons. And I lie to him so that he will not suspect that I am lying to him. I assume that he feels and does the same" (McCarry 1974, 11–12).

6. Sarah Emma Edmondson describes undergoing a phrenological examination prior to her acceptance as a Union agent: "Next came a phrenological examination . . . and finding that my organs of secretiveness, combativeness, etc. . . . were largely developed . . . the oath of allegiance was administered" (1864, 106).

Chapter 2

1. Ekman 1985. As an example of the fictional treatment of subtle behavioral clues, consider the following from Dorothy Uhnak's *The Investigation*: "The trick of the game, according to Williams, was proper selection of the jury. No matter which of his offices he operated from . . . he made the same point to his staff: the key to a successful trial rested, to an incredible degree, on the ability to accurately read a prospective juror. He maintained, and I believed him, that he could interpret the meaning of and reason for every gesture, twitch, cough, facial and bodily adjustment; could interpret character as revealed by selection of color and style of clothing, hairstyle, makeup (women), mustache, sideburn or beard (men), type of eyeglass frame. He had a sharp ear and could pick out otherwise hidden evidence of ethnic heritage and then conclude certain ingrained prejudices and leanings. Aside from the usual standard considerations of sex, age, marital and parental status, occupation, height, weight and appearance, Jay T. Williams could read the soul of an individual as revealed by the condition of hands, fingernails, shiny or unshined shoes, eager or reticent mannerisms, broad or abrupt gestures, grudging, constrained or inappropriate laughter" (1977, 135). This may sound rather like Sherlock Holmes reading a man's history from the condition of his hat, but Uhnak spent fourteen years with the New York City police. Readers familiar with the 1995 murder trial of O. J. Simpson will recall the prominent and essential role played by Simpson's jury consultant, Jo Ellan Dimitrios, who monitored jurors' responses throughout the trial.

2. Like the historian, the detective must put events in their proper (causal) sequence, attribute motives accurately, and weigh testimony critically in terms of the speaker's interests. In mystery fiction, the past matters and "Everything must have a reason. Nothing was done without a cause." The thoughts are Jim Chee's in Hillerman (1982), but the sentiment pervades the genre.

3. The consequences of understanding others intimately are well illustrated by the following. In a story about Christopher Darden, who helped prosecute O. J. Simpson for murder in 1995, William Booth writes of defense attorney Johnnie Cochran's understanding of his prosecutorial adversary: "Millions watched Dar-

den on television, scowling, pouting, sulking, grimacing. Some saw immaturity, others intensity. But Cochran knew—with the precision of a surgeon—exactly how to rattle his younger, less experienced opponent." Darden, a former colleague is quoted as saying, "is highly emotional and he wears his feelings on his sleeve," leaving himself open to manipulation ("A Simpson Prosecutor Becomes Odd Man Out," *Washington Post*, 6 October 1995: A4).

4. These stories have received extensive discussion from Poe specialists as well as from historians and critics of detective fiction. Among the more useful are Silverman (1991); Hoffman (1972, 104–36); Irwin (1994); Thompson (1993, 43–59); and Van Dover (1994).

5. Eco and Sebeok (1983) remains the essential starting point for any consideration of Holmesian method. See also Truzzi and Morris (1971), Norden (1967).

6. On Buchan, see Smith (1979); Atkins (1984, 31–39); Masters (1987, 15–34).

7. For an alternative reading of *The Maltese Falcon* from the point of view of the problem of Other Minds, see Rifelj (1992, 65–86). On Hammett, see Metress 1994; Wolfe 1980; Spicer 1983.

Chapter 3

1. On Chandler, see Chandler (1981); Durham (1963); Gardiner and Walker (1962); MacShane (1978); Spier (1981); and Van Dover (1995).

2. On Macdonald, see Spier (1978); Schopen (1990); Carter (1973); and Mahan (1987).

3. Chee prepares himself for the novel's final confrontation, which he expects will be dangerous, and may require him to use deadly force, by performing a traditional ceremony, the Stalking Way: "If one was to hunt deer, the Stalking Way repeated the ancient formula by which man regained his ability to be one with the deer. One changed the formula only slightly to fit the animal. The animal, now, was man. . . . Through it all, verse by verse, the purpose was the same as it had [always been] . . . [to] be as one with the hunted animal, sharing his spirit, his ways, thoughts, his very being" (1983, 185–86).

Chapter 4

1. The commentary on espionage fiction, like the commentary on mystery fiction more generally, is dominated by literary critical approaches (Palmer 1979; Merry 1977; Panek 1981; Atkins 1984; Denning 1987a).

2. As if to underscore the inadequacy of Latimer's stance, Ambler resurrected the character thirty years later in *The Intercom Conspiracy* (1969). Latimer uncovers the details of a clever plot by the intelligence chiefs of two small European countries to fund their retirement by blackmailing the CIA and KGB. He not only reconstructs their plot but incautiously hints at exposing it and them. For that bit of folly, Latimer pays with his life.

3. Bingham's service in MI5, during and after World War II, is described by Masters (1987, 173–87).

4. Two important nonliterary treatments of Le Carré's work are Dobel (1988) and Boyer (1989). See also Barley 1986, Wolfe 1987, Lewis 1985, Monaghan 1985, and Beene 1992. Le Carré's association with intelligence work is discussed by Masters (1987, 229–56). Atkins (1984) devotes two chapters to Le Carré.

5. Cf. Allbeury (1981). "Kim" Philby, who defected to the Soviet Union in 1963, wants to come home to England to die. British and Soviet intelligence both have an interest in understanding his true motives and determining whether he can do either side any harm, if he is allowed to return.

6. Dick Francis, whose heroes are notable for their unflappability, describes one as having "a head cool enough to calculate a ship's position for a Mayday call by dead reckoning at night, after tossing around violently for four hours in a force-ten gale with a hole in the hull and the pumps packed up, and get it right" (Francis 1978, 72).

Chapter 5

1. Among contemporary writers of mystery fiction, no one in my experience makes the separation between reason and emotion as sharply as Adam Hall does in the series of espionage novels featuring Quiller. A characteristic passage from *The Warsaw Document* illustrates the point. Quiller has briefly returned to the British embassy to send a cable: "The cowled lamps threw a lot of back glare and I could feel needles in my eyes. It wasn't exactly fatigue: the organism had started panicking because some of the brain think had filtered through and it was squealing to know what I intended to do about its survival" (1972, 251).

Chapter 6

1. John Bingham, a career counterespionage officer in Britain's MI5 and for a time Le Carré's superior, disparaged Le Carré's depiction of the "Circus," and in the preface to his novel *The Double Agent* (1966) rebutted negative views of the British intelligence services: "There are currently two schools of thought about our Intelligence Services. One school is convinced that they are staffed by murderous, powerful, double-crossing cynics, the other that the taxpayer is supporting a collection of bumbling, broken-down layabouts. It is possible to think that both extremes of thought are the result of a mixture of unclear reasoning, ignorance and possibly political or temperamental wishful thinking."

2. On the history of the concept, see Thompson (1990, 28–73). Also useful are: Geertz 1973, Jehlen 1986. Murphey (1979,) does not refer to ideology, but his analysis of the uses of knowledge in modern society is relevant and valuable. Studies of an ideological dimension of mystery fiction include: Knight 1980; Porter 1981; Denning 1987a; and Winston and Mellerski 1992.

Chapter 7

1. Press (1994, 221–45) usefully summarizes recent sociological work on audience reception (see also Radway 1984, and her new introduction to the 1991 edition; Long 1986, 1987; Steig 1989; Davidson 1989; Hermes 1995; Suleiman and Crosman 1980; and Rogers 1991). Ethnographic approaches to audience research, in the wake of the recent crisis in ethnographic theory, are discussed in two important works (Morely 1992; Ang 1996). Both focus on television audiences, but have implications for empirical research on readers, as does Thompson (1995). Olson (1994) offers a broad historical account of the conceptual and cognitive implications owing to the development of reading.

2. Fictional works can convey information only if fiction can be said to make or contain genuine assertions. For a spirited defense of that view against the "anti-assertionist" view that works of fiction can refer only to a world of fiction, can only seem to convey information, and therefore can never contain logical propositions, see Graff (1984): "Briefly put, the arguments [for rejecting the anti-assertionist view] are that authors intend assertions and readers can scarcely help looking for them" (1984, 105). Claims that mystery fiction can be a source for historical research rest on the assumption that it contains accurate statements: see for example Beschloss (1996, 1), and Amy E. Schwartz: "Murder-mystery plots move forward on an engine of exact observations, the more exact the better, and it's hard to think of a more alert way to be guided through the thicket of [real-world] behaviors too new to have hardened into norms" (1996, A23). See also Searle 1975; Juhl 1980; Keller and Klein 1990.

3. To preserve anonymity in quoting from DorothyL, I have noted only the date of the digest in which a given posting was listed. I retain printouts of those digests.

References

Alcott, William. 1834. *The Young Man's Guide*. Boston: Lilly, Wait, Colman, and Holden.

Allbeury, Ted. 1981. *The Other Side of Silence*. New York: Scribner's.

Alpert, Hollis. 1962. The Ian Fleming. *Saturday Review of Literature*, 26 May, 37+.

Ambler, Eric. 1939. *A Coffin for Dimitrios*. New York: Dell.

———. 1969. *The Intercom Conspiracy*. New York: Atheneum.

———. 1985. *Here Lies: An Autobiography*. London: Weidenfeld and Nicholson.

American readers love a mystery. 1986. *Publishers Weekly*, 21 November, 17+.

Ang, Ien. 1996. *Living Room Wars: Rethinking Media Audiences for a Postmodern World*. London and New York: Routledge.

Anthony, Carolyn. 1994. Many ways to mayhem. *Publishers Weekly*, 17 October, 43+.

Ashton-Wolfe, H. 1932. The debt of the police to detective fiction. *Illustrated London News*, 27 February, 320–28.

Atkins, John Alfred. 1984. *The British Spy Novel: Styles in Treachery*. London: Calder.

Aubrey, Arthur S. Jr., and Rudolph R. Caputo. 1980. *Criminal Interrogation*. 3d ed. Springfield: Thomas.

Aydelotte, William O. 1976. The detective story as a historical source. In *Dimensions of Detective Fiction*, edited by Larry N. Landrum, Pat Browne, and Ray B. Browne, 68–82 (Bowling Green, Ohio: Bowling Green State University Popular Press). First published in *Yale Review* 39 (1949).

Bagley, Desmond. 1973. *The Mackintosh Man*. 1971. Greenwich, Conn.: Fawcett. [Original title: *The Freedom Trap*.]

Bailey, F. G. 1991. *The Prevalence of Deceit*. Ithaca, N.Y.: Cornell University Press.

Barley, Tony. 1986. *Taking Sides: The Fiction of John Le Carré*. Milton Keynes: Open University Press.

Barnes, J. A. 1994. *A Pack of Lies: Towards a Sociology of Lying*. Cambridge: Cambridge University Press.

Bedell, Jeanne F. 1982. A sense of history: The espionage fiction of Anthony Price. *The Armchair Detective* 15, no. 2: 114–18.

Beene, LynnDianne. 1992. *John Le Carré*. New York: Twayne.

Bennett, Tony, and Janet Woollacott. 1987. *Bond and Beyond: The Political Career of a Popular Hero*. New York: Metheun.

Berg, Stanton O. 1970. Sherlock Holmes: Father of scientific crime detection. *Journal of Criminal Law, Criminology and Police Science* 61: 446–52.

Berger, Peter. 1967. *The Sacred Canopy: Elements of a Sociological Theory of Religion*. Garden City, N.Y.: Doubleday.

Berger, Peter, Brigitte Berger, and Hansfried Kellner. 1973. *The Homeless Mind: Modernization and Consciousness*. New York: Random House.

Berger, Peter, and Thomas Luckmann. 1966. *The Social Construction of Reality*. Garden City, N.Y.: Doubleday.

Berkhofer, Robert. 1989. A new context for a new American studies? *American Quarterly* 41: 588–613.

Berman, Marshall. 1982. *All that Is Solid Melts into Air: The Experience of Modernity*. New York: Simon and Schuster.

Beschloss, Michael. 1996. President Jack Ryan. Review of *Executive Orders*, by Tom Clancy. *Washington Post Book World*, 18 August 1996, 1.

Bingham, John. 1969. *A Fragment of Fear*. 1966. New York: E. P. Dutton.

———. 1967. *The Double Agent*. New York: E. P. Dutton.

Bledstein, Burton. 1976. *The Culture of Professionalism: The Middle Class and the Development of Higher Education in America*. New York: W. W. Norton.

Boucher, Anthony. 1973. *Multiplying Villainies: Selected Mystery Criticism, 1942–1968*. Edited by E. Robert Briney and Francis M. Nevins Jr. [n.p.]: A Bouchercon Book.

Bowles, Scott. 1996. Real estate agents say caution is key in showing homes. *Washington Post*, 14 December, B2 +.

Boyer, Allan D. 1989. Agents, lovers, and institutions: John Le Carré as legal critic. *Notre Dame Law Review* 65: 78–106.

Brainard, Dulcey. 1994. Marcia Muller: "The time was right." *Publishers Weekly*, 8 August 1994, 361–62.

Brewer, Priscilla J. 1984. The Shaker decline. *Journal of Interdisciplinary History* 15: 31–52.

Buchan, John. 1963. *The Thirty-nine Steps*. 1915. New York: Popular Library.

Burke, Kenneth. 1957. *The Philosophy of Literary Form: Studies in Symbolic Action*. Revised ed., abridged by the author. New York: Vintage Books.

Burke, Sean. 1992. *Death and Return of the Author: Criticism and Subjectivity in Barthes, Foucault, and Derrida*. Edinburgh: Edinburgh University Press.

Campbell, Robert. 1986. *The Junkyard Dog*. New York: Signet.

Carr, John Dickson. 1936. *The Murder of Sir Edmund Godfrey*. London: Hamish Hamilton.

Carter, Steven R. 1973. Ross Macdonald: The complexity of the modern quest for justice. In *Mystery and Detection Annual*, edited by Donald Adams, 59–82. Beverly Hills: Donald Adams.

Cawelti, John. 1969. The Spillane phenomenon. *Journal of Popular Culture* 3, no. 1: 9–22.

Chandler, Raymond. 1964. *Farewell, My Lovely.* 1940. New York: Pocket Books.

———. 1981. *Selected Letters of Raymond Chandler.* Edited by Frank MacShane. New York: Columbia University Press.

———. 1995. The simple art of murder. In *Later Novels and Other Writings.* New York: Literary Classics of the U.S.

Childers, Erskine. 1952. *The Riddle of the Sands.* 1903. New York: Penguin.

Christie, Agatha. 1940. *Murder in the Calais Coach.* 1934. New York: Pocket Books. [British title: *Murder on the Orient Express*]

Clancy, Tom. 1989. Interview with Ken Adelman. *Washingtonian*, January, 67–73.

Columbia surveys the pleasure of mystery reading. 1941. *Publishers Weekly*, 26 April, 1714.

Cornwell, Patricia. 1993. *All that Remains.* 1992. New York: Avon.

———. 1995. *From Potter's Field.* New York: Scribner.

Csere, Csaba. 1987. Audi agonistes. *Car and Driver*, June, 51–55 + .

Daly, John Carroll. 1934. Ticket to murder. *Dime Detective*, 1 October, 8–45.

Davidson, Cathy. 1986. *Revolution and the Word: The Rise of the Novel in America.* New York: Oxford.

Davidson, Cathy, ed. 1989. *Reading in America: Literature and Social History.* Baltimore: Johns Hopkins University Press.

De Borchgrave, Arnaud, and Robert Moss. 1980. *The Spike.* New York: Crown.

———. 1983. *Monimbo.* New York: Simon and Schuster.

Deighton, Len. 1995. *Faith.* New York: HarperCollins.

de la Torre, Lillian. 1945. *Elizabeth Is Missing.* New York: Alfred A. Knopf.

Denning, Michael. 1987a. *Cover Stories: Narrative and Ideology in the British Spy Thriller.* London: Routledge.

———. 1987b. *Mechanic Accents: Dime Novels and Working-Class Culture in America.* London: Verso.

Dobel, J. Patrick. 1988. The honorable spymaster: John Le Carré and the character of espionage. *Administration and Society* 20: 191–215.

DorothyL. LISTSERV@KENTVM.KENT.EDU.

Doyle, Sir Arthur Conan. 1927. *The Complete Sherlock Holmes.* New York: Doubleday.

Durham, Philip. 1963. *Down These Mean Streets a Man Must Go: Raymond Chandler's Knight.* Chapel Hill: University of North Carolina Press.

Eames, Hugh. 1978. *Sleuths, Inc.: Studies of Problem Solvers.* Philadelphia: Lippincott.

Ebert, Theresa. 1992. Detecting the phallus: Authority, ideology, and the production of patriarchal agents in detective fiction. *Rethinking Marxism* 5: 6–28.

Eco, Umberto, and Thomas A. Sebeok, eds. 1983. *The Sign of Three: Dupin, Holmes, Peirce.* Bloomington: Indiana University Press.

Edmondson, Sarah Emma. 1864. *Nurse and Spy in the Union Army.* Hartford, Conn.: n.p.

Ekman, Paul. 1985. *Telling Lies*. New York: Norton.

Fisher, Jacob. 1948. *The Art of Detection*. New Brunswick, N.J.: Rutgers University Press.

Francis, Dick. 1978. *In the Frame*. 1976. New York: Pocket Books.

Freemantle, Brian. 1977. *Charlie M*. New York: Doubleday.

Gallup polls mystery readers, finds Gardner most popular. 1950. *Publishers Weekly*, 25 November, 2267.

Gardiner, Dorothy, and Katherine Sorley Walker, eds. 1962. *Raymond Chandler Speaking*. Boston: Houghton Mifflin.

Geertz, Clifford. 1973. Ideology as a cultural system. In *The Interpretation of Cultures*, 193–233. New York: Basic Books.

Geherin, David. 1982. *John D. MacDonald*. New York: Ungar.

Giddens, Anthony. 1987. Action, subjectivity, and the constitution of meaning. In *The Aims of Representation: Subject/Text/History*, edited by Murray Krieger, 159–174. New York: Columbia University Press.

———. 1990. *The Consequences of Modernity*. Stanford: Stanford University Press.

———. 1991. *Modernity and Self-Identity: Self and Society in the Late Modern Age*. Stanford: Stanford University Press.

Gilbert, Elliot L. 1976. McWatters' Law: The best kept secret of the Secret Service. In *Dimensions of Detective Fiction*, edited by Larry N. Landrum, Pat Browne, and Ray B. Browne, 22–36. Bowling Green, Ohio: Bowling Green State University Popular Press.

Goffman, Erving. 1959. *The Presentation of Self in Everyday Life*. Garden City, N.Y.: Doubleday.

———. 1971. *Relations in Public*. New York: Basic Books.

Gorney, Cynthia. 1987. Hillerman & his Navajo mysteries. *Washington Post*, 29 January, C2.

Graff, Gerald. 1984. Literature as assertions. In *American Critics at Work: Examinations of Contemporary Literary Theories*, edited by Victor A. Kramer, 81–110. Troy, N.Y.: Whitston.

Hall, Adam. 1972. *The Warsaw Document*. New York: Pyramid.

Halttunen, Karen. 1982. *Confidence Men and Painted Women: A Study of Middle-Class Culture in America, 1830–1870*. New Haven, Conn.: Yale University Press.

Hammett, Dashiell. 1964. *The Maltese Falcon*. 1930. New York: Vintage Books.

Hanson, F. Allen. 1993. *Testing Testing: Social Consequences of the Examined Life*. Berkeley: University of California Press.

Hardin, Russell. 1993. The street-level epistemology of trust. *Politics & Society* 21: 505–29.

Harris, Neil. 1973. *Humbug: The Art of P. T. Barnum*. Boston: Little, Brown.

Harvey, David. 1990. *The Condition of Postmodernity: An Enquiry into the Origins of Cultural Change*. Oxford: Blackwell.

Haycraft, Howard, ed. 1941. *Murder for Pleasure: The Life and Times of the Detective Story*. New York: Appleton-Century.

———. 1946. *The Art of the Mystery Story: A Collection of Critical Essays*. New York: Simon and Schuster.

Healy, Jeremiah. 1990. Plot and structure in the mystery novel. *The Writer*, November, 11+.

———. 1994. *Act of God*. New York: Pocket Books.

———. 1996. DorothyL. LISTSERV@KENTVM.KENT.EDU. 2/3 January.

Heinze, Andrew R. 1990. *Adapting to Abundance: Jewish Immigrants, Mass Consumption and the Search for American Identity*. New York: Columbia University Press.

Hendrickson, Paul. 1996. The CIA's indelible man. *Washington Post*, 7 May, D1.

Hermes, Joke. 1995. *Reading Women's Magazines: An Analysis of Everyday Media Use*. Cambridge: Polity Press.

Hillerman, Tony. 1983. *The Dark Wind*. 1982. New York: Avon.

———. 1986. *Skinwalkers*. New York: Harper and Row.

———. 1995. Interview with Hamlin Hill. *South Central Review* 12: 31–42.

Hoffman, Daniel. 1972. *Poe Poe Poe Poe Poe Poe Poe Poe*. New York: Doubleday.

Hogan, John C., and Mortimer D. Schwartz. 1964. The manly art of observation and deduction. *Journal of Criminal Law, Criminology and Police Science* 55: 157–64.

Hollis, Martin. 1985. *Invitation to Philosophy*. Oxford: Blackwell.

———. 1987. *The Cunning of Reason*. Cambridge: Cambridge University Press.

———. 1994. *The Philosophy of Social Science*. Cambridge: Cambridge University Press.

Hood, William. 1982. *Mole*. New York: W. W. Norton.

———. 1990. *Cry Spy*. New York: W. W. Norton.

Houseman, John. 1965. Lost fortnight or 'The Blue Dahlia' and how it grew out of Raymond Chandler's alcoholic dash for a deadline. *Harper's*, August, 55–61.

Hutton, Charles. 1812. *A Course of Mathematics. For the Use of Academies, as Well as Private Tuition*. New York.

Irwin, John T. 1994. *The Mystery to a Solution: Poe, Borges, and the Analytic Detective Story*. Baltimore: Johns Hopkins University Press.

Jehlen, Myra. 1986. Introduction: Beyond transcendence. In *Ideology in Classic American Literature*, edited by Sacvan Bercovitch and Myra Jehlen, 1–18. Cambridge: Cambridge University Press.

Juhl, P. D. 1980. *Interpretation: An Essay in the Philosophy of Literary Criticism*. Princeton, N.J.: Princeton University Press.

Kalbfleisch, Pamela J. 1992. Deceit, distrust and the social milieu: Application of deception research in a troubled world. *Journal of Applied Communication Research* 20: 308–34.

Katzenbach, John. 1996. *The Shadow Man*. 1995. New York: Ballantine.

Keefer, T. Frederick. 1985. Albert Camus' American disciple: John D. MacDonald's existentialist hero, Travis D. McGee. *Journal of Popular Culture* 19, no. 2: 33–48.

Keller, Joseph, and Kathleen Gregory Klein. 1990. Detective fiction and the function of tacit knowledge. *Mosaic* 23, no. 2: 45–60.

Kelly, R. Gordon. 1974. Literature and the historian. *American Quarterly* 26: 141–59.

———. 1976. The precarious world of John D. MacDonald. In *Dimensions of Detective Fiction*, edited by Larry N. Landrum, Pat Browne, and Ray B. Browne, 149–61. Bowling Green, Ohio: Bowling Green State University Popular Press.

Kenniston, Kenneth. *The Uncommitted: Alienated Youth in American Society.* 1970. New York: Dell.

King, Nina, with Robin Winks and others. 1997. *Crimes of the Scene: A Mystery Novel Guide for the International Traveler.* New York: St. Martin's.

Klockars, Carl. 1985. *The Idea of Police.* Beverly Hills, Calif.: Sage.

Knight, Stephen. 1980. *Form and Ideology in Crime Fiction.* Bloomington: Indiana University Press.

Landrum, Larry, Pat Browne, and Ray B. Browne, eds. 1976. *Dimensions of Detective Fiction.* Bowling Green, Ohio: Bowling Green State University Popular Press.

Le Carré, John. 1964. *The Spy Who Came In from the Cold.* New York: Coward-McCann.

———. 1968. Introduction. In *The Philby Conspiracy*, by Bruce Page, David Leitch, and Phillip Knightley, 1–16. Garden City, N.Y.: Doubleday.

———. 1970. *Call for the Dead.* 1962. New York: Pocket Books.

———. 1974. *Tinker, Tailor, Soldier, Spy.* New York: Alfred A. Knopf.

———. 1980. *Smiley's People.* New York: Alfred A. Knopf.

Levin, Doron P. 1989. Audi gets a lift from safety study. *New York Times*, 11 March, Late City Final Edition, Section 1, 35.

Lewis, Michael, and Carolyn Saarni, eds. 1993. *Lying and Deception in Everyday Life.* New York: Guilford.

Lewis, Peter. 1985. *John Le Carré.* New York: Ungar.

———. 1990. *Eric Ambler.* New York: Continuum.

Littell, Robert. 1973. *The Defection of A. J. Lewinter.* New York: Popular Library.

Long, Elizabeth. 1986. Women, reading, and cultural authority: Some implications of the audience perspective in cultural studies. *American Quarterly* 38: 591–612.

———. 1987. Reading groups and the postmodern crisis of cultural authority. *Cultural Studies* 1: 306–27.

Lowndes, Robert A. W. 1970. The contributions of Edgar Allan Poe. In *The Mystery Writer's Art*, edited by Francis M. Nevins Jr., 1–18. Bowling Green, Ohio: Bowling Green State University Popular Press.

MacDonald, John D. 1963. *The Deep Blue Good-by.* Greenwich, Conn.: Fawcett.

———. 1964. How to live with a hero. *The Writer*, September, 14–16+.

———. 1965. *A Deadly Shade of Gold*. Greenwich, Conn.: Fawcett.

———. 1968. *Pale Gray for Guilt*. Greenwich, Conn.: Fawcett.

Macdonald, Ross. 1960. *The Galton Case*. 1959. New York: Bantam.

———. 1964. *The Zebra-Striped Hearse*. 1962. New York: Bantam.

———. 1969. A preface to *The Galton Case*. In *Afterwords: Novelists on Their Novels*, edited by Thomas McCormack, 147–59. New York: Harper and Row.

———. 1970a. Foreword. In *Archer at Large*, vii–xi. New York: Alfred A. Knopf.

———. 1970b. The writer as detective hero. In *The Mystery Writer's Art*, edited by Francis M. Nevins, Jr., 295–305. Bowling Green, Ohio: Bowling Green State University Popular Press.

———. 1970c. *The Instant Enemy*. 1968. New York: Bantam.

———. 1971. "Introduction." In *Kenneth Millar/Ross Macdonald*, compiled by Matthew Bruccoli. Detroit: Gale.

———. 1972. *The Underground Man*. 1971. New York: Bantam.

———. 1976. Interview with Sam L. Grogg Jr. In *Dimensions of Detective Fiction*, edited by Larry N. Landrum, Pat Browne, and Ray B. Browne, 182–91. Bowling Green, Ohio: Bowling Green State University Popular Press.

MacInnes, Helen. 1967. *The Double Image*. 1966. Greenwich, Conn.: Fawcett.

MacShane, Frank. 1978. *The Life of Raymond Chandler*. New York: Penguin.

Mahan, Jeffrey. 1987. Investigations of Lew Archer. *Clues* 8, no. 2: 1–39.

Mandel, Ernest. 1984. *Delightful Murder: A Social History of the Crime Story*. Minneapolis: University of Minnesota Press.

Marks, Paula. 1989. *And Die in the West: The Story of the O. K. Corral Gunfight*. New York: Morrow.

Masters, Anthony. 1987. *Literary Agents: The Narrator as Spy*. Oxford: Blackwell.

Maugham, W. Somerset. 1943. *Ashenden*. 1928. New York: Avon.

McCarry, Charles. 1974. *The Miernik Dossier*. 1973. New York: Ballantine.

———. 1975. *The Tears of Autumn*. New York: Saturday Review Press.

———. 1994. Between the real and the believable. *Washington Post Book World*, 11 December, 1+.

McWatters, George S. 1871. *Knots Untied; or, Ways and By-ways in the Hidden Life of American Detectives*. Hartford, Conn.: Burr and Hyde.

Means, Howard. 1991. Heart of darkness. *Washingtonian*, July, 65–67+.

Merry, Bruce. 1977. *Anatomy of the Spy Thriller*. Montreal: McGill-Queen's University Press.

Metress, Christopher, ed. 1994. *The Critical Response to Dashiell Hammett*. Westport, Conn.: Greenwood.

Misztal, Barbara. 1996. *Trust in Modern Societies*. Cambridge: Polity Press.

Mitchell, Robert W., and Nicholas S. Thompson, eds. 1986. *Deception: Perspectives on Human and Non-human Deceit*. Albany: State University of New York Press.

Monaghan, David. 1985. *The Novels of John Le Carré: The Art of Survival*. New York: Blackwell.

Moore, Lewis D. 1994. *Meditations on America: John D. MacDonald's Travis McGee Series and Other Fictions*. Bowling Green, Ohio: Bowling Green State University Popular Press.

Morgan, Ted. 1980. *Maugham*. New York: Simon and Schuster.

Morley, David. 1992. *Television Audiences & Cultural Studies*. London and New York: Routledge.

Most, Glenn, and William W. Stowe, eds. 1983. *The Poetics of Murder: Mystery Fiction and Literary Theory*. San Diego: Harcourt.

Muller, Marcia. 1991. *Trophies and Dead Things*. 1990. New York: Mysterious Press.

———. 1994. *Wolf in the Shadows*. 1993. New York: Mysterious Press.

Murphey, Murray. 1979. The place of beliefs in modern culture. In *New Directions in American Intellectual History*, edited by John Higham and Paul K. Conkin, 151–65. Baltimore: Johns Hopkins University Press.

———. 1986. Explanation, causes, and covering laws. *History and Theory* Beiheft 25: 43–57.

———. 1987. Signs, acts and objects. *Social Science History* 2: 211–32.

———. 1994. *Philosophical Foundations of Historical Knowledge*. Albany: State University of New York Press.

Nevins, Francis M. Jr., ed. 1970. *The Mystery Writer's Art*. Bowling Green, Ohio: Bowling Green State University Popular Press.

Nixon, Joan Lowery. 1977. *Writing Mysteries for Young People*. Boston: The Writer.

Nordon, Pierre. 1967. *Conan Doyle: A Biography*. Translated by Frances Partridge. New York: Holt, Rinehart, and Winston.

O'Brine, Manning. 1976. *No Earth for Foxes*. 1974. New York: Dell.

Olson, David R. 1994. *The World on Paper: The Conceptual and Cognitive Implications of Writing and Reading*. Cambridge: Cambridge University Press.

Oram, Malcolm. 1974. Eric Ambler. *Publishers Weekly*, 9 September, 6–7.

Ostrom, John Ward. 1948. *The Letters of Edgar Allan Poe*. 2 vols. Cambridge: Harvard University Press.

Palmer, Jerry. 1979. *Thrillers: Genesis and Structure of a Popular Genre*. New York: St. Martin's Press.

Panek, LeRoy L. 1981. *The Special Branch: The British Spy Novel, 1890–1980*. Bowling Green, Ohio: Bowling Green State University Popular Press.

Paretsky, Sara. 1988. *Bitter Medicine*. 1987. New York: Ballantine.

———. 1995. *Tunnel Vision*. New York: Dell.

Pederson-Krag, Geraldine. 1983. Detective stories and the primal scene. In *The Poetics of Murder: Detective Fiction and Literary Theory*, edited by Glenn W. Most and William W. Stowe. New York: Harcourt Brace Jovanovich. First published in *Psychoanalytic Quarterly* 18 (1949): 207–14.

Pinkerton, Allan. 1886. *Thirty Years a Detective*. New York: n.p.

Poe, Edgar Allan. 1845. *Tales*. New York: Wiley and Putnam.

———. 1938. *The Complete Tales and Poems*. New York: Random House.

Porter, Dennis. 1981. *The Pursuit of Crime: Art and Ideology in Detective Fiction*. New Haven, Conn.: Yale University Press.

Press, Andrea L. 1994. The sociology of cultural reception: Notes toward an emerging paradigm. In *The Sociology of Culture*, edited by Diana Crane, 221–45. Oxford: Blackwell.

Price, Anthony. 1975. *Other Paths to Glory*. Garden City, N.Y.: Doubleday, for the Crime Club.

———. 1986. *The Labyrinth Makers*. 1970. New York: Mysterious Press.

———. 1988. *Our Man in Camelot*. 1975. New York: Mysterious Press.

Pyrhonen, Heta. 1994. *Murder from an Academic Angle*. Columbia, S.C.: Camden House.

Radway, Janice. 1984. *Reading the Romance: Women, Patriarchy, and Popular Literature*. Chapel Hill: University of North Carolina Press.

Raskin, Richard. 1992. The pleasures and politics of detective fiction. *Clues* 13, no. 2: 71–113.

Reybold, Malcolm. 1976. *The Inspector's Opinion*. New York: Warner.

Reynolds, William. 1986. The labyrinth maker: The espionage fiction of Anthony Price. *The Armchair Detective* 19, no. 4: 350–58.

Rifelj, Carol de Dobay. 1992. *Reading the Other: Novels and the Problem of Other Minds*. Ann Arbor: University of Michigan Press.

Rogers, Mary F. 1991. *Novels, Novelists, and Readers: Toward a Phenomenological Sociology of Literature*. Albany: State University of New York Press.

Sammons, Jeffrey. 1977. *Literary Sociology and Practical Criticism*. Bloomington: Indiana University Press.

Sanders, William B., ed. 1974. *The Sociologist as Detective: An Introduction to Research Methods*. New York: Praeger.

———. 1977. *Detective Work: A Study of Criminal Investigations*. New York: Free Press.

Schopen, Bernard. 1990. *Ross Macdonald*. Boston: Twayne.

Schwartz, Amy E. 1996. The ABCs of popular culture. *Washington Post*, 9 May, A23.

Searle, John R. 1975. The logical status of fictional discourse. *New Literary History* 6: 319–32.

Shapin, Steven. 1994. *A Social History of Truth: Civility and Science in Seventeenth-Century England*. Chicago: University of Chicago Press.

Short, Sharon Gwynn. 1994. *Past Pretense*. New York: Fawcett.

Sicherman, Barbara. 1989. Sense and sensibility: A case study of women's reading in late-Victorian America. In *Reading in America: Literature and Social History*, edited by Cathy Davidson, 201–25. Baltimore: Johns Hopkins University Press.

Silver, Allan. 1985. "Trust" in social and political theory. In *The Challenge of Social Control: Citizenship and Institution Building in Modern Society*, 52–67. Norwood, N.J.: Ablex.

Silverman, Kenneth. 1991. *Edgar A. Poe: Mournful and Never-ending Remembrance*. New York: HarperCollins.

Skinner, Quentin. 1988. A reply to my critics. In *Meaning & Context: Quentin Skinner and His Critics*, edited by James Tully, 231–88. Princeton, N.J.: Princeton University Press.

Smith, Janet Adam. 1979. *John Buchan and His World*. New York: Scribner's.

Sokolow, Raymond A. 1971. The art of murder. *Newsweek*, 22 March, 101–8.

Span, Paula. 1995. Aww, write it right, willya? *Washington Post*, 24 July, B1.

Spicer, Christopher. 1983. A hard-boiled philosophy of human nature: Understanding people according to Spade, Marlowe, and Archer. *Clues* 4, no. 1: 93–104.

Spier, Jerry. 1978. *Ross Macdonald*. New York: Ungar.

———. 1981. *Raymond Chandler*. New York: Ungar.

Stearns, Peter N. 1994. *American Cool: Constructing a Twentieth-Century Emotional Style*. New York: New York University Press.

Steig, Michael. 1989. *Stories of Reading: Subjectivity and Literary Understanding*. Baltimore: Johns Hopkins University Press.

Suleiman, Susan, and Inge Crosman, eds. 1980. *The Reader in the Text*. Princeton, N.J.: Princeton University Press.

Symons, Julian. 1985. *Dashiell Hammett*. San Diego: Harcourt Brace Jovanovich.

———. 1993. *Bloody Murder: From the Detective Story to the Crime Novel: A History*. 3d ed., revised. New York: Mysterious Press.

Talburt, Nancy Ellen. 1981. Josephine Tey. In *10 Women of Mystery*, edited by Earl Bargainnier. Bowling Green, Ohio: Bowling Green State University Popular Press.

Tey, Josephine. 1959. *The Daughter of Time*. 1951. New York: Berkley.

Thomas, Francis-Noel. 1992. *The Writer Writing: Philosophic Acts in Literature*. Princeton, N.J.: Princeton University Press.

Thomas, Ross. 1985. *The Briar Patch*. 1984. New York: Penguin.

Thompson, John B. 1990. *Ideology and Modern Culture*. Stanford, Calif.: Stanford University Press.

———. 1995. *The Media and Modernity: A Social Theory of the Media*. Stanford, Calif.: Stanford University Press.

Thompson, Jon. 1993. *Fiction, Crime, and Empire: Clues to Modernity and Postmodernism*. Urbana: University of Illinois Press.

Thompson, Josiah. 1989. *Gumshoe: Reflections in a Private Eye*. 1988. New York: Ballantine.

Thornton, Susan. 1992. In pursuit of the state: Uses of the detective novel form in recent South African fiction. *The Griot* 11: 29–39.

Tompkins, Jane. 1985. *Sensational Designs: Cultural Work in American Literature, 1790–1860*. New York: Oxford.

Trachtenberg, Alan. 1982. *The Incorporation of America: Culture and Society in the Gilded Age*. New York: Hill and Wang.

Truzzi, Marcello, and Scot Morris. 1971. Sherlock Holmes as a social scientist. *Psychology Today*, December, 63 +.

Tully, James. 1988. *Meaning & Context: Quentin Skinner and His Critics*. Princeton, N.J.: Princeton University Press.

Uhnak, Dorothy. 1977. *The Investigation*. New York: Simon and Schuster.

Van Dover, J. K. 1994. *You Know My Method: The Science of the Detective*. Bowling Green, Ohio: Bowling Green State University Popular Press.

Van Dover, J. K., ed. 1995. *The Critical Response to Raymond Chandler*. Westport, Conn.: Greenwood Press.

Walbridge, E. F. 1954. Ross Macdonald. *Wilson Library Bulletin*, 26 July, 334.

Walsh, John Evangelist. 1967. *Poe the Detective: The Curious Circumstances Behind the Mystery of Marie Roget*. New Brunswick, N.J.: Rutgers University Press.

Weibel, Kay. 1976. Mickey Spillane as a fifties phenomenon. In *Dimensions of Detective Fiction*, edited by Larry N. Landrum, Pat Browne, and Ray B. Browne, 114–23. Bowling Green, Ohio: Bowling Green State University Popular Press.

White, Jean M. 1974. Helen MacInnes: Romance, intrigue and a good story. *Washington Post*, 27 January, E1 +.

White, Robb. 1963. The whirlpool. In *The Boys' Life Book of Mystery Stories*, selected by the editors of *Boys' Life*, 25–43. New York: Random House.

Wiebe, Robert. 1967. *The Search for Order, 1877–1920*. New York: Hill and Wang.

———. 1975. *The Segmented Society*. New York: Oxford University Press.

Williams, Juan. 1987. Man in a trap. *Washington Post Magazine*, 1 March, 37 +.

Williams, Raymond. 1977. *Marxism and Literature*. Oxford: Oxford University Press.

Winks, Robin, ed. 1969. *The Historian as Detective*. New York: Harper and Row.

———. 1982. *Modus Operandi: An Excursion into Detective Fiction*. Boston: Godine.

———. 1988a. *Detective Fiction: A Collection of Critical Essays*. Woodstock, Vt.: Countryman.

———. 1988b. Review of Ted Allbeury, *The Judas Factor*. *Washington Post Book World*, 21 February, 1 +.

———. 1993. Spy fiction; spy reality. *Soundings* 76: 221–44.

Winston, Robert P., and Nancy C. Mellerski. 1992. *The Public Eye: Ideology and the Police Procedural*. New York: St. Martin's Press.

Wolfe, Peter. 1980. *Beams Falling: The Art of Dashiell Hammett*. Bowling Green, Ohio: Bowling Green State University Popular Press.

———. 1987. *Corridors of Deceit: The World of John Le Carré*. Bowling Green, Ohio: Bowling Green State University Popular Press.

————. 1993. *Alarms and Epitaphs: The Art of Eric Ambler*. Bowling Green, Ohio: Bowling Green State University Popular Press.

Wood, L. A. 1986. American readers love a mystery. *Publishers Weekly*, 21 November, 71+.

Wuthnow, Robert. 1984. *Cultural Analysis: The Work of Peter L. Berger, Mary Douglas, Michel Foucault and Jurgen Habermas*. Boston: Routledge and Kegan Paul.

Index

Abduction, in Holmes stories, 43, 196
Abel, Rudolph, 151
Access points, 4, 5, 7, 133
Accuracy. *See* Realism
Act of God, 81–82, 130, 145, 146, 147, 148, 151
Acting: as impression management, 18; detective's skill at, 29, 45, 49–51, 58, 78–79, 101, 122–24
Action, 137; explanation of, as rule governed, 30–31; model of, 110; problem of interpreting, 74, 106. *See also* Mystery fiction, as action
"Adventure of the Blue Carbuncle, The," 152
"Adventure of the Copper Beeches, The," 128
"Adventure of the Dancing Men, The," 46
"Adventure of the Speckled Band, The," 44, 45, 155
Advice books, in antebellum period, 14, 24
Aesthetic, operational, 15
After Babel, 19
Agent provocateur, 21
Alcott, William, 11
Allbeury, Ted, xix, 83, 95, 111, 129, 154, 178, 202; *The Other Side of Silence*, 142
Alpert, Hollis, 149
Amateur, 47, 83, 92, 93, 98, 154, 155, 156
Ambler, Eric, xvi, 52; *Background to Danger*, 85; *A Coffin for Dimitrios*, 85–89, 93, 102, 134, 201; *Cause for Alarm*, 85; *The Dark Frontier*, 85; *Epitaph for a Spy*, 85; *The Intercom Conspiracy*, 201; *Journey into Fear*, 85; Anthony Boucher on, 181, 182
Analysis, in Poe's stories, 32
And Then There Were None, 61
Ang, Ien, 203
Annotated Sherlock Holmes, The, 184
Anthony, Carolyn, 140
Archer, Lew, 63–70, 75, 119, 129, 131, 195
Argument, mystery fiction as, xix, 110, 141–43, 148, 149, 196
Art of Detection, The, 132
Ashenden, 83–85
Ashford, Jeffrey, 184
Ashton-Wolfe, H., 47
Atkins, John Alfred, 83, 201, 202
Aubrey, Arthur S., and Rudolph R. Caputo, 106
Audi automobiles, 4
Audience, for mystery fiction, 166–68. *See also* Readers; Reading
Aydelotte, William, 164, 165, 168

Background to Danger, 85
Bagley, Desmond, 155
Bailey, F. G., 108
Barley, Tony, 202
Barnes, J. A., 199
Barr, Nevada, 173
Barzun, Jacques, 183, 184

Bedell, Jeanne F., 96
Beene, LynnDianne, 202
Belief, attribution of. *See* Interpretation
Beliefs, and socio-economic status. *See*
  Ideology
Beliefs, of writers, 156
Bennett, Tony, 110
Bentley, E. C., 154
Berg, Stanton O., 47
Berger, Peter, 8, 10, 17, 25, 195
Berger, Peter, Brigitte Berger, and Hans-
  fried Kellner, *The Homeless Mind,*
  8–10, 17, 25, 195, 199
Big Sleep, The, 59
Bingham, John, 202; *A Fragment of*
  Fear, 93–94
Bitter Medicine, 130, 131, 150
Blackwood's, 47
Bledstein, Burton, 199
Bleek, Oliver (Ross Thomas), 134
Bloody Murder, 181
Boesky, Ivan, 186
Bond, James, 149
Booth, William, 200
Boucher, Anthony, 168; as reviewer,
  181–84
Bowles, Scott, xi
Boyer, Allan D., 202
Boys' Life Book of Mystery Stories,
  The, 107
Brainard, Dulcey, 78
Brewer, Priscilla, 199
Briar Patch, The, 123–24, 150
Brother Cadfael's Penance, 173
Buchan, John, xvi, 27, 83, 89, 129,
  139, 155; *The Thirty-nine Steps,* 47–
  52, 54, 143
Bureaucracy, 8–9
Burke, Kenneth, xv, 197
Burke, Sean, 199

Cain, James M., 59
Call for the Dead, 151

Campbell, Robert, *The Junkyard Dog,*
  75–78, 113, 116, 130, 131
Cannell, Dorothy, 178
Capitalism, 160
Carr, John Dickson, 142
Carter, Stephen R., 201
Case, and the detective, 21
Casual Notes on the Mystery Novel,
  61, 153
Caudwell, Sarah, 173
Cause for Alarm, 85
Cawelti, John, 110
Chain of Fools, 174
Chandler, Raymond, xvii, 27, 55, 66,
  113, 120, 121, 149, 151, 181; and
  conventions of mystery fiction,
  59–61; and problem of other minds,
  61, 63; importance of honesty in, 61;
  The Big Sleep, 59; *Casual Notes on*
  the Mystery Novel, 61, 153; *Fare-*
  well, My Lovely, 59, 62, 129, 131,
  152; *The High Window,* 60; *The*
  Long Good-bye, 59; "The Simple Art
  of Murder," 60–61, 113, 120–21,
  131
Character: importance of likeability for
  readers of mystery fiction, 178–79; in
  antebellum American society, 11–13;
  in mystery fiction, 171–73
Chee, Jim, 70–74, 201
Childers, Erskine, *The Riddle of the*
  Sands, 83, 139, 140
Chill, The, 182
Christie, Agatha, xvi, 61, 175, 181;
  Murder in the Calais Coach, 145,
  147, 148
Christilian, J. D., 173
Churchill, Jill, 173
City, as locus of modernity, 11
Civil inattention, 4
Clancy, Tom, 169–70
Clues: behavioral, in Poe, 33; in mys-
  tery fiction, 28–29

lem," 42, 46; "The Greek Interpreter," 42; *The Hound of the Baskervilles,* 42, 44; "The Redheaded League," 44; "The Reigate Puzzle," 42; "A Scandal in Bohemia," xvi, 41, 45, 58, 119, 134; "The Stock-broker's Clerk," 41
Dulles, Allen, 17
Dupin, C. Auguste, 31–40, 46, 47, 106, 111, 134, 138, 195
Durham, Philip, 201

Eames, Hugh, 60, 86
Ebert, Theresa, 156–59, 160
Eco, Umberto, and Thomas Sebeok, 201
Edmondson, Sarah Emma, 200
Effects, of mystery fiction, 164, 175–76, 180, 183, 185–87
Ekman, Paul, 19, 20, 28, 200
Elkins, Aaron, 150
Emerson, Ralph Waldo, 197
Emotion: control of, xiv, 5–8, 17, 45, 46, 51, 105–06, 118, 133–34, 143, 155, 193, 196; leakage of, 32. *See also* Acting
End of the Night, The, 182
Epitaph for a Spy, 85
Expert, 4, 5, 7; investigator as, 47; trained capacities of, 196. *See also* Professional
Expert systems, defined, 2, 5–7

Face, as index to character, 13
Facts: accuracy of, 149–53; as constraints on writers, 149–53; as structuring readers' expectations, 151, 175, 176–78; relativity of, 152–53
Fair play, in mystery fiction, 61, 153, 154, 163, 181, 182
Faith, 154
Far Side of the Dollar, The, 184
Farewell, My Lovely, 59, 62–63, 129, 131, 152

Fechheimer, David, 185
Final Design, 172
"Final Problem, The," 42, 46
Firestorm, 173
Fisher, Jacob, 132
Flannery, Jimmy, 75–78, 113, 130, 131
Fleming, Ian, 110, 149
Flitcraft episode (in *The Maltese Falcon*), 52–53, 59, 139; Josiah Thompson's reading of, 185
For the Record, 153
Fowler, Orson, and Lorenzo Fowler, 19
Francis, Dick, 150, 176, 184, 185, 186, 202
Freeling, Nicholas, 184
Freeman, R. Austin, 154
Freemantle, Brian, xix, 154, 176; *Charlie M,* 94–96
From Potter's Field, 136, 143, 145, 147

Gall, Franz Joseph, 18
Galton Case, The, 65–70, 114, 115, 122, 129, 131, 142, 193
Game, as means to identify with others, 36
Gardiner, Dorothy, and Katherine Sorley Walker, 60, 61, 62, 153, 201
Gash, Jonathan, 150
Geertz, Clifford, 202
Geherin, David, 116
Giddens, Anthony, 199; *The Consequences of Modernity,* xv, 1–7, 10, 15, 18, 25, 190–92
Gift, The, 32
Gilbert, Elliot L., 22
Gilpatrick, Noreen, 172
Goffman, Erving, 4, 6, 23; *Relations in Public,* 15–20, 27, 85, 94, 128, 192, 193
Gorney, Cynthia, 140
Graff, Gerald, 203
Grafton, Sue, 120
"Greek Interpreter, The," 42

Juggernaut, as image of modernity, 2, 3, 191–92
Juhl, P. D., 203
Junkyard Dog, The, 75–78, 113, 116, 130, 131
Justice, in mystery fiction, 55, 76–77, 110, 140–49. *See also* Disposition

Kalbfleisch, Pamela J., 199
Katzenbach, John, xi–xiii, xv, xx
Keefer, T. Frederick, 116
Keller, Joseph, and Kathleen Gregory Klein, 203
Kellerman, Jonathan, 176
Kelly, R. Gordon, 107
Kenniston, Kenneth, 9–10, 17, 195
Key to the Suite, A, xvii
Killer.app, 177
Kind of Anger, A, 182
King, Nancy, and Robin Winks, 176
Kirst, Hans Helmut, 182
Kiss Before Dying, A, 182
Klockars, Carl, 20–21, 133
Knight, Stephen, 202
Knots Untied, 21–23, 24, 106
Knowledge: of others, xi–xiv, xvi, xx, 2, 3, 4, 5, 7, 20, 27, 28, 29, 31, 32–36, 39, 40, 41–43, 51, 52, 54, 55, 56, 61, 73, 74, 75, 77–78, 82, 83, 84, 87, 94, 96, 98, 105, 106, 108, 110, 118, 122, 132, 134, 162, 192, 193, 196, 197; and power, 29, 132–33; possessed by investigators, 105–06. *See also* Interpretation; Other minds
Knox, Fr. Ronald, 153

Labyrinth Makers, The, 124, 126, 143
Last One Left, The, 184
Le Carré, John, 17, 83, 105, 112, 126, 128, 140, 154, 178, 186, 202; *Call for the Dead,* 151; *Smiley's People,* 98–102, 112, 126, 141; *The Spy Who Came in from the Cold,* 120;

Tinker, Tailor, Soldier, Spy, xix, 99, 130, 141; Anthony Boucher on, 182
Leon, Donna, 176
Levin, Doron P., 4
Levin, Ira, 182
Levin, Meyer, 183
Lewis, Michael, and Carolyn Saarni, 199
Lewis, Peter, 86
Littell, Robert, *The Defection of A. J. Lewinter,* 102–05, 134
Long Good-bye, The, 59
Long, Elizabeth, 172, 203
Lowndes, Robert, 55
Ludlum, Robert, 177
Lying, 13, 19, 20, 28; and the detective, 22, 23, 24, 57, 67, 75, 78, 79, 82, 112, 113, 116, 186
Lyotard, Jean-Francois, 192

McBain, Ed, 184; Anthony Boucher on, 181
McCarry, Charles, 83, 129, 153, 169, 178; *The Miernik Dossier,* 200; *The Tears of Autumn,* 142
McClure, James, 177
McCone, Sharon, 78–81, 119–20, 125, 128, 134, 148, 151, 172, 192, 195
MacDonald, John D., xvi, xix, 116, 119, 148; *A Deadly Shade of Gold,* 152; *And Then There Were None,* 61; *The Deep Blue Good-by,* xviii; *The End of the Night,* 182; "How to Live with a Hero," xvii–xviii; *A Key to the Suite,* xvii; *The Last One Left,* 184; *Pale Gray for Guilt,* 122, 127; *Slam the Big Door,* xvi
Macdonald, Ross (Kenneth Millar), xvi, 55, 63–64, 110; on Raymond Chandler, 64–65; *The Chill,* 182; *The Galton Case,* 65–70, 114, 115, 122, 129, 131, 142, 193; *The Far Side of the Dollar,* 184; *The Instant*

Enemy, 70; *The Underground Man,* 122; *The Zebra-Striped Hearse,* 67, 121; on use of conventions, 65–66, 138; on qualities of investigators, 67

McGee, Travis, xviii, xix, 116–17, 119, 122–23, 126, 134, 148, 152

MacInnes, Helen, xvi, 52, 150–51, 155, 177; *Above Suspicion,* 89; *The Double Image,* 89–93, 139, 140, 141

Maclean, Donald, 142

MacShane, Frank, 201

McWatters, George S., 21–23, 24, 25, 29, 94, 106, 112, 132–33

Mahan, Jeffrey, 201

Maltese Falcon, The, 52–54, 59, 73, 113, 120, 129, 139, 143, 193–94; Josiah Thompson's use of, 185–87; Raymond Chandler on, 60

Mandel, Ernest, 156–59, 160

Marks, Paula, 199

Marlowe, Philip, xvii, 60–63, 113, 121, 129, 131, 152

Martineau, Harriet, 13

Masters, Anthony, 83, 201, 202

Mathews, Francine, 173

Maugham, W. Somerset, 169; *Ashenden,* 83–85

Meaning: and mystery fiction, 154; as problem of modernity, 25–26

Means, Howard, 142

Means, related to ends in investigation, 23, 40

Melville, Herman, 15

Merry, Bruce, 201

Metress, Christopher, 201

Millar, Margaret, 64, 182

Millhone, Kinsey, 120

Ministry of Fear, The, 182

Misztal, Barbara, 2

Mitchell, Robert W., and Nicholas S. Thompson, 199

Modern consciousness, 8–10

Modernity, xi, xv, 1–10, 160, 161; and modern personality, 7, 9–10, 195

Modus Operandi: A Writer's Guide to How Criminals Work, 151

Monaghan, David, 202

Money, 130

Monimbo, 139

Monteilhet, Hubert, 183

Moore, Lewis D., 116

Morely, David, 203

Morgan, Ted, 83

Muller, Marcia, xvi, 119, 128, 172; and use of experts, 150; *Trophies and Dead Things,* 125; *Wolf in the Shadows,* 78–81, 125, 132, 148, 150, 151

Mum's the Word, 178

Murder at God's Gate, 174

Murder, crime of, 21, 109

Murder in the Calais Coach, 145, 147, 148

Murder One, 176

Murders in the Rue Morgue, The, 15, 31–35, 39, 40, 75, 103, 109

Murphey, Murray, 25, 27, 29–31, 62, 202

Mystery fiction: and modernist fiction, 174; appeal of, 162–65; as action, 139, 140, 141, 144, 158; as argument, xix, 110, 141–43, 148, 149, 196; conventions of, 66, 134, 137, 138, 167, 194; as cultural evidence, 158; as model for being in the world, xiii, xx, 47, 108, 135, 137, 144, 194, 196; as solutions to technical problems, 47–52, 143–44; as source of knowledge, 166, 175–77, 180, 194; audience for, 166, 167, 168; effects of reading, 162, 164, 175–77; experience of reading, 162, 166, 167, 168, 169, 170–80; explanations of popularity, 162–64; prototypes of, 28; readers' criteria for judging, 170–75; mystery fiction, rules for, 121, 149, 153, 163, 164; trends in, 140

Mystery of Marie Roget, The, 32, 35, 142

Nevins, Francis M., Jr., 64
Night of the Generals, The, 182
Nixon, Joan Lowery, 107
No Earth for Foxes, 141
Norden, Pierre, 201
Normal appearances, 16, 17, 23, 24, 50–51, 87

O'Brine, Manning, *No Earth for Foxes*, 141
Observation, 41
Odds Against, 184
Olson, David R., 203
Opacity, 29, 44, 52, 74, 75, 87, 118, 120, 134; investigator's skills in creating, 105–06. *See also* Acting; Lying
Oram, Malcolm, 86
Ostrom, John, 35
Other minds, problem of, xii, xx, 27, 28, 31, 63, 70, 74, 81–82, 83, 94, 96, 192, 193. *See also* Interpretation
Other Paths to Glory, 143
Other Side of Silence, The, 142
Our Man in Camelot, 96–98, 143, 155

Pale Gray for Guilt, 122–23, 127
Palmer, Jerry, 201
Panek, Leroy, 201
Paretsky, Sara, xvi, 109, 116, 120, 175; and use of experts, 150; *Bitter Medicine*, 130, 131, 150; *Tunnel Vision*, 125–26, 128, 150
Past Pretense, 112
Pederson-Krag, Geraldine, 163, 168
Perkins, Edward J., 166, 194
Peters, Ellis, 173
Philby Conspiracy, The, 140
Philby, H. A. R. (Kim), xix, 141, 142
Phrenology, 18, 19, 28
Pinkerton, Allan, 20, 40, 106, 128, 193; *Thirty Years a Detective*, 23–24, 132
Pinkertons, Hammett on, 138
Planners, strategic, qualities of, 195

Planning, strategic, xii, xiv, xviii, xxi, 37, 52, 73, 78, 88, 97, 101, 102, 104, 107, 123, 155, 189–97. *See also* Prediction
Pluralism, as feature of modernity, 25
Pocket Full of Rye, A, 181
Poe, Edgar Allan, xii, xvi, 15, 27, 31, 32, 47, 51, 52, 66, 75, 103, 106, 109, 111, 134, 135, 138, 139, 197; *The Murders in the Rue Morgue*, 15, 31–35, 39, 40, 75, 103, 109; *The Mystery of Marie Roget*, 32, 35, 142; *The Purloined Letter*, 32, 36–38, 75, 111, 138, 197; and power derived from knowledge of others, 52
Poirot, Hercule, 145
Police informer, 20
Polls, of mystery fiction readers, 168
Porter, Dennis, 202
Postmortem, 136
Power, from knowing others, xi, xii, xvi, 5, 9, 19, 20, 29, 31, 40, 52, 86, 108, 110, 111, 112, 117, 125, 130, 131, 192, 197
Prather, Richard, 119
Prediction, xii, xiii, xiv, xx, 30, 31, 33, 36, 45, 53–54, 72–73, 76–77, 97–98, 103, 104–05, 108; and professionalism, 155; related to cultural rules, 30–31
Presence of mind, xiv, 17, 23, 24. *See also* Emotion
Press, Andrea, 203
Price, Anthony, xvi, 142, 150; knowledge of others, 97–98; professionalism, 98; *The Labyrinth Makers*, 124, 126, 143; *Other Paths to Glory*, 143; *Our Man in Camelot*, 96–98, 143, 155
Private sphere, 6, 25, 118, 186
Probabilities, weighing of, xiii
Problem solving, 8, 9, 15
Production: context of, 162, 165; tech-

nological, and modern consciousness, 8
Professional, 2, 4, 5, 6, 7, 11, 21, 47,
95, 98, 131, 132, 133, 181, 185,
193; as cultural category, 154;
trained capacities, 155–56; versus
amateur, 98
Public sphere, 6, 25, 118, 186
Purloined Letter, The, xvi, 32, 36–38,
52, 75, 111, 138, 197
Pyrhonen, Heta, 165

Quiller, 156, 202

Radway, Janice, 140, 203
Raskin, Richard, 163–64
Rationality, 25; legitimation of, 133–35
Rayle, Larry, 151
Readers, and meaning, 158
Reading experience. *See* Mystery fiction
Reading others. *See* Other minds
Reading the Romance, 140, 203
Reagan, Nancy, 153
Realism, in mystery fiction, 92, 140,
149–50, 169–74, 176–78, 180,
183–85
Reason, and emotion, 119, 143
Reception: context of, 162, 165; texts
of, 166, 168
"Red-headed League, The," 44
Regan, Donald T., 153
"Reigate Puzzle, The," 42
Relations in Public, 15–20, 27, 85, 94,
128, 192, 193
Resources, cultural, 117
Reybold, Malcolm, *The Inspector's
Opinion,* 142
Reynolds, William, 96
Riddle of the Sands, The, 83, 139, 140
Rifelj, Carol de Dobay, 201
Risk, xi, xiii, xiv, xvi, xviii, xx, 3, 5, 7,
13, 14, 16, 31, 54, 56, 57, 61, 67, 80,
93, 94, 98, 105, 155, 187, 190, 191,
193, 196, 197

Road to Hell, The, 183
Robinson, Lynda, 174
Rodell, Marie, 153
Rogers, Mary F., 203
Roles: knowledge of, 105; in Poe,
36–37; in Hillerman, 70–71; in
Campbell, 77
Rules, cultural, 29–31

Sammons, Jeffrey, 149
Sanders, William B., 29, 189
Sayers, Dorothy L., 170, 175
"Scandal in Bohemia, A," xvi, 41, 45,
58, 119, 134
Scarlet Women, 173
Scarpetta, Kay, 136, 143, 148
Schopen, Bernard, 201
Schwartz, Amy, 203
Scott, Shell, 119
Searle, John, 203
Security, ontological, 7
Sensational Designs, xv, 159–60
Setting, and the reading of mystery fic-
tion, 173–74
Shadow Man, The, xi, xii–xv, xx
Shapin, Steven, 2
Short, Sharon Gwyn, 112
Sicherman, Barbara, 167
Silver, Allan, 2
Silverman, Kenneth, 201
"Simple Art of Murder, The," 60–61,
113, 120, 131
Simpson, O. J., trial of, 151, 200
Sincerity, 12, 13
60 Minutes, 4
Skepticism, 39, 121, 127, 128–29, 190,
192
Skin Tight, 175
Skinner, Quentin, 169, 199
Skinwalkers, 70–75
Slam the Big Door, xvii
Smiley, George, 99–102, 105, 130, 134,
140, 151, 192, 193, 195